Don't Blame the Parents

Don't Blame the Parents

Positive Intentions, Scripts and Change in Family Therapy

Rudi Dallos

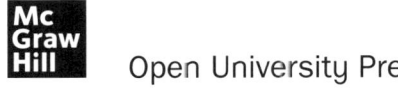
Open University Press

Open University Press
McGraw-Hill Education
8th Floor, 338 Euston Road
London
England
NW1 3BH

and Two Penn Plaza, New York, NY 10121-2289, USA

First published 2019

Copyright © Open International Publishing Ltd, 2019

All rights reserved. Except for the quotation of short passages for the purposes of criticism and review, no part of this publication may be reproduced, stored in a retrieval system, or transmitted, in any form or by any means, electronic, mechanical, photocopying, recording or otherwise, without the prior written permission of the publisher or a licence from the Copyright Licensing Agency Limited. Details of such licences (for reprographic reproduction) may be obtained from the Copyright Licensing Agency Ltd of Saffron House, 6–10 Kirby Street, London EC1N 8TS.

Senior Commissioning Editor: Hannah Kenner
Development Editor: Tom Payne
Editorial Assistant: Karen Harris
Content Product Manager: Ali Davis

A catalogue record of this book is available from the British Library

ISBN-13: 9780335243457
ISBN-10: 0335243452
eISBN: 9780335247950

Library of Congress Cataloging-in-Publication Data
CIP data applied for

Typeset by Transforma Pvt. Ltd., Chennai, India

Fictitious names of companies, products, people, characters and/or data that may be used herein (in case studies or in examples) are not intended to represent any real individual, company, product or event.

Printed in Great Britain by Bell and Bain Ltd, Glasgow

Praise for this book

"This book offers a compassionate approach to understanding how blame and responsibility entrap parents within transgenerational family patterns. Rudi's honest reflections on his intentions to be a better parent than his own break down therapeutic barriers between 'us and them', opening collaborative space to apply clinical theory. Integrating systemic and attachment processes he explores the influence of corrective and replicative scripts in parents' active choices to do their best. The central dilemma for parents is liberating. How can the complexities of parenting seemingly go wrong while we are striving so hard to get things right; a classic systemic conundrum!"

Dr Jacqui Stedmon, Plymouth University, UK

"Rudi Dallos offers us a thoughtful and helpful deconstruction of the crucial ethical and therapeutic differences between blame and responsibility in family life. Drawing on his integration of trauma theory and attachment theory with systemic theory and practice, he explores the vexed questions of causality, context and intergenerational influences in the understanding and alleviation of distress in close relationships."

Arlene Vetere, Professor of Family Therapy and Systemic Practice,
VID Specialized University, Oslo, Norway

"Rudi Dallos bravely addresses the controversial question of the extent to which parents could be responsible for the development of psychological difficulties in their children, claiming that this could be the case without them necessarily being to blame. He is impatient with resorting to psychiatric diagnosis of difficulties as illnesses, with its apparent exoneration of parents in contributing to these difficulties. Instead, he draws on attachment theory and proposes a role for the patterns of interaction that we all experience as a result of how we were parented ourselves. Not all will agree with his proposals but the book will be a useful vehicle for stimulating discussion of this important debate. Dallos is concerned to give voice to the participants in his research and his willingness to share and reflect on his own struggles in his difficult family history will warm the hearts of many readers."

Prof Harry Procter PhD, Consultant Clinical Psychologist

"This book is for practitioners working with families where children display behaviours which attract a mental health diagnosis, often with profound effects on families, and where the recommended 'treatment' includes family therapy. It addresses the interface between the professional and societal systems, each with vastly different world views, which must be navigated by such families. Following the thread of the twin phenomena of responsibility and blame it examines how parents are viewed and view themselves in relation to children's difficulties. Importantly it links the internal and the external: attachment narratives and how we process information about comfort and danger with family scripts and the culture we live in. It fills an important gap in our theory and knowledge. It is rooted in the author's vast experience. It will go straight onto the reading list at the Institute of Family Therapy."

Dr Chip Chimera, Director of CPD and Innovation,
Institute of Family Therapy

Acknowledgements

I want to thank Becky for her tireless support and enthusiasm for this project including reading scrappy drafts in the dazzling heat of our holiday house in a sleepy Hungarian village. Thanks to my children Tim, Alex and Jas for what you have taught me and I hope that the accounts of our experiences can be helpful for others.

My appreciation also for Arlene Vetere and Harry Procter who have been inspirational over many, many years. Also my appreciation for Tom Payne who was exemplary in his editing for his energy, commitment and intelligence to shaping the first draft of the book.

Finally, a thank you to all of the families that I have had the privilege of working with over the years and their generosity in letting me share their experiences.

Contents

	List of figures and tables	viii
	Introduction	1
1.	**Don't blame the parents: Blame and responsibility in families**	12
2.	**The dominance of psychiatry: Diagnosis and formulation**	33
3.	**The development of problems in families: Attachment, narratives and systemic therapy**	53
4.	**Attachment and family scripts**	71
5.	**Autonomy and attachment: Corrective and replicative scripts**	88
6.	**Trauma and scripts**	109
7.	**Therapy with families: Trauma, scripts and intentions**	133
8.	**Discussion and reflections**	153
	Appendix	161
	Adult Attachment Interview	166
	References	170
	Index	181

List of figures and tables

Figures

Figure 3.1	Escalating pattern of insecurity in a family	59
Figure 3.2	Attachment as a triadic process	61
Figure 4.1	Internal working model of attachment	72
Figure 4.2	Types of scripts	77
Figure 4.3	Different attachment patterns shown by parents towards a child	82
Figure 4.4	The child caught up in parental conflicts: Attachment triangulation	82
Figure 5.1	Attachment styles and intentions: A triadic process (the structure)	100
Figure 5.2	Attachment styles and intentions: A triadic process (the split)	105
Figure 6.1	Trauma: Stress and cortical integration	113
Figure 6.2	Trauma: A relational response to danger	114
Figure 6.3	Interaction between trauma and scripts	120
Figure 6.4	Scripts, intentions and trauma	121
Figure 6.5	Genogram: Dan and his family	122
Figure 6.6	Competing and contradictory attachment scripts	129
Figure 6.7	Trauma and scripts and the interactive model	130
Figure 7.1	Double sense of failure of corrective scripts	134
Figure 7.2	Genogram: Denise and her family	140
Figure 7.3	Denise and Tina's drawings	144
Figure 7.4	Genogram: Robin and his family	146
Figure 7.5	Tracking an attachment sequence	149
Figure 7.6	Relational dynamic in maintaining ineffective intentions	150

Tables

Table 4.1	Insecure attachment scripts	79
Table 6.1	Summary of core reactions	112

Introduction

To paraphrase the poet Philip Larkin, 'Your parents, they fuck you up'. Alan Bennett, in referring to this quote, mentioned that as a writer, if your parents in fact *did not* 'fuck you up' – if they had instead been stable, nice and supportive – your parents left you with very little to write about: they 'really fucked you up good and proper' (2009: 7).

We have all been children, and most of us also become parents. So, most of us have seen the two sides of the coin: how exasperated, upset, angry, mad, crazy we can become about our parents, but also how unfair it can seem that our children do not seem to appreciate what we have tried so hard to do for them, the sacrifices we have made, the money we have spent, the things we gave them that we never had. In Alan Bennett's whimsical quote, we see how the gift of love and kindness from our parents can even be experienced as a curse!

In some training workshops, I used to ask participants the rather obvious question of 'why did you choose to have children?' It transpired that many of these people, who were professional therapists, psychologists and clinicians, had not thought about this all that deeply before embarking on parenthood. Their answers were also often not as predictable as I had imagined. For example, they stated things like, 'I was responding to my biological clock', 'my friends were all having children', 'I was drunk', or referenced family expectations, pressure from parents, it being 'just what you do'. The mention of receiving love and affection from our children was much less frequently expressed than I had expected.

The role of blame and responsibility

This book arises from my experiences of working clinically and engaging in research with many families over a span of over 40 years. It also arises from my own experiences in my own family. In particular, I have found the themes of *blame* and *responsibility* to be central features of the experiences of the families with which I have worked and of my own life. These themes are central to people's experience, but discussing them in clinical work can be fraught with difficulties and risks.

We use the terms 'blame' and 'responsibility' every day: but what do they mean? The former is invoked solely when we have appeared to do or cause something bad; the latter is invoked when we appear to do or cause something good as well as bad. For example, being 'blamed' or 'responsible' for making the family late for an important occasion, but only being 'responsible' for developing a new invention or taking care of someone we recognised as being in need. Attribution theory has added some perspectives to this in the finding that people are more likely to claim self-responsibility (that is, internal agency and causation) for successes and good actions, but attribute failure to external causes (Kelley 1967; Stratton 2003). Things are never quite so simple. For instance, people diagnosed as suffering with depression appear to find it harder to consider that they have achieved any success and instead may blame themselves for things they cannot have caused, such as being abused as a young child by their parents (Beck 2002; Stratton 2003).

The concept of blame implies that people have acted deliberately in ways that have caused their problems or those of others. It implies that punishment or retributions of various sorts may be appropriate responses to their actions. Responsibility can also imply some deliberate intention, but does not assume such an active and deliberate process. For example, we might consider that 'blame' is appropriate to speak about a parent who has deliberately abused their child, but might consider 'responsibility' to be more appropriate to discuss how the arguments between the parents, unwittingly witnessed by their child, may have had a negative impact on their upbringing. These distinctions are complex and debatable but have important implications for therapy, especially with families. In relation to the example of arguing in front of our children (or even within earshot), parents may quickly feel that a discussion of the impact of their arguments suggests that they are to blame. This potentially has a paralysing and negative effect on therapy so that important causes for their child's anxiety or fearful states are not discussed and the child's condition becomes framed as a form of illness – we might call this the medical model of the causation of problems in families, that they are caused by medical conditions inherent in the child. More broadly, this concern about the potential consequences of discussing responsibility of the parents for problematic behaviours exhibited by their children or problems in the family has resulted in a virtual embargo of research into the causal effects of family dynamics on the development of problems such as anorexia, self-harm, depression or autism (Keen 1999).

How are problems caused?

Before we can answer this question, let's first consider what is meant by 'problems'. Problems might be understood as any child behaviour that is experienced by parents as conducive to stress, anxiety or concern. These are sometimes described in terms that suggest the problems are inherent to the child, and sometimes they seem inherent in the family's interpersonal dynamics. We should note here that a child may not share the view that they 'have' a 'problem', and we need to think about what their rights are in this process of defining what is a problem and for whom it is problematic.

One core issue with writing a book on how we should explain the causation of problems in families is that it runs the risk of it being experienced by parent readers as yet another unsympathetic book that blames them for causing their problems, whether these are emotional, behavioural, social or something else entirely. For this reason, family therapy and other forms of clinical practice have debated the issue of how we refer to 'problems' (Dallos and Draper 2015; Dallos 1991). One approach that I find helpful is the idea that all of us experience difficulties in our families, but whether these result in *problems* is determined by the reactions or the solutions that are attempted to solve the problems (Watzlawick, Weakland and Fisch 1974). In psychiatry, in contrast, there is reference to terms such as psycho-pathology, illness, symptoms and so on, which derive from concepts from medical science. There is an increasing debate in psychiatry and psychotherapy about whether such medical terminology is appropriate and what assumptions and evidence it is based upon (Timimi 2005; Boyle and Johnstone 2014). The position that will be adopted in this book is that people in families experience distress, trauma, loss, conflict, pain – as well as joy and satisfaction. These *are* real, but they may be explained in varying ways. One of the most dominant forms of explanation is to see some of these forms of distress and difficulty as indications of an underlying illness. A lot of attention has been given to this biomedical model along with massive investment in research to establish its validity and to develop pharmaceutical treatments based upon it. This approach is experienced as helpful by some individuals and families. But I will argue that good science is about keeping an open mind and not shutting the door on research and clinical practice that also considers how the relationships we are in may exacerbate or ameliorate distress or problems. Here, I do not seek to dismiss biomedical models of the cause of distress, but argue that they are not proven and claims about their validity have been exaggerated. Furthermore, my position does not dismiss the use of medication to assist families. We all use medication – coffee, tea, beer, wine, analgesics and so on. Unfortunately, there is a danger that they are overused – for example, Calpol (paracetamol suspension) has been found to be used excessively to medicate and control children (Bennin and Rother 2015). Similarly, despite current trends, medications used in psychiatry, such as methylphenidate, were intended to provide a window of opportunity to use alongside other interventions such as psychotherapy for children diagnosed with attention deficit hyperactivity disorder (ADHD). So medical interventions can be used *in addition to* psychological interventions to help ameliorate distress and difficulties. This does not necessarily mean, however, that what is being treated is an *illness*.

I hope this starts to illustrate some of the conceptual issues. But I also want to start from a personal position in revealing some of my own experience as a parent and a child. If I could turn the clock back, I would do many things differently and not do some of the things that I did as a parent, especially when my three children were young.[1] I have regrets about some of my behaviour to which I exposed my children. I have frequently engaged in blaming myself, but no longer think this is helpful,

---

[1] I have three adult children from two different marriages and have asked them for permission to share some memories from their childhood for this book.

either for me or my children; but I do feel *responsible*. I deeply regret that I engaged in heated and angry arguments with my children's mothers – arguments they could hear. At times, they were clearly frightened and upset, and it makes me very sad to recall this. But I also understand some of the reasons why I acted like this, including my own childhood and witnessing many arguments and some violence. I intended never to expose my own children to such anger, but realise how one's intentions may misfire or be frustrated. This notion of unintended consequences and actions resulting from interactional processes – how we interact in a family setting – will be a central aspect of the book. What I find helpful is to be offered a sympathetic view of my actions, but also to recognise that it *did* affect my children. I have talked with them about this, and I am hopeful these frank discussions have had a more positive influence than my denying any responsibility. Unfortunately, in order not to *blame* parents, the therapeutic and research exploration of *responsibility* has diminished.

As a young parent, I think I was also overly preoccupied at times with my own needs and having fun and friends, at the expense of taking care of my family. I but regret that I could not resolve the problems in the relationships with their mothers, resulting in divorce, which I think is always a painful experience for children however much we try to alleviate the pain and how amicably we think we have separated. As I write this, I imagine that one of my children might angrily say I am minimising how bad things sometimes were and how badly I acted; however, the others may be more forgiving. It is very hard to admit to my failings and the urge to start to defend myself is almost overwhelming. I remember talking with one of my sons when he had become an adult and apologising for the upset caused by divorcing from his mother. He offered me the reassurance that, from his experience with a girl he had just broken up with, he could understand that sometimes relationships cannot work and it is best for everyone involved to end the relationship. This forgiving statement felt like a massive boulder of guilt and failure being lifted off my shoulders. However, the concern that my actions had some negative influences on my children lingers.

How can I try to explain and justify how I behaved to myself and to my children? Also, how should I do this without sounding like I am making excuses to exonerate myself? One way is to turn to my own childhood and some of the difficult experiences that shaped the person and parent that I became. I was born in Hungary in 1948; my parents divorced when I was about 4 years old. My younger sister stayed with my father's family, partly due to their view that my mother was the guilty party. My mother remarried and I lived with her and my two half-brothers until the Hungarian Uprising, which led to a bloody suppression by the Red Army. My father meanwhile remarried and fled to Canada, and I came with my mother, stepfather and two half-brothers to the UK.

Though I did not hold the concept of a *corrective script* until much later when I came across the writing of John Byng-Hall (1995), I had resolved to be a father who was available, there for his children, and who never lost contact with them. My personal experiences have contributed to my curiosity about how problems arise in families, such as how positive intentions can perversely play a role in aggravating problems, as well as the potential for positive changes across the generations. In reading John Byng-Hall's book, I experienced resonances in my own life: *but despite my wishes*, I have separated from my children and not been as available as I had intended. Nor, sadly, have I been able to be as close to them as I would like. In my experience, parents almost always act out of positive intentions, but often inexplicably find themselves reverting to the behaviours in their own parents that they had wanted to avoid. Perhaps most painfully of all, I desperately want my children to understand that I have wanted to do things better than had been my experience. But of course, this is very hard to understand, especially for a young child. They were not there in my childhood and it can be hard to imagine how my experiences shaped me as a parent to them. They may even think it is unfair that my traumas impacted on them or, even more, that I should have resolved these before choosing to become a parent. I know how hard such forgiveness can be from the other side of the coin. Though my father and I were eventually reunited, I felt resentful that he had not appeared to try harder. Some years after this first reunion I confronted him about this, and he tearfully explained that my mother had humiliated him and her personality made it difficult for him to see me. Also, he had made a new life and a new family and was therefore preoccupied. As he talked, these seemed to me like excuses when I wanted a simple apology, which seemed very hard for him to offer. Despite all my training as a clinical psychologist and family therapist, and rationally understanding that wars fracture families, I still felt like an abandoned child – I still wasn't able to move beyond blaming him for his actions and the problems I believed he had caused in my childhood. I think he also felt so guilty that justifications came to the fore rather than dealing with our emotional loss and pain.

It would be a simple solution if an apology from our parents was enough to remove the desire to blame. Perhaps this can be helpful, resulting in a feeling of reconciliation or reassurance, but it is often more complex than this – there are many characters shaping such family dramas and such feelings and attempts at repair, including apologies, occur in the context of the wider family system of relationships. One very positive thing that my mother did was to always speak highly of my father. She constantly told me that he was a good, honest, kind, sensitive and intelligent man – so much so that it made me wonder why they had ever broken up! This made it easier to forgive his absence but, in many families, the continuing conflict between separated parents makes this process harder and sometimes impossible. Further, in forgiving one parent, the child may be seen as disloyal to the other.

Though wars and the resultant fragmentations of families and becoming refugees can have severe negative consequences, they also offer a clear indication of the causes of problems. In a sense, my father and perhaps myself had less to feel guilty about because events were out of our control. But for many families, the causes and problems are not so clear, and identifying some possible causes, such as family conflicts, may be experienced as implying blame. If, unfortunately, our children develop problems, a search for explanations typically ensues. This may trigger feelings of self-blame and, not infrequently, accusations and counter-accusations in families that the other parent is to blame. A classic example is where we see our child's faults as predominantly coming from their other parent and their good qualities from ourselves. But this process of blaming is highly painful and destabilising for a family. It is tempting to try to resolve these contradictory feelings by seeing problems as resulting from some form of 'illness' in a child, as in the medical model – for example, as resulting from ADHD, anorexia or autism.

My clinical experience with families is that turning exclusively to a medical model of their child's difficulties – viewing all problems as 'illnesses' – is often associated with an experience of loss and sadness towards the happy, healthy child they had hoped for. Additionally, appearing to prematurely challenge this explanation by offering an alternative account of their child's problems, or even one that may draw on the medical model but also offers other, more nuanced causal accounts, can be extremely distressing for parents. Bowlby (1988) suggested that a therapist can limit these negative affects by becoming a transitional attachment figure for family members. This means becoming like a temporary parent for the family – or a benevolent uncle or auntie (Minuchin 1974) – who is a potential source of security and trust and the subject of their vulnerability and anger. Part of this vulnerability comes from the family's sense that they have failed. They are desperate for some reassurance and acknowledgement of their positive intentions. This sense of failure and desperation can become so overwhelming that it can cloud their ability to see the many features of a child that can be seen as positive and 'normal', rather than pathological. By becoming a transitional attachment figure, the therapist can work alongside a family so that they can explore possible alternative explanations and possibilities. This becomes possible when the family feels reassured that the therapist will not blame them. In my early work with families, I used the concept of 'reframing', which was to offer 'new' ways of understanding their difficulties (Palazzoli 1974). I now consider that families typically hold many ways of understanding their problems, but feel constrained and unsure about considering many of them until they feel sufficiently safe – in a secure relationship with the therapist – to do so.

Throughout this book, I will illustrate examples of ways that we can sympathetically assist families to consider their responsibility in relation to the development of problems without feeling blamed and, alongside this, their potential to promote positive changes. Key to this is promoting recognition of positive aspects of their child and what as parents they can take credit for. A useful exercise for helping families to explore their understanding of any problems they may be facing, and to consider alternatives to solely relying on a medical model, can be to map and compare the apparently problematic and non-problematic aspects of their child. To illustrate: I worked with a family with a young child with a diagnosis of autism. I asked them to draw two overlapping pictures of themselves and colour in how much of them was 'autism' and how much of their 'normal' self was left. They said their hands, arms, legs and eyes are not autistic, but their mouth and brain is. Then, we drew how much of their brain was not autistic. They described that dreaming and reading were not autistic, but sometimes speaking and when they interacted with others was. They also mentioned that the balance between their normal self and autism varied at different times and places – for example, that it was more at school and less at home. It is likely that as the child's mother listened to them talking, feelings of anxiety arose for her. Such questioning could imply that it was not really an illness and, hence, was her fault – that the child's mother was to blame.

As a therapist, it is extremely compelling in responding to these anxieties to offer reassurance that we believe it *is* an illness and it *is not* caused by parenting. However, though it can be difficult, it may be more helpful to explore these feelings of guilt and responsibility. It is often the first thing that families want to talk about, but it often ends up as the last, or is completely avoided. This activity is called 'Self-autism Mapping' (SAM) (McKenzie and Dallos 2017) and has the aim of helping members of the family to gain a better understanding of each other's understandings of autism. It is also intended to foster a less rigid and more multilayered perception of what the condition means. To repeat, this connects with an idea that will be central to this book: families nearly always have multiple understandings of perceived problems and how they are caused. The medical model – the view that the problems are diagnosable and fit a medically based condition – is one of several explanations they may hold. Alternative views may have become subjugated to the dominant medical explanation, and in this activity they may come a little closer to the surface. An important implication for the child with the diagnosis and the rest of the family is that this can open up different, more productive possibilities of action. For example, rather than seeing a child's 'special interest' and attention to detail as a feature of their disability or disorder, they may view it as a potential strength when nurtured in the right environment; this can help them to shrug off the social values regarding acceptable, neurotypical behaviours. The focus of interventions can then move – the earlier the better – to alleviate more clearly problematic behaviours (e.g. disruption or aggression) and to support those possible strengths (e.g. methodological tendencies). This should mean that families do not have to wait until they receive a diagnosis before they receive any help and reduce the risk that distress and difficulties escalate. This can lead to a reduction in feelings of exasperation about the child's differences, frustration and a sense of failure about 'managing' them, a sense of exclusion for the child from their siblings, and so on.

From responsibility and blame to causation and intention

Perhaps taking a wider historical view here can help elaborate on these feelings of guilt and responsibility. Psychology and psychotherapy are new phenomena. The confessional has a much longer history, and ideas of blame, responsibility and culpability are deeply embedded in cultures and their discourses, which influence our clients and the families we work with. Foucault (1967) argued that the explanations we employ in ascribing responsibility can be seen to be embedded in our language and in turn located in our cultural histories of religious, scientific, artistic and legal discourses. These discourses operate most powerfully when they are tacit, implicit, and have the status of taken-for-granted 'common sense' (Gergen 1999). As Coulter and Rapley (2011) illuminate, not to acknowledge that these discourses are part of common, everyday thinking leads to an inauthentic stance with families. A lack of this acknowledgement may also lead to condemning children in families to a lifetime of being labelled as flawed and subject to unnecessary medication – we have to acknowledge where our drive to blame comes from before we can move beyond this causal line. Core to such explanations, which draw on wider cultural factors, are questions of *causation*, especially questions about why people act as they do, and, importantly, this revolves around the issue of *intention* as we saw in our discussion of blame and responsibility.

Outline of the book and pedagogy

This book is written with the intention of giving voice to the families with whom I have conducted research and clinical work. They have shared with me their hopes and their anxieties about the problems that have faced them, and I have been struck by their courage and wisdom, especially in terms of how they have struggled with understanding and trying to resolve their difficulties. Inextricably woven into their struggles have been the issues of responsibility and blame, and how their problems have come about. In order to illustrate how these are played out in their lives, I have employed a substantial number of extracts from therapy and research with families. By offering these 'therapy extracts', extended 'case studies' and 'pause for thought' boxes, I invite you to consider whether alternative explanations of the problems are possible – and no doubt there will be instances where you interpret them differently to me.[2] I hope this makes the book more alive.

All of the families have explicitly and formally given permission for the extracts to be used for teaching and publications. I have changed their names and some details of their circumstances for anonymity. However, since the context of their lives is important to understand the challenges they face, I have tried to keep close to their circumstances.

Finally, there is the matter of the term 'mother'. Throughout the book, 'mother' will refer to the primary carer in the family relationship, unless specified otherwise. There are many family arrangements, and attachment figures can be grandparents, step-parents, adoptive parents, foster-parents, nannies, same-sex partners, siblings, to name a few.

The content of the chapters is outlined here:

1. *Don't blame the parents: Blame and responsibility in families* This chapter will set the scene for the book in considering issues of blame and responsibility, broadly in relation to problems of mental distress and, specifically, in families. It will distinguish between responsibility and blame with the view that responsibility for our actions and their consequences is embedded in cultural discourses, including the legal systems and mental health professions.
2. *The dominance of psychiatry: Diagnosis and formulation* This chapter will explore how systemic family therapy initially posed a challenge to the psychiatric orthodoxy of 'illness' models of problems, and it will review

---

[2] I am always happy to hear from readers and my email address is appended at the end of the book.

the subsequent critiques of systemic models as family blaming. It will go on to discuss the contemporary dominance of psychiatric diagnosis and will describe how diagnoses and illness identities can serve to alleviate a sense of blame and responsibility in families, which is temporary, illusory, and may – in the long term – hold negative consequences for families, especially in terms of fostering pathological identities.

3. *The development of problems in families: Attachment, narratives and systemic therapy* This chapter will offer an overview of systemic family therapy models of the nature and development of problems in families. This will include an overview of research and clinical evidence from the early communicational approaches, structural family therapy, as well as the contemporary social constructionist and narrative attachment models. It will also an overview of key systemic conceptualisations, which inform family therapy formulation and practice, including feedback, escalation, conflict detouring, triangulation and communication. The chapter will focus on how meanings regarding problems are constructed in families and the drift towards problem-saturated conversations that focus on explanations that emphasise problems, failure and helplessness.

4. *Attachment and family scripts* This chapter will offer an overview of how an attachment perspective can be combined with systemic approaches to offer an understanding of how narratives develop in families. This will include an exposition of how the family system evolves from the internal working models that the parents bring to their relationships. How attachment strategies shape the nature of narratives will be described, along with how these relate to particular forms of family dynamics, such as conflict avoidance or escalation.

5. *Autonomy and attachment: Corrective and replicative scripts* This chapter will set out the central part of this book, which is that our narratives and attachment representations can embody choice. Scripts and internal working models contain not only representations of past events but our anticipations of the future and strategies for coping. A key feature of these models is intentions to repeat or change aspects of our childhood experiences of how we were parented. This shapes how we act as parents towards our own children and contains ideas regarding intimate relationships with our partners and other family relationships, such as grandparenthood and being a step-parent. This chapter draws on the seminal concept of scripts from John Byng-Hall (1995), but elaborates how their influence can operate at conscious or unconscious levels (i.e. via representational systems – embodied, verbal and reflective). A key point of emphasis is that the scripts contain 'positive intentions' – either to do things better or to repeat what we experienced as positive. This allows a consideration of parental responsibility for how a child develops without necessarily implying blame. The chapter will end with a discussion of representational systems and how, for example, a corrective script can be a conscious semantic intention that is in conflict with embodied or procedural representation.

6. *Trauma and scripts* This chapter will consider the influence on scripts of unresolved traumas and losses. It will describe how unresolved states can lead to scripts becoming inflexible and non-adaptive. For example, a mother who has experienced domestic violence in her childhood may hold an intense corrective script regarding conflict in her own family. As a consequence, she may become highly sensitive and vigilant regarding expressions of anger and conflict such that these expressions become blocked in the family and expressed through various forms of symptoms. Examples from research and clinical practice will be offered illustrating how dissociative processes underlie such rigid scripts such that people are not aware of what drives their commitment to correct or repeat aspects of their own experiences. The chapter will also discuss the extremely painful consequences of the *failure* of corrective scripts. This will be illustrated by research and clinical examples of such escalating cycles – for instance, of parents desperately wishing to do things better for their own child and believing that they have worked hard to overcome their own negative experiences. When their positive intentions appear to be failing, a temptation can be to 'do more of the same' and apply the scripts more strongly and rigidly. It will be discussed how this pattern of repeated failure increases negative arousal and a sense of failure, making it harder for the parent to reflect on the failure of the script and to apply modifications.
7. *Family therapy: Responsibility within a non-blaming approach* This chapter will describe the clinical implications of the book. This will include a discussion of how the idea of scripts driven by unresolved traumatic states offers important clinical implications in terms of the formulation of a variety of problems, research areas and clinical interventions. It will suggest that this model offers the basis for an alternative to medical diagnostic systems and that a variety of problems may be 'caused' by family dynamics that are based in the parents' childhood attachment histories. However, instead of 'blaming' families, the chapter will attempt to show how this approach is sympathetic in regarding them as trying desperately to do the best for their children and their family relationships generally. Further, it suggests a compassionate approach to the frustration that they feel and recognises that family members, despite family therapists adopting a stance of neutrality or a non-blaming approach, frequently do feel responsible and that not acknowledging this runs the risk of a slippage in medical diagnosis, which essentially locates the problems in one person.
8. *Discussion and reflections* This chapter will draw together the content of the preceding chapters and summarise how a therapeutic position can be adopted with families where discussions of responsibility and blame can take place. The chapter will also offer suggestions for why family dynamics and their relationship to the development of problems is important for the development of theory and clinical practice.

Appendix

An outline of the Adult Attachment Interview (AAI), indicating its structure and the specific questions that are asked, and examples from AAIs illustrating how narratives indicate different attachment strategies. There are also some examples of the kinds of responses people give regarding their conscious (corrective and replicative) intentions. The appendix is intended to assist in the assimilation of the book's ideas.

1 Don't blame the parents: Blame and responsibility in families

Introduction

> This chapter will begin by exploring the distinctions between blame, responsibility, influence and intention. It will do so with the view that responsibility for our actions and their consequences is deeply embedded in cultural discourses, including the legal systems and mental health professions. It will then explore how systemic family therapy (SFT) has changed our understanding of key terminology through the emergence of a non-blaming framework and mutual influence, and how this has been received by parents and families alike. Next, it will consider how families experience the emergence of problems in the family unit and how this can generate feelings of guilt, responsibility and a longing for forgiveness. It will then discuss in greater depth the role of guilt in blame, therapist approaches to addressing blame (including the medical model and narrative therapy) and how these feelings are framed within what I will call the dominant 'constellations of explanations' regarding problems: notably the medical model. Differences between family members in their understanding of these problems and constellations will also be discussed to explore the challenges families and therapists face in addressing problematic occurrences.

Is it our fault? Blame, responsibility, influence and intention

The terms 'blame' and 'responsibility' are often used interchangeably. Sometimes, however, ascertaining who was responsible for an action or an event is a precursor to and prerequisite for assigning blame. 'Influence' can also form part of the process of considering and assigning responsibility in that if a person was seen to exert influence over the occurrence or course of an event, they may be seen as having as much responsibility as they had influence. For example, a parent may ask, 'was this anything to do with you, Rudi?', enquiring into whether Rudi had any influence over the event. To the extent that Rudi did have such an influence, he might be held responsible and, depending on the nature of the event, whether good or bad, he may be blamed. It might be useful to think of these terms – blame, responsibility and influence – as located along a continuum, with influence holding a neutral position in terms of blame or responsibility. Related to these distinctions is also the question of *intention*. In legal parlance, there is a distinction between premeditated action, as in murder, and non-premeditated action, arsing in the 'heat of the moment' as an outburst of emotion, as in assault on a drunken night out. Premeditated transgressions are typically awarded higher levels of punishment than, for example, a thoughtless or careless action, even in some cases when the negative consequences of the latter are more severe – intention, then, is seen to incur greater blame and responsibility, even if it influences a less severely negative outcome.

These concepts are widely employed in the lives of families. Though parents are not (usually) judges or lawyers, they inadvertently draw subtle distinctions between the intentions behind their children's actions when evaluating familial problems and problematic behaviours (see the preliminaries for a discussion of 'problems'). I am likely to be more concerned if my child deliberately hurts and bullies someone than if they spontaneously lose their temper, for instance. (Though it would be concerning if they repeatedly lost their temper and appeared to lack reasonable self-control.) The concept of influence is also widely used in the family unit – for example, when we observe siblings influencing each other, a younger child wanting to be like an older sister, siblings copying each other or 'winding each other up'. Influence may also be seen as good or bad, whether exerting a bad influence by encouraging a sibling to be naughty or encouraging them to work hard and be respectful. These concepts are not only applied to children, however. Parents hold each other to account for their actions towards each other and towards children, and this can form the kindling for arguments, conflicts and even violence between parents.

From influence to mutual influence

The differences between these terms could be expanded into an entire book in itself but, instead, I want to focus on some of the implications that the development of systemic family therapy (SFT) has held for these concepts. That is, how has SFT altered our understanding of blame, responsibility, influence and intention?

SFT is a form of therapy that involves working together with multiple family members to consider how the family can employ its resources to ameliorate problems. Usually, one member has been perceived to have a problem, but a key assumption of SFT is that if the overall family system is able to make positive changes the problems in the identified person will also improve. A core concept in SFT, therefore, is that of *mutual* influence. Mutual influence proposes that members of families and other close relationships are continually influencing each other in the everyday interactions that shape the family unit. This has also been called *circular* causality, placing it in opposition to *linear* causality, which focuses on how one persona causes or makes another do or feel something. For example, moving away from how the father affects the son and towards how the father and son influence one another in a complex milieu of wider familial and intimate relationships, whether with friends, other relatives, significant carers or other close relations. Within this framework, family therapists do not ask 'who' causes some thing or problem to happen, but 'how' a problem is located within a cycle of mutually influencing interaction in a family. Family therapy has been around for over 60 years, from the late 1950s (Jackson 1957; Dallos and Draper 2015), but at its inception, the concept of mutual influence was seen as radical departure from traditional conceptualisations of how problems arise or traditional causal models (Watzlawick, Weakland and Fisch 1974; Dallos and Draper 2015; Dallos 1996). At a stroke, it was seen to remove the spectre of blame for parents regarding the arising of problems and even the idea of vulnerable or inadequate individuals being prone to different problems, such as psychosis. Everyone in a family was seen to be influencing everyone else and no one was singled out as responsible or blameworthy. Instead, families were seen as having become trapped in unhelpful patterns of actions that were maintaining problems – patterns that might be ironed out. This presented a radical challenge to orthodox psychiatry and psychology, which saw problems as aspects of individual personality, genetic heredity and neurological deficiencies – the foundation of the medical model (see the preliminaries) (Timimi, Gardner and McCabe 2011).

Unfortunately, though family therapists came to regard problems in this non-blaming manner, some parents came to see this as moving the focus of blame away from the children and onto them or the whole family. For some, working with families – even the term 'family therapy' – became uncomfortable since the term 'therapy' appeared to imply to parents that there was something that needed to be fixed or changed, a problem for which they might be blamed or at least culpable. Many of us sought to use the term 'systemic therapy' instead to navigate around this issue, but a problem was that families did not understand what this meant and, when it was explained to them, it sounded very like family therapy! Consequently, some families, especially the parents, worried that this 'systemic therapy' still implied that they were to blame and culpable for the problems and distress that had become manifest in their children.

Within the family therapy movement, some critical voices were raised regarding the concept of a neutral, non-blaming stance. For example, it was suggested that children might experience abuse at the hands of parents and, more generally from feminism-inspired therapists and researchers, that typically men held more power than women and were more likely to exert coercive forms of control, such as through threats or violence. Further, unease about blame was fuelled by various parent support groups like the Schizophrenia Society of Canada and the National Alliance on Mental Illness (Keen 1999), who reacted strongly to research and clinical practice that appeared to suggest that problems such as anorexia were 'caused' by problematic forms of family processes. One consequence of this revolt – one that is still felt today – is that parents are unsure about family therapy and whether it involves them being blamed, which often centres on mothers feeling blamed. This is, in part, due to research on family dynamics tending to focus on difficulties in mother–child relationships (Bateson et al. 1956; Bettelheim 1967; Bruch 1973; Dallos and Draper 2015; Dallos 2015). There is also a risk that men may feel blamed for unwittingly abusing their patriarchal positions of power, which may be part of the reason, alongside others, why typically men are much less likely to attend family therapy (Dallos and Draper 2015).

Interestingly, similar suggestions in favour of a non-blaming framework that upheld the notion of mutual influence were being made about family life by John Bowlby (1988), who described types of communicational and emotional processes in families that could lead to severe and complex attachment insecurity and the development of problems. Bowlby talked about the processes in families regarding children's experiences where children 'forget' significant distressing and painful events because their parents persuade or even coerce them into doing so. Like R. D. Laing (Laing and Esterson 1964), Bowlby noted many cases of parents encouraging children to forget painful episodes in the genuine belief that this would somehow protect their child's sanity. However, despite their intentions being benign, the consequences of such a process of distortion could lead children to experience confusion, insecurity and a fragmented sense of self and reality. Bowlby and Laing, as well as Bateson – who we will encounter later – all shared a belief that families needed to be able to engage in open and undistorted communicational transactions and that significant problems arise when patterns of distortion, deception and denial become central to the family's functioning.

The experience of emerging problems in families

Blame, guilt, responsibility, influence, intention and a need for forgiveness are arguably some of the most important issues in family life. They impact on everything in the family unit, from the most mundane actions, like washing the dishes, to supporting the mental well-being of an adolescent child. But when families engage in blaming each other in a therapy setting, it triggers feelings not just among family members but also in family therapists. For instance, blame may prompt anxieties that there may ensue an unhelpful escalation of negativity or a chaotic and uncontained process. This connects with our personal preferences for dealing with conflicts in our own families, which may shape which orientations of family therapy we feel most comfortable adopting.

This passage illustrates how parents may develop a sense of their family disintegrating and below problems as escalating, dangerously. Instead of responding positively to the affection they had tried to provide for him, Carl exhibited problematic behaviours and Mark and Brenda experienced these as rejecting them, as their adoptive son 'going off the rails'. They expressed that they were at their wit's end about what to do to help address these problems and that wanting to help him was tinged with anger at what they felt he was putting them through – they were resentful and were enticed towards blaming Carl for his conduct. This therapy extract also illustrates that perhaps for adoptive parents some of the dilemmas are even

Therapy extract 1.1:[3] Feelings of failure and self-blame

I saw Mark, an adoptive father, and his family in an early intervention family therapy service where I was working as part of a team of therapists. Referrals to the service were usually through a general practitioner or, in some cases, self-referrals by a family. My conversation with Mark and his family illustrates the sense of failure and self-blame that we regularly encounter in families and the powerful emotions that are present when accusations and blame start to permeate a family session.

The family background was that Carl, then an adolescent, and his younger brother had been adopted by Brenda and Mark when he was 6 years old. Carl's life in his family of origin had been very difficult and featured neglect, alcoholism, and violence between his parents and towards him. Referral to family therapy was made because Brenda and Mark, the adoptive parents, were concerned and worried about Carl's behaviour and feared that he was heading for trouble, including criminal activities. They were also upset that he was emotionally disengaged from them and no longer seemed to care about them or his brother.

RD: (to Mark) *'Do you feel that sometimes Carl thinks you don't care or don't love him?'*

Mark: (to RD) 'I don't know. I know that I am extremely pissed off with him. Because it's eight years we have had him, seven years of absolute crap <with tears in his voice, Brenda touches his knee for comfort>. Police, police, running away, phoning social services, stealing, smoking, drinking, drug dealing …'

Mark: (to Carl) 'I've tried to talk to you. I'm peed off, unhappy, I love you, I don't think you want to be part of the family <tearful>. Take charge of yourself, otherwise you're gonna be on drugs, in jail and probably dead. And there ain't anything I can do. I'm angry <nodding his head>.'

RD: (to Mark) *'Thanks for being honest.'*

Mark: (to RD) 'I am honest. I just don't know what to do <tearful>.'

RD: (to Mark) *'Is it like this at home when you have this conversation?'*

---

[3] Except where stated otherwise, this and other therapy extracts, research interviews and case studies are based on real-world scenarios, therapy interactions or research interviews. The sessions and research were carried out and documented in accordance with all requisite ethical regulations, whether university ethics committees or NHS regulatory committees. While the scenarios and illustrations are based on real-world interactions, all effort has been taken to anonymise the clients, to remove identifiable details and to ensure explicit consent has been gained for this use. Some of the details are therefore fictional, but the themes and the experiences outlined are indicative of the family therapy experience and illuminate the outcomes of key research studies.

Mark: (to RD) 'Yes, I am angry with him.'

Carl: (to RD) 'We don't really talk.'

Mark: (to RD) 'We don't talk, we don't do nothing.'

Carl: (to RD) 'I push people away …'

Brenda: (to RD) 'I don't know how much goes back to the early years … was told he needs a strong male model. Wish I could get into his head. He needs me most, when I'm angry with him <tearful> … when he's done something wrong and I'm shouting, that's when I should be able to go to him, tell him he's wanted. But I can't do it, and I don't know how to do it – and I know I should.'

Source: Adapted from author's personal clinical work and research.

---

sharper than they are for biological parents: Brenda and Mark appeared to feel that they had got things wrong with Carl and made mistakes with how to parent him, and that consequently maybe they were to blame for adopting him into a family that couldn't provide for his needs. For example, Brenda remarked that she felt she does the opposite of what she rationally thinks she *should* do, which is to show Carl love when he has done something wrong, instead finding herself angrily shouting at him. This is all very hard to bear given that they wanted to be kind in helping disadvantaged young people. They wanted to show these young people more care and affection than their biological parents had. They had been thoughtful about the best ways to act, in this case reading psychological books on parenting and taking advice from professionals – not least myself.

Pause for thought 1.1

- What conversations have you engaged in or heard regarding the explanations that people develop problems in families when they start to notice that something seems to be going 'wrong'?
- What has been your experience of how the person who is identified as having problems responds to this?

Frequently in my clinical work, a child starts to be identified as having some problems by parents, carers, teachers or other relatives. The child may not understand what the concerns are and may not see themselves as having a problem. In a piece of research I supervised, we talked with children about their experience of family therapy (Strickland-Clark, Campbell and Dallos 2000) and they described that they had felt compelled to attend, judged and blamed by the adults, preferred to attend with their other siblings or even with their friends, and often did not know why they were there. In the following extract from another piece of research that I supervised (Research Interview 1.1), we found that the mothers in families typically took responsibility and guided this initial process. It also appeared that often they felt confused about how to explain the difficulties, felt caught between mediating conflicts in the family, and frequently felt to blame.

Research interview 1.1: Responding to guilt and blame

This example is drawn from a piece of research I conducted exploring families' experience of having a child with a diagnosis of anorexia. I worked with a research assistant and we met with the families, employing a collaborative research process where we invited them to act not only as research participants but as consultants to advise us how to develop our research protocol and shape the questions we should focus on (Dallos and Denford 2008).

RD: (to the families) *'We are going to interview families: what things do you think we should ask them? What would you be interested in us asking them?'*

George (father): 'We felt as though we were guilty. You know, we didn't know what we'd done wrong, if we were guilty, and I wonder whether other people felt the same way.'

Source: Dallos and Denford 2008

Like George, guilt and blame appear to have been central to many of the families I have worked with clinically and in research. Either explicitly or implicitly, they ask: 'Where did we go wrong? It cannot be our fault, we tried so hard? Other parents have not been as good as us and yet their children are OK'. On the other side of the coin, children may worry that they caused their parents' problems, were unreasonable, or even that they caused them to split up. There may be significant differences of opinion within a family about what the problems are and what should be done about them. Family members are continuously trying to make sense of their lives, their own and each other's thoughts, feelings and actions. An important part of this meaning-making process is an attempt to figure out each other's intentions: 'Why did she do it?', 'What was her reason?', 'What was behind that remark or that look?' These processes may become increasingly negatively toned and problematic as problems surface in families. It is also possible that there is a mutual process – a mutual influencing – in that we do not simply respond to emerging problems, but that the way we think and talk about each other's actions in turn constructs problems. Conversation can become 'problem-saturated' so that a pervasively negative view grows where most aspects of a family's life come to be seen as problematic (Anderson, Goolishan and Windermand 1986).

Therapy extract 1.2: Responsibility, blame and explaining away problems

In this example, we will discuss Kathy, a young adult in the Andrews family. Kathy had experienced problems with her eating, which had come to be diagnosed as anorexia. We can see some of the processes of searching for explanation and meanings in the following conversation as the family discussed the development of anorexia in their daughter. This example also illustrates the ways that feelings of responsibility and blame seem to bounce like a rubber ball between family members.

George (father): (to RD and Mandy) 'We've often thought, if we'd had Kathy when we were younger, things might have been different. But we were in middle age and totally engrossed in our work, and did that have a factor? Because the other three lads, they just grew up with us and we hardly noticed a problem, did we?'

Mandy (mother): (to RD) 'You think you're doing the right thing by working and getting a decent job.'

Kathy (daughter): (to parents) 'Yeah, they're not saying you're *wrong* . . . If you hadn't have worked and we'd had no money, something else could have happened.'

Mandy: (to Kathy) 'No, I know, it's just . . .'

Kathy: (to RD) 'It's just, why was it food? Why wasn't it something else I used as my coping mechanism?'

George: (to RD) 'Why wasn't it drugs?'

Kathy: (to parents) 'I got a lot of attention when I was younger through food, didn't I? A lot. Maybe that had something to do with it? . . . I subconsciously knew that, um, kind of, people took notice of me for food and, like, I just got all the attention from food, didn't I, really?'

Mandy: (to Kathy) 'I didn't realise that . . . and that was before you were even 16 . . . when I was staying with your Nana, she asked straight away: "How's Kathy eating now?"'

Kathy: (to Mandy) 'But it was made such a big issue, though, wasn't it? When I was going to someone's house, you'd have to tell them beforehand that I wouldn't eat anything and stuff, and it was made such a big thing all the time.'

Mandy: (to RD and Kathy) 'But then, you think you're helping when you're doing it.'

Kathy: (to Mandy) 'I *know* . . . I was always very fussy with food, wasn't I? . . . I used to give half of it to the dog.'

Source: Adapted from author's personal clinical work and research.

In this short therapy extract, each family member appears to be proportioning blame to themselves and/or deflecting blame from others, rather like a rubber ball bouncing between them. George starts with thinking about whether because of their busy jobs, they may have ignored Kathy's needs and consequently had not noticed the emergence of her problems. Her mother, Mandy, connects with this story to lament that, though she was trying to do the 'right' thing, it may have been detrimental to their daughter's well-being. Kathy, as many children I have seen in families, then steps in to reassure her parents that they are not being blamed, and that they are not to blame for causing her anorexia. Her reassurance includes a somewhat fatalistic view that if not anorexia, then some other problem would inevitably have arisen, even if they had not been so busy with work. Her father accepts this apparently benign invitation and suggests that instead of anorexia 'it might have been drugs'. Kathy then helpfully takes responsibility and blame further unto herself – 'I got a lot of attention'. She develops this story to suggest a hint of blame, claiming that it did not help for her eating to be made such a big issue by Mandy and her Nana. This remark appears to spark her mother to recede into blaming herself again – 'you think you're doing the right thing'. Kathy then helpfully appears to try to alleviate their sense of blame by her remark, 'I know', which appears to acknowledge her parents' good intentions. Finally, she adds that perhaps it was all about her problems – 'I was always very fussy with food, wasn't I?' Blame and mutual influence are at play throughout this interaction, each family member influencing the other in a complex causal network.

In my work with the family, almost every session involved an episode of Mandy crying and showing concern about her parenting. Alongside this, she let it be known that she had not been happy in the marital relationship, which carried the implied possibility that she wanted to divorce George, and the family would have been fractured. Likewise, George remarked he and his wife used to quarrel: 'We used to argue a lot when Kathy was young, and she used to hear it, and it upset her . . . I think maybe we have come to pay a price for that?' Here, George appeared to be implying that their arguments may have caused or contributed to Kathy's problems with eating. Kathy perhaps captured this in the following quote, which appears to contain some of the parents' worst fears:

> The only thing I ever hear them talking about is me and if I didn't have this [(anorexia)] it's kind of like, would everything fall apart, at least it's keeping them talking. And they won't argue while I've got this because it might make me worse. So um . . . that's kind of bought, sort of like, I'm not in control as such but I've got more control over the situation that way . . .

Kathy's family came voluntarily for family therapy, intending to work together. What struck me during my work with them was that they were well-intentioned and wanted to understand what the problems were and how to resolve them. What was also interesting was that they knew about the dominant discourses of anorexia as a medical 'illness', but were not satisfied with this categorisation. They were concerned that their family dynamics may have exerted an influence on the development of Kathy's problems and that perhaps their own childhood experiences had made some aspects of parenting difficult for them. Neither George nor Mandy felt that they had positive models of parenting to draw on nor experience of a secure and comforting family. Above all, they came to agree that they were not working in a united way to help Kathy, in part because of their own marital problems, but also in part due to their past experiences. They decided to work with the family therapists to try and resolve the problems in their relationship and this appeared to have a positive effect of ameliorating Kathy's anorexic symptoms.

Why do parents typically feel blamed when problems emerge?

Responsibility and blame are embedded in our own and other cultures. Parents have historically been held responsible for raising their children and expected to prepare them to be adjusted for playing a positive part in their culture. In relation to mental health, this has taken a convoluted path. There are a number of influential strands of research and explanations that now seem to be held in our collective consciousness as explicit forms of blaming of families for causing serious pathologies in their children.

One of these explanations is the model of anorexia proposed by Hilda Bruch (1980) in which she described family environments characterised by overprotection, intrusiveness and control as 'causal', with few opportunities for self-expression. Bruch argued that these family interactions led to the development of a highly compliant 'false self', and self-starvation was a rebellion against such parental impingement. Anorexia was seen as a form of covert communication of protest and attempt for autonomy, which typically emerged in adolescence. Since the most influential and causal interaction was seen to be between the women in the family – girls and women are ten times more likely than boys and men to suffer from anorexia or bulimia (Royal College of Psychiatrists 2019) – this model was experienced by many as gendered and as 'mother-blaming'. A similar model can be seen in the double-bind theory of schizophrenia in which Bateson and his team (1956) argued that mothers engage in confusing and contradictory processes of communication with their children. At the verbal level, a mother may say that she wants affection from her son, but non-verbally expresses disgust and gives a message that this confusion must not be commented on since it might challenge the relationship, hurt her, and so on. Bateson et al. (1956) strongly implied that the ambivalent and contradictory communication arose out of a deep fear of potential rejection. Bateson et al. (1956) and Bateson (1972) suggested in his description of double-bind situations that these were driven by anxieties and insecurities:

> The *need of the mother to be wanted and loved* . . . prevents the child from gaining support from some other person in the environment – a teacher, for example. A mother with these characteristics would feel threatened by any other attachment of the child and would sabotage any competing

relationship in order to [break it up and] bring the child back closer to her with consequent *anxiety* when the child became *dependent* on her.

(Bateson 1972: 215; emphasis added)

Bateson's theory is typically considered as focused on communicational dilemmas that emerge between a parent and a child. However, it is evident in this quote that the communicational problem as such is seen to be located in underlying anxieties and a fear that the mother will lose her attachment to the child. Arguably, in the example of Kathy and her family, her mother and father also appeared to be highly anxious that Kathy was rejecting her. As with Bruch's model, an unfortunate reaction to this formulation was the impression that it was 'mother-blaming'. This view became so strongly established that it obscured later reformulations as a mutual and even a triadic process. Weakland (1976) argued further that such patterns could be better seen as a triangular double-binding process, typically where the mother is, or feels, disempowered. A third, and perhaps even more powerful, example comes from Kanner and Eisenberg's (1956) theory of autism, which drew attention to what they saw as a lack of parental warmth and attachment to autistic children, either causing or acting as a catalyst for autism. They attributed autism to a pervasive lack of emotional warmth from mothers that led to the concept of the 'refrigerator mother' – a parent who had difficulty in responding to their child's emotions and requests for comfort and reassurance. Their ideas have produced widespread criticism and rejection by parents of children diagnosed with autism, people with this diagnosis and professionals working with these families.

Autism is a powerful example of some of the difficulties facing parents. Concepts such as schismogenic or refrigerator mothers not unsurprisingly can lead parents to feel blamed and misunderstood. A consequence can be that research on the causation of problems and the parents' attempts to gather information may be short-circuited to accept biologically based models as proven fact. Apart from the wide disparity in research findings about the genetic component of a condition such as autism, it is made all the more confusing by the fact that diagnosis may be unreliable and it encompasses a massive range, from children and adults with severe intellectual impairment to those with superior intellectual functioning. Also, the definitions shift so that Asperger's has now been deleted as a separate condition from the fifth edition of the *Diagnostic and Statistical Manual of Mental Disorders* (DSM-5). Generally, parents are informed quite categorically that autism is a neurologically based vulnerability, but without clear evidence of genetic indicators for this and equivocal findings from research on inherited genetic components in twin studies (Timimi, Gardner and McCabe 2011). An influential approach with autism, and previously schizophrenia, is the stress–vulnerability model (Zubin and Spring 1977). This frames problems as an interaction between a genetically based vulnerability that might be triggered and particular triggering environmental factors, and it may appear to offer a compromise between biological and psychological explanations. However, it still ignores the possibility that the vulnerabilities may have developed from complex family or relational dynamics rather than adding to a genetically based vulnerability. It can, however, provide a useful starting point to discuss with families without appearing to be blaming what aspects of their life may be aggravating as opposed to assisting the problems they are encountering.

Blame and the role of the mother

When we discuss family factors and potential causation in relation to the emergence and maintenance of problems, this is often synonymous with a focus on the role of mothers, and sometimes explicit mother-blaming. O'Reilly and Lester (2015) suggest that blame is widespread in cultural discourses of mothering and women are expected to fit an idealised view of motherhood. As a consequence, they are frequently subject to evaluations and negative judgements when they access services for their children and carry a burden of responsibility and blame when they do so.

In the previous therapy extracts, the central dynamics could be seen as focused primarily on the relation between the mother and child, whether between Brenda and Carl or Mandy and Kathy. But a view of family systems as related to 'problems' is broader than this. The fundamental unit of analysis is seen to be triadic: it is between *both* parents and the child. The idea of children as becoming entangled in their parents' distress and conflicts has been central to family therapy, though interestingly research has lagged behind clinical intervention and has focused on *triangulation* – the process whereby a child can be destructively drawn into the parents' conflicts. Recent research supports the view that triadic conflicts can relate to the aetiology of problems in children (Dubois-Comtois and Moss 2008; Dallos et al. 2015). Though a triadic formulation is not blaming of any one person in a family, it can still be experienced as blaming of the parents collectively. Systemic perspectives therefore strongly advocate a stance of neutrality such that in triadic processes, no one is to blame and all feel that they play a part in maintaining the processes. Despite this, it is of course tempting to think that there are fundamental inequalities in how much parents as opposed to an infant can construct the family relational system – that is, how much *influence* each player makes to the overall family dynamics. Parents can be extremely distressed at the implication that they have caused serious problems to have developed in their children. In Research Interview 1.1, George indicated regret that their marital conflicts may have negatively impacted on their daughter.

Approaches to addressing blame, responsibility and guilt

How should a family therapist respond when family members blame, accuse and demand justifications from each other?

Friedlander, Heatherington and Marrs (2000) suggest that, despite a non-expert and non-directive stance, most therapists operate within a fundamental and pervasive assumption that blame is unhelpful or counterproductive. It may appear obvious that families that engage in blame and conflict are likely to degenerate into serious problems, but Minuchin argued that where this is compulsively avoided, in 'conflict-avoidant' families (1974: 52), this can cause significant, if not greater, problems.

Friedlander, Heatherington and Marrs (2000) conducted research into the process of how therapists responded to episodes of blaming by family members and noted a number of frequent strategies. They highlighted examples of actions illustrating ignoring/diverting, acknowledging/challenging, and reframing and found that the most frequent code of conduct was focusing on the positive. (Nevertheless, therapists often used multiple codes in a single episode of blaming.)

In Therapy extract 1.1, we saw how I employed two of these strategies: I attempted to reframe Mark's (the adoptive father) anger and sadness as honesty and I attempted to divert the conversation by asking if this is how things were at home. I might add that, at the time, I was not aware of consciously using these strategies. Alongside these strategies, we hopefully recognise and communicate to families our awareness of the underlying softer emotions of sadness, vulnerability, frustration and failure that they may be feeling. It is also clear that these parents were well-intentioned. (Acknowledging the underlying intentions is one of the core themes of this book and will be explored in Chapter 5.)

Models of family therapy

Models of family therapy have tended to focus on patterns and processes in families and subsequently on the beliefs and explanations that shaped these. But family life is also *emotional*. Different families show emotions in different ways but especially during moments of blame, accusation or requests to justify actions – that is, when responsibility enters the room. Blaming may even shift to threats and intimidations if adequate justifications for 'wrong' actions are not offered.

Attachment theory (Byng-Hall 1995; Dallos 2006; Dallos and Vetere 2009) suggests that patterns of blame and accusation vary in families. For some, this is seen as highly dangerous and to be avoided at all costs. In other families, preoccupation with blaming, quarrels, and accusations are a common and expected feature of family life. In yet others, there appears to be a balance such that responsibility for actions is sought but negative escalations of blaming or complete avoidance do not result.

Studies employing attachment measures suggest that adults looking back on their childhoods tend to tell two kinds of stories. In the so-called *dismissing* orientations, they try to see things from their parents' perspectives, dismiss difficulties, excuse their parents' actions and portray a rosy, idealised version of events. In contrast, some people employ an angry or *seething* version of events where the parents did very little 'right' and were largely to blame for most of the difficulties they faced. These may seem like caricatures, but they are repeatedly found in Adult Attachment Interviews (Solomon and George 1999; Crittenden and Landini 2011). (Exploration of attachment, blaming and responsibility will be the focus of Chapter 4.)

The purpose of paying attention to these models is not simply to attempt to justify them, though emerging research supports aspects of the models (Dallos and Denford 2008; Read and Gumley 2008), but to consider some broader implications for science and clinical practice.

Pause for thought 1.2

- What do models like this feel like for families and parents?
- How do you imagine families approach 'family therapy' or, if you or someone you know has experienced it, what were your/their anticipations about what it would feel like?
- To what extent did you or they expect to feel judged, criticised or blamed?
- What do you think is a helpful stance for therapists to adopt to address this issue?
- Do you think it might be helpful to discuss such feelings at the first meeting?

In the context of work, for example with families presenting with anorexia, I have found that many families approached therapy with a high level of anxiety (Dallos and Draper 2015). They often communicated what felt like a reluctance to talk about their relationships as in any way connected to the problems they experienced. I initially felt some irritation at what seemed like deliberate obstructiveness, but gradually developed a sense that the parents were doing their best but were struggling to draw on positive experiences from their childhoods. They also appeared to be terrified that they might have *caused* the problems.

Labelling and the relief of guilt: The medical model

Given the pervasiveness of medical models of problems, such as anorexia, it is compelling for parents to turn to illness labels ('anorexia' or 'ADHD', for example) to alleviate their sense of blame. This has been extensively discussed as the beneficial effects of an illness diagnosis by Grunebaum and Chasin (1978). They suggest that in some cases, a pathological label such as 'depression' can generate a sense of relief that helps to mitigate cycles of blaming and anguished searching for responsibility. They also argue that families employ various explanations to account for problems:

> In some families, the situation for some may be better for all if a member is labelled as psychotic in the health frame rather than stubborn in the moral frame.
>
> (1978: 454)

This view seeks to consider that illness labelling can function to alleviate blame from seeing a member as 'obnoxious and intolerable' to that of 'being ill and in need of help'. However, alongside the sense of relief for family members can be a related closure (Kleinman 1988; Crix et al. 2012) whereby alternative and familial explanations are eliminated. This may not have serious consequences if 'ill' is seen as a condition that is relatively temporary and subject to amelioration, but unfortunately it implies a longer-term, lifelong disability. Typically, this is seen to require medication in the form of psychoactive drugs.

Breggin and Breggin (1994) suggest that psychiatric diagnoses can lack a scientific basis and pigeonhole children. Instead, where possible, we should attempt an individual-oriented approach where we try to understand and meet the psychosocial and educational needs of each individual child. Breggin and Breggin go on to argue that associated with a diagnosis is likely to be recourse to long-term, if not permanent, psychoactive medication. Similarly, in my research on ADHD, I frequently observed a dynamic in which mothers, in particular, felt caught between the competing demands of school, partner and their child.

> **Research interview 1.2: Responding to ADHD**
>
> The following is an illustrative dialogue based on research I supervised as part of a project exploring how families made sense of the problems that had resulted from what had been diagnosed as ADHD (Lewis-Morton et al. 2014). What follows is a typical conversation in the families responding to a question about how they explain and try to deal with what they regarded to be characteristic symptoms of ADHD exhibited by their son, Ben.
>
> **Mother:** 'We try and keep things calm, don't we, Ben?'
>
> **Ben:** 'Yeah, but it doesn't help when grandad shouts at me.'
>
> **Mother:** 'Well, he doesn't really shout . . .'
>
> **Ben:** 'Yes, he does, he keeps telling me not to touch anything in the front room.'
>
> **Mother:** 'Well, I'm trying to keep things as calm as I can . . .'
>
> **Ben:** 'Grandad winds me up.'
>
> **Mother:** 'I don't think he means to . . .'
>
> **Ben:** 'Then why does he do it?'
>
> **Mother:** 'Well this is a bit of a surprise to me – I thought you liked him living with us?'<laughs>
>
> **Ben:** 'I don't.'
>
> **Mother:** 'Oh, OK. Are you sure you don't?'
>
> **Ben:** 'I'm sure!'
>
> Source: Adapted from author's personal clinical work and research.

It appeared repeatedly in these research interviews with parents, as with Ben's mother (and similarly with other parents in my wider research samples and clinical experience), that mothers frequently attempted to consider and eliminate alternative possible explanations for Ben's behaviour. Instead, there was a momentum towards attributing everything she regarded as problematic to his ADHD diagnosis. In this extract, this appeared to have been driven by her feeling triangulated – caught in the middle of conflicts in the family. (In this case, this was between her son and his grandfather.) In this illustrative research interview extract, Ben expresses that he does not get on with his grandfather. His mother understandably finds this difficult to accept since she wants to be close to both her son and her father and wants to believe that difficulties in their relationship are not causally linked with or contributing to Ben's diagnosed condition. Reassurance from a professional that the child's problems might be due to an organic condition, treatable with medication, can be seen to have a strong appeal. Some of the alternatives are that Adam is a wilfully difficult boy, that the stepfather is not a good parent and, by implication, that she has 'got it wrong' as a mother for raising a 'difficult' boy and choosing an unsuitable stepfather to satisfy her own 'selfish' needs.

Therapy extract 1.3: How questions are perceived

The process whereby blame is managed by recourse to diagnosis is not a linear process of just the parents labelling a child. It can also actively involve the young person in the family. Returning to Kathy and her parents, who we met in Therapy extract 1.2, we can see how the use of a diagnosis to detour blame can be introduced as much by the child or person displaying the problems as the other family members. This passage illustrates how the parents may feel a sense of preoccupying blame for having caused their daughter's problems with eating and that professionals are implying this in their questions.

George: 'You know, we didn't know what we'd done wrong, if we were guilty, and I wonder whether other people felt the same way . . .'

Mandy: 'That's the way you do feel. You stop and think, "is it what we did?"'

Kathy: 'They didn't make you feel guilty though, you felt guilty.'

George: 'Well, some of the questions made you feel guilty . . .'

Kathy: 'When I was in hospital, one of the nurses was telling me that someone they had in there was diagnosed as anorexic and then, when they did a brain scan, she had a tumour on part of her brain and once they took it away she was eating normally. And the nurse who was talking to me reckons that proves it's just something in your brain.'

Kathy, appearing to sense her parents' distress, steps into this process to tell the story of a tumour as appearing to have caused anorexia. In supporting this view, she can be seen to be trying to protect her parents from feelings of blame. An illness diagnosis, a recourse to the medical model, also protects Kathy from an implication that *she* is to blame.

RD: 'Looking back, what were your memories of mealtimes?'

> **Kathy:** 'Um. When I was very young, I hated them, really. I was so fussy. I used to give most of it to the cat . . . very fussy . . . I can only remember one roast dinner, which I was so annoyed to have to go to because I was playing outside and I would prefer to be playing than eating that, and then I'd be left there with "you've gotta eat your meat". And everyone would be on my back with "oh, you've gotta eat your greens". I was so fussy, wasn't I?'
>
> *Source:* Adapted from author's personal clinical work and research.

An alternative to an illness label may be the implication that a child is wilfully manipulative, destructive, difficult and causing problems in the family. This can be accompanied by a discourse that it is related to personality traits, in this case that Kathy was a fussy person. Kathy checks for confirmation about this with her parents, seeking reassurance that she really was fussy. However, this position, though taking away some of the blame from the parents, also places it back on Kathy. Families can be seen to be caught in a catch-22 dilemma: to blame themselves is painful, but an alternative to blame their daughter is also painful. Possibly, one of the reactions of professionals is that in wanting to absolve both of them – the child and parent – from blame, the notion that it is an illness is constructed. Now no one is blamed – it is just an illness. An unfortunate consequence of this approach is that it can set the family on a path where the idea of their problems as being a product of an illness becomes the dominant or even the exclusive explanation. This has a range of negative implications, for example that, as in Kathy's case, her position of being caught up (triangulated) in the conflicts between her parents is not addressed. Without recognising the potential influence of this, it increasingly focuses attention on her 'eating problems' and there is the risk that Kathy is, in a sense, compelled to maintain, or even escalate, the problems in order to ameliorate the tensions between her parents. She remarked in one interview how she felt that her 'anorexia' ensured that her parents stayed in communication with each other and they did not argue so much for fear that it might make her 'illness' worse. In fact, her parents agreed to engage in marital therapy and, as they were able to resolve some of their problems, Kathy's eating problems decreased. Of course, it is important to recognise that her parents were desperately anxious that she was becoming 'ill' and struggled to find ways to help her. In my experience, it is important to be sympathetic to the parent's explanation that their child has an 'illness' but at the same time to gently support and encourage exploration of alternative, relational factors that might be relevant.

Relational approaches and the relief of guilt: The narrative response

The outcome of the boiling pot of emotions, pain, hurt and anger in families can be a tendency to search for narratives that do not blame the parents or the child or young person: maybe it all goes back to their early years, maybe it is their temperament (bad blood) and, most compellingly for many families, that they have a form of dysfunction or illness. The idea that families hold a range of competing narratives regarding the nature of their problems is, unsurprisingly, most commonly associated with the narrative school of family therapy (White and Epston 1990). This views each family as unique and each member's story as equally valid – as one among many possible constructions of their lives. However, it also recognises that dominant narratives may take hold, for example illness and genetically based theories of anorexia or ADHD. In my experience, this is frequently the case and parents come to desperately hold to a view that the problems are due to some form of illness. This raises problems for how to work alongside a family and develop a trusting relationship with them when we hold a contrasting formulation to their preferred one. As Friedlander et al. wrote:

> If therapists want to avoid confronting their clients' versions of reality, what should they do when family members engage in mutual blame? Indeed, the expression of blame provides therapists who espouse a 'not-knowing, non-expert' ideology with a curious dilemma since it is generally agreed and has been empirically demonstrated that blaming conversations are not healthy ones.
>
> (2000: 139)

In Carl's case (Therapy extract 1.1), some candidates for labels might be personality disorder, sociopathic personality or ADHD. We should also note that Carl starts to buy into diagnosis in his remark that 'I push people away', implying perhaps that he thinks there is something wrong with him and, combined with the diagnosis identifying something intrinsic to him, there is little he can do to help this.

Next, we will consider how family therapists and families have sought to explain problems in the family unit: the dominant constellations of explanations.

Dominant constellations of explanations

The development of SFTs represented a major step in how we understand problems and difficulties. A key change was in the idea that problems do not reside *inside* people, are not simply reducible to biologically based 'illnesses', but instead arise out of *patterns of interactions* in families (Watzlawick, Weakland and Fisch 1974; Dallos and Draper 2015). Central to this perspective was the idea that people in families and other established relationships are continually influencing each other. No one person is seen to have control of this process, to be liable to blame or as solely responsible for the patterns that develop. SFTs increasingly came to develop a focus on the patterning of actions in families, holding the view that these were driven by the family members' understanding and explanations of their problems. These changes were fuelled by social constructionist perspectives, which held that the stories we developed about our lives do not merely describe our experience but construct the choices we make. This led to the idea that the explanations and stories we hold are shaped by dominant ideas that are held in our culture (White 1995; Gergen 1999). In my work with families and in research conversations with them, I have discerned a number of core explanations that families consider and that shape the members' conversations with each other. Their understandings can be seen to arise from their family histories over generations, their own life experiences and, importantly, the dominant ideas in their culture. The following list is not exhaustive but represents some of the dominant constellations of explanations that they employ:

1. *That the difficult actions represent some form of wilful action.* This frequently involves negative views, for example that 'he is trying to intimidate me', 'she is being manipulative', 'he is attention seeking' or 'she is thoughtless and disregarding of other people's feelings'. These carry a strong sense that the person is responsible and even sometimes that they need to be disciplined or punished for their 'bad' behaviour.
2. *That the difficulties are caused by some form of dispositional or personality factors, which may be inherited.* For example, that 'she is highly strung', 'he is very extravert', 'she is boisterous' or 'he has an addictive personality'. These are typically less blaming, and responsibility is softened by implication that it is not their fault that they were born this way. Sometimes parents describe how a child takes after their dad or is just like their grandmother, that there is something in the family genes.
3. *That there are psychological processes or traumas and events that are causing or triggering their actions.* For example, that a child has been bullied at school, experiences a rejection or is struggling with school work. The events can be relatively immediate (e.g. what happened at school today) or more distant in terms of their influence (e.g. best friend moved away last year).
4. *That there are relevant relational or family processes.* For example, that the child may be responding to the parents' arguments, conflicts between siblings or communicational problems in the family. This may also contain ideas of poor or inappropriate parenting, which in turn may trigger explanations of why this might be the case, for instance that 'we were distracted by Father's illness', 'we were too concerned with our work' or 'we became parents too early'.
5. *That the problems are due to some form of underlying pathology or illness.* This is perhaps the most common or pervasive set of explanations. The lexicon of diagnostic labels has expanded dramatically – for example, DSM-5 contains over 300 diagnostic codes. Searching for biologically based explanations is also widely featured in the media and is supported by the pharmaceutical industries in advertising drugs to cure depression, anxiety and psychosis, many of which have become common knowledge (e.g. Prozac).

It is likely that families go through the gamut of these potential explanations and we might expect that the diagnosis of an underlying 'illness' is a last resort. However, it is also becoming increasingly evident that labelling and diagnosis have become so pervasive that in some instances they may arise very early on in families' considerations rather than occurring subsequent to the gradual elimination of other explanations. There may also be significant differences between family members regarding which of these explanations they prefer.

Such differences in how family members understand their difficulties has been the foundation of many schools of family therapy. For example, in relation to eating disorders, Minuchin (1974) suggested that frequently parents displayed widely different ideas about the cause of their child's refusal to eat. He argued that this was not simply a response to the diagnosed illness of anorexia but that the parents' conflictual explanations led to inconsistent attempts to assist and help the child to manage their life. Not infrequently, one parent argued that the child was upset or ill and needed sensitive understanding. In contrast, another parent would suggest that the child needed firm guidance, clarity and a demand to eat, suggesting that they were otherwise at grave risk. This in turn could be experienced as confusing and served to escalate the difficulties.

Summary and reflections

An unfortunate consequence of developments in SFTs has been that sometimes parents come to regard this framework as 'blaming' them. Drawing on the ideas of John Byng-Hall (1995) and Tomm (1988), this chapter suggested that in Minuchin's (1974) example, both parents are acting out of good intentions – they want the best for their child, but unfortunately what they are trying to do is not working as they would wish.

Much of my work has been with families where the focus of the concern – the 'identified patient', to use the professional language – has been a child. The experiences of the child, and specifically their ideas about blame and responsibility, can often become invisible. In some ways, displaying a problem may constitute a removal from the sphere of consideration. Again, this may be well-intentioned – for example, they are too upset or 'ill' to be able to give an account or offer an explanation of their problems. One young woman who had been engaging in self-harming responded to a question in a research interview with me about her explanations of why she self-harmed by saying, 'Well, if I knew why I was self-harming, I wouldn't be doing it, would I?'

This may seem a self-evident statement, but it can also be seen to reveal many layers. Alongside such statements, young people often tell me that parents and others 'don't listen to [them]', so they give up trying to say what is going on. Sometimes children also tell me that in their families the parents are often angry, upset and distressed with each other – and so preoccupied with their own relationship that they disappear and the children 'become invisible'. Family therapy approaches have likewise discussed how such relational contexts shape and constrain what children feel they are able to say. In more extreme situations, for example where there is violence in the family, children might feel fear and dare not articulate their sense of who might be responsible or to blame events in the family, including violence of abuse towards them. Apart from differences within families, there are a variety of influences that shape the paths that these thoughts and feelings take and how they develop, escalate or attenuate. For example, grandparents, uncles and aunties, close friends, and even neighbours often have opinions and ideas about the family's dynamics. Not infrequently, I hear that grandparents take a view that a child showing problems needs 'clear guidance and discipline'. In contrast, the parents may be concerned that they are seeing the emergence of some form of illness or diagnosable dysfunction. These differences of opinion can foster tensions and anxieties that contribute to an escalation of problems.

2 The dominance of psychiatry: Diagnosis and formulation

Introduction

> This chapter will explore some of the assumptions of diagnosis and the functions these serve for families and professionals. It will suggest that *formulation* offers an alternative to diagnosis and that systemic family therapy (SFT) embodies one of the most valid alternatives to the medically oriented diagnosis. The chapter will explore how the issue of blame operates differently in relation to diagnosis and formulation and how the latter offers a less-blaming orientation. The chapter will outline SFT formulation and offer some critiques of SFT models that can appear to be family-blaming. It will discuss how this sense of blaming may make family members vulnerable to embracing psychiatric diagnosis instead. The idea that diagnosis offers a temporary sense of relief from blame will be explored along with potential disadvantages in the shutting down of alternative understandings and avenues for change.

History of diagnosis and formulation

When family therapy arose in the late 1950s, it was heralded to offer a major philosophical and moral position regarding the conceptualisation and treatment of what had come to be called 'mental health problems'. It aimed to shift the focus from diagnosing individuals to understanding clinical problems as issues in living together with our intimate family members. It has therefore had a somewhat uncomfortable co-existence alongside the process of diagnoses, which, rather than abating in the light of SFT theories, has expanded almost exponentially. The range of diagnosable conditions in the fifth edition of the *Diagnostic and Statistical Manual of Mental Disorders* (DSM-5) is in the region of 330 and appears to expand with each revision.

Diagnosis obviously has a long and respected tradition in medicine. There are many examples of diagnosis but to take one: the diagnosis of cholera involved identifying a consistent set of symptoms. In particular, cholera-related diarrhoea comes on suddenly and may quickly cause dangerous fluid loss – as much as a quart (about 1 litre) an hour – and has a pale, coconut, milky consistency. Nausea and vomiting occur, especially in the early stages of cholera, and may persist for hours at a time. Dehydration can develop within hours after the onset of cholera symptoms. Signs and symptoms of cholera include: dehydration irritability, lethargy, sunken eyes, a dry mouth, extreme thirst, dry shrivelled skin that's slow to bounce back when pinched into a fold, little or no urine output, low blood pressure, and arrhythmia. This profile constitutes a pretty clear and easily measurable set of symptoms. Importantly, it is also associated with a clear idea of *causation*, discovered by John Snow in 1954, namely that it is a bacterial disease usually spread through contaminated water. Treatment is also clear and effective. The development of sanitation and clean water supplies has virtually eliminated cholera from many parts of the world except where there are wars, extreme poverty or similar challenges.

Since the science of medicine has produced astonishing results and saved millions of lives, it is understandable that many believe this highly impressive medical approach, involving accurate diagnosis, could be applied to our understanding and treatment of mental distress. The framework of identifying clearly observable and causal factors that create various problems has been transported from medicine into the realm of psychology and human mental experience. Central to this was the development of the concept of 'mental health', which suggests that mental states can similarly be described and understood within a concept of health. This implies the idea of a 'healthy' mind or healthy mental states as opposed to unhealthy ones, which leads to the view that certain types of mental experience become designated as 'unhealthy'. For example, bizarre or delusional thoughts. This approach equates aspects of human existence – the mind, emotions, even what used to be called the soul – with medical models. It is as if we are waiting, as with cholera, to discover the treatable bacteria that will help eliminate mental ill health. Hopes were raised that such breakthroughs would occur when it was discovered that syphilis was caused by a bacterium that was treatable with penicillin. The symptoms were initially thought to be intimately related with the mental symptoms of psychosis – obsessions and fixed ideas, phobia, increasing anxiety and risk of suicide, all of which were responsible for large numbers of mental hospital (or asylum) admissions. Soon, it was believed, similar causes would be discovered for all the other forms of clinical problems (Sadock and Sadock 2010). However, this is arguably putting the cart before the horse because we are assuming that all problems of the mind, emotions and so on can be viewed as a form of 'illness'. This is to suggest that they are similar to physical illness in having a clear biological cause, profile of symptoms, predictable progression and duration, and admit of prescriptions for treatment or cure. For example, in the diagnoses of cholera and syphilis, the reason for the symptoms is clarified by the diagnoses. In psychiatric diagnoses, in contrast, the diagnoses typically only fulfil the first part, that is to say a description of the symptoms, not the reason for the symptoms.

The problems with diagnosis

We should note that in the history of now well-understood illnesses, such as cholera, there have been widely differing explanations of and folklore around the causes and suggested remedies. Many of the older remedies were based on the miasma theory – that the illness was due to a noxious form of air. Some also believed that abdominal chilling made one more susceptible, so flannel and cholera belts were routine in army kits. *Mothers' Remedies*, by Ritter (1917), even listed tomato syrup as a remedy! It was clear that these remedies did not work and eventually obvious what the causation and treatment should be. But the felt requirement to move beyond a description of the symptoms to a clear understanding of aetiology and the application of aetiological treatments does not apply for the majority of the DSM-5 diagnostic categories (Boyle 1990; Timimi, Gardner and McCabe 2011).

Conditions such as attention deficit hyperactivity disorder (ADHD), depression, anorexia, schizophrenia and even autism do not have a clear, biologically based causes. Much of the research suggests that there is a genetic and inherited component to such conditions and the most prevalent view is that people have a genetically based *vulnerability*. This proposed vulnerability is typically accompanied by an assumption that eventually such clarity of causation and treatment will occur and is in fact just around the corner (Boyle 1990; Bentall 2003; Boyle 2011; Boyle and Johnstone 2014).

Though this concept of a genetically based vulnerability has some appeal, it leads to an assumption that it has been reliably proven that such vulnerabilities exist. This is not in fact the case. For example, it is suggested that autism is based on the interaction between a range of vulnerabilities that make children susceptible to certain environmental stressors, but it is not at all clear what these vulnerabilities are. It is also unclear whether vulnerabilities have developed due to various psycho-social process, including stress and trauma. One of the difficulties that bedevils these issues is that the diagnosis of these conditions is neither clear nor consistent. The issue is not that the various symptoms do not exist but that it is an assumption that the grouping of a range of symptoms represent some distinct medical condition, for example autism or ADHD. The diagnosis leads to an assumption that something (e.g. ADHD) exists over and beyond a cluster of apparently connected symptoms. In fact, the diagnosis is merely a grouping of these symptoms in a particular way, it is an idea not a proven condition. Researchers differ in how clearly the diagnostic criteria are used and these alter regularly, like shuffling a pack of cards in different ways. For example, Asperger's has been dropped from DSM-5 because it could not be reliably diagnosed and it was not clear that it represented a clear sub-type from autism. This also leaves many families and people with the diagnosis confused, since they have come to think about themselves within this framework, which like a wisp of smoke has now vanished in front of their eyes. In short, we do not know whether these conditions do have biological bases, but the medical diagnostic discourse assumes that this evidence is imminently forthcoming in future research (Timimi and Timimi 2015). Further, we do not know whether the grouping of the symptoms together into clusters with names like autism or ADHD is meaningful and valid and represents something that exists over and beyond a cluster of symptoms. A typical research approach is to compare groups, for example children with a diagnosis of ADHD and a control group who do not have this diagnosis, and try to identify whether there are differences in various aspects of brain functioning. As an example, a study by Thapar et al. (2013) claimed to find significant differences in rare chromosomal deletions and duplications in ADHD. They found that 15 per cent of the ADHD-diagnosed group had large and rare variations in their DNA, compared with 7 per cent in the control group. This was statistically significant, but how is it that 85 per cent of children diagnosed with ADHD did not have this abnormality and why did the 7 per cent in the control group not have ADHD? This is just one example, but similar claims that a neurological basis has been found on such controversial evidence are rife. To have found a clinically meaningful causal link, we would expect that something like 90 per cent of the children with the diagnosis of ADHD would have this abnormality and then we would be curious why even a small percentage did not show this. Close inspection of the neurological evidence for conditions such as ADHD and autism shows a similar pattern of over-exaggerated, inconsistent or even erroneous findings and conclusions (Timimi and Timimi 2015; Simon 2019).

Related to this question are wider ones regarding *co-morbidity*, namely that the symptoms that are taken to constitute various form of diagnosis are distinct. For example, autism and anorexia both typically also involve symptoms of anxiety, while autism and obsessive-compulsive disorders (OCD) share a preoccupation with details, routines and anxieties regarding uncertainty. This critique of diagnosis is not intended to suggest that the various symptoms are not 'real'. The conditions of distress and suffering are real but lumping them together into diagnostic categories might not add anything to our understanding of the mechanisms of their causation, nor help to guide their treatment (Boyle 1990; Bentall 2003; Timimi and Timimi 2015).[4]

Diagnosis operates so that the reality of the symptoms that constitute a diagnosis are used to imply that a condition such as depression, bipolar disorder or ADHD really exists. There is then a circular argument that this condition (e.g. depression) somehow causes the symptoms (e.g. low mood). Nested in here is a muddled assumption that the second two features of a diagnosis – the causes and the appropriate treatments – are known and have an objective status. In fact, they are neither known nor do they have an objective status, and it is more conjecture or a wish that the understanding of the neurobiology is just around the corner. This can also be described as a process of 'reification' whereby something that is a proposition or a theory takes in the form of a substantiated concrete reality, ideas, theories and conjectures become real things. Unfortunately for family therapy, an implication is that these conditions assume the form of realities in the lives of individuals and their families. This can imply, as we saw in the previous chapter, that families start to exclude other possibilities, such as that the problems may be due to traumatic

---

[4] There is not room to fully develop the critique of diagnosis here, so I recommend following the critiques that have been fully articulated by Timimi, Bentall and Boyle cited here.

experiences or family dynamics. As White and Epston (1990) describe, these can become dominant narratives that exclude others and stop the search for other possible explanations. They can even encourage narratives that suggest that even to look for other explanations, for example, that autism may be influenced by family dynamics, is disrespectful blaming and should be discouraged, excluded or even framed as unprofessional. These dominant narratives can also promote 'in-the-corner' lifestyles, for example a belief that one is schizophrenic and this will reduce and restrict aspects of one's life. This has been considered in terms of self-fulfilling and family-fulfilling prophecies. Once a person and their family come to accept and believe in the diagnosis, they may come to increasingly view all of the person's actions in this way. The diagnosis thereby appears to gather supporting evidence. Moreover, once one believes one *is* the diagnosis, one may inadvertently become drawn into acting like or performing being, for example, a schizophrenic. What might this look like? There are various depictions of conditions such as schizophrenia in the media – for example, hearing voices, hallucinating or acting in bizarre ways – and unfortunately often depictions as being dangerous. Perhaps Ken Kesey's book and film, *One Flew Over the Cuckoo's Nest*, nicely captures the extent to which illness identities become absorbed. After encouraging his fellow inmates in the asylum to escape, Randle McMurphy discovers that he is the only involuntary patient – the others could walk out free at any time.

In my work with families with a child with a diagnosis of autism, a process of absorption can be seen. For example, one mother told me that her son's brain was 'wired differently'. Also, I frequently hear the diagnosis being generalised to other family members – for example that they now understand that the child's father and uncle 'has it'. In effect, it becomes a pervasive and inclusive lens through which people's actions become interpreted. The young people I work with also increasingly come to describe themselves as autistic or 'aspy' (Asperger's) and explain their difficulties in terms of what they understand to be indications of the condition. As an example, they may say that they are suffering because of 'sensory overload' as part of their 'sensory issues'. An alternative explanation might be that they are experiencing emotional stress in a similar way that most people would in the circumstances they are describing.

Self and family diagnosis

Frequently, the considerations regarding diagnosis focus on the role of the medical profession and pharmaceutical companies in perpetuating and escalating the development of diagnosis – but it can be seen as a much more subtle and complex process. For individuals and their families, there may be numerous reasons for seeking medical diagnoses. As we considered in the previous chapter, families may feel blame and guilt over the problems they are experiencing. But even more broadly, problems that arise in our lives may be highly confusing, distressing, debilitating and difficult to understand. A medical diagnosis can help to give some sense and meaning to what might appear to be a confusing mess of complaints and symptoms that are ted or mysterious. A diagnosis can appear to transform this swarm ⸺oubles into something organised and understandable.

⸺ illustrate the implications for family therapists of families seeking a ⸺.∪ical diagnosis, allow me to recount an anecdote from some psychiatry registrars whose research I was supervising. There was a mother who was seeking a prescription of methylphenidate (Ritalin) for her adolescent son who she was experiencing as troublesome. After examining the boy, they explained to her that his condition was very borderline but also that he was displaying facial tics, possibly related to Tourette's Syndrome, which were counter-indicated for use of methylphenidate. In these circumstances, they did not want to offer a prescription. The mother listened patiently and then enquired if, however, it would be possible to prescribe 'just a lower dosage'. They were not highly medically oriented psychiatrists but described how they frequently felt pressure from families to offer a diagnosis and medical prescriptions as the solution.

Diagnosis frequently starts with reference to some knowledge about different kinds of psychiatric conditions. It is now easy to read up about these on the internet, to watch YouTube clips of 'sufferers' talking about their condition and even professionals explaining, in authoritative ways, what the symptoms of particular mental illnesses are. This may mean that individuals and families are not predominantly seeking an *assessment* for a diagnosis but *confirmation* of a diagnosis that they have already formed. When this is given added legitimacy by a medical practitioner or person in authority, often through the internet, it is not surprising to see people embracing medicalisation. These arguments are not intended to put all of the responsibility for diagnosis back on individuals and their families. It is a surprise to many people that, for example, what they assume to be neutral websites and forums for people with conditions such as psychosis or ADHD are supported financially by pharmaceutical companies (Bentall 2003; Timimi 2005; Timimi, Gardner and McCabe 2011). They may also contain a preponderance of parents who have developed, as a response to their own family dynamics, a commitment to medical models, producing a kind of echo chamber that reinforces these models in website visitors. The process of making choices is thereby shaped for people in ways of which they may be unaware. It is perhaps salutary to note that various form of media, including television, tend to show a preference for medical models of clinical conditions and rarely consider alternatives to diagnosis in the discussion of mental health issues. The idea that diagnosis is about something 'real' seems to exist as the basic starting position for consideration of clinical problems. A powerful example is the rise of the diagnosis of adult ADHD (Timimi 2005). In this case, the diagnosis is embraced and promoted by the people who receive it and appears to be sought out by the very people to whom it is to be applied. This may signal a shift to a consumerism of diagnosis, with people attempting to attain their diagnosis of choice (Conrad and Potter 2000).

Illness versus disability

Illness and medical models imply that problems can have predictable pathways and timescales for recovery. For example, if I have the flu, a recognised illness,

I expect that I will exhibit certain symptoms and recover in a few weeks. However, medical diagnosis of mental conditions is often closer to a *disability* model than an illness or medical model: many of the diagnoses suggest that the condition is genetic and lifelong and that there is little prospect of recovery (Timimi, Gardner and McCabe 2011). (In fact, in some cases, such as schizophrenia, it was assumed that if there was a full recovery, it cannot have been schizophrenia in the first place! [Boyle 1990; Keen 1999]) This has also been seen in the case of autism where Rutter et al. (2007) found high incidence of autism diagnoses in Romanian orphanages. However, when removed from these deprived environments, the children significantly recovered. This became known as 'quasi' (as opposed to 'real') autism.

The person and their family are informed that it is a lifelong condition and that what they will receive will not be therapy, or even treatment, but management of the symptoms. This usually involves the use of medication, which it is hoped will produce some 'control' of the symptoms – though this is not control in the sense of some agency but control, in effect, from the outside by the influence of medication that is administered. This is problematic for two key reasons, however. First, these regimes often further curtail any sense of control, since a frequent issue is that the person should 'comply' with their medication. Second, it becomes the task of parents to help ensure this compliance, while raising questions about other possible causes can be seen to interfere with assisting with this compliance since it might confuse the issue. Family members may even feel that they will get a 'telling off' from the professional or other family members if they dare to question the use of medication, as it may 'confuse' the person.

Coming to accept a diagnosis, therefore, may imply that the person adopts a relatively depressed view of their life and opportunities (Bassman 2007). It typically implies that the person and their family accept a gloomy outlook with the implication of lifelong dependency on psychiatric treatment, use of medication and little chance of recovery from the problem. It has been described as a process of loss or grieving that the person and their family may experience (Boyle 1990; Bassman 2007). There have been attempts to counter this by suggesting, for example, that autism is not a disorder but a state of neuroatypicality that contains some positive features that should be celebrated. Likewise, there have been attempts to consider schizophrenia as susceptibility to hearing voices rather than some form of underlying illness. Developing such arguments might imply that we do not need these diagnostic labels. For some, rejecting the diagnosis may be understood as a positive way of coping with the implications of the diagnosis for personal identity.

Formulation and systemic family therapy

All forms of therapy have ideas about how problems arise and what can be done to assist people to feel less troubled and more able to live fulfilling lives. SFT offers a way of looking at problems and distress that differs from other approaches. Instead of having the person and their internal states as the initial focus, SFT views distress and problems experienced as intimately bound up with *relationships*[5]. As it has evolved, there have also been changes and shifts within SFT as to how we explain problems. In the first phase, problems and their resolutions were seen in terms of family organisational structures and patterns of behaviour. There was later, in the second and third phases, a shift to a focus on the creation of meanings and culturally shared language processes.

How does such understanding or theory inform our clinical practice? There have been extensive debates in the psychotherapies concerning whether clinical practice involves intuition and can become overly intellectualised with theory or, conversely, overly vague and in need of the precision of theory to guarantee effectiveness. This interface between theory, research evidence and clinical practice has been labelled *formulation*. More specifically in SFT, it has been referred to as *hypothesising* and later as *curiosity* (Eells 1997; Green and Latchford 2012; Johnstone and Dallos 2013).

Formulation can be broadly defined as the process of:

- putting together an understanding of the difficulties;
- combining information about the problems;
- observation;
- conversations with the family together with theory;
- clinical experience; and
- the therapist's own personal experiences.

Essentially, this formulation puts together a local theory about the causes of the problems, what may be maintaining them and what might assist in facilitating change. Formulation therefore helps to create explanations and ideas or guides for therapists' actions. This emphasis has also been spurred on by the guidelines that have evolved on clinical practice for a variety of physical and psychological conditions. For example, recent guidelines have appeared for the diagnosis and treatment of ADHD (The National Institute for Health and Care Excellence [NICE] 2018). The guidelines based on formulation recommend a tailored approach whereby treatment is specific to each unique case. The guidelines vary in the advice offered regarding assessment and diagnosis. In some cases, the assessment is recommended simply to be conducted by a consultant psychiatrist, which appears to frame this condition as largely within a medical domain (see NICE [2014] guidelines for psychosis and schizophrenia). These guidelines have predominantly been based on an illness or medical model and feature the use of diagnosis to detect the presence of symptoms to draw up a diagnosis. In contrast, formulation does not assume an underlying medical illness, but attempts to provide an analysis of a wide range of potentially relevant social, psychological and biological factors (The Division of Clinical Psychology 2011; Johnstone and Dallos 2013). At a simple level, formulation can become an attempt to match the treatment to the type of problem based on the research evidence. In practice, it is much more complex than this and formulation embodies

---

[5] See Chapter 1 for more on the role of relationships and mutual influence in SFT.

the idea of fitting the treatment closely to an ongoing detailed exploration with families of their problems. Formulation also helps to clarify communication and understanding between various professionals and between them and families. Importantly, formulation offers an alternative to psychiatric diagnosis. It instead offers an understanding based on psychological processes, including thoughts and feelings, and the impact of environmental events.

It is increasingly recognised that formulation needs to be considered as a dynamic and collaborative process whereby the therapist and family work together to co-construct a shared understanding of the difficulties (Green and Latchford 2012; Johnstone and Dallos 2013; Hudson, Dallos and McKenzie 2017). Both the therapist and the family have their formulations about the nature and causes of the problems, and many families come to therapy with entrenched ideas influenced by medical theories. For example, families claim that their child 'has' ADHD and this is what is 'causing' the problems. There may also be differences among family members about what the problems and causes are. A typical case with reconstituted families may be that the step-parent sees their partner's child as deliberately difficult and spoilt, as opposed to the child's birth mother who sees their difficulties as related to the stress and losses they have witnessed and the conflicts they have experienced through separation and divorce. Families may attempt to resolve such differences through recourse to a medical illness model. Siblings can adopt an interesting position in relation to this and be much more likely to view their brother or sister as responsible, manipulative and deserving of censure or punishment for their actions.

Therapy extract 2.1: Differences of opinion

Here is an extract of a family discussing the older sister Rose's symptoms of fibromyalgia. Lucy is the younger sister and Ryan is Rose's boyfriend. This therapy extract illustrates, somewhat humorously, the differences of opinion that we encounter in therapy and that are also present in professional systems.

Lucy: 'Like, one second she's really happy and then really moody and then like being horrible to all my friends, so I don't want to invite anyone over ever 'cause she'll—she's always horrible.'

Rose: 'And what about me being [gestures inverted commas with fingers] "lazy", as you call it?'

Lucy: 'Yeah, well, some days you're like, "arhh I can't move". And if Ryan calls, you're like, "Oh, I'm going to see Ryan".'

Rose: 'I'm not always like that.'

Lucy: 'Yeah, you are, so she's—if there's something to do with Ryan, "oh I'm better now".'

Source: Reproduced with permission and adapted from Crix et al. 2012: 18

Formulation typically takes place in a context where colleagues who work together may hold different theories and ideas about problems. For example, psychologists, psychiatrists and social workers frequently work alongside each other in clinical work with children but, in order to facilitate communication, it is important to be clear and explicit about one's different understandings and explanations. Often in multidisciplinary family therapy teams, my experience has been that, though myself and the other team members share a systemic perspective, there are layers of differences shaped by our particular professional discipline. For example, one member of the team might be focused on the impact of a bereavement of one of the grandparents, another on the difficulties in communication between the parents, and another on the beliefs and explanations the family members hold about the causes of the child's difficulties in concentrating and aggressive behaviour.

Formulation allows each team member to hold their own variation of a formulation regarding a family or system, but also to move towards an understanding of points of agreement and, importantly, of difference. These differences can then be employed as useful and creative tensions rather than covert feelings and, later, obstacles to collaborative working. Formulation can be seen to offer an alternative to diagnosis in that it attempts to develop specific explanatory models for different conditions that may or may not include a focus on biological or hereditary factors. Within the psychotherapies, we can see that each holds different frameworks, which they bring to develop formulations or explanations of problems and related ideas about what treatments should follow (Johnstone and Dallos 2013).

Systemic theory: Formulation and formulating

In the rest of this chapter, I would like to focus on *systemic* formulation. Systemic theory adopts the view that problems do not reside in individuals but emerge out of the ebb and flow of family interactions. This arguably offers one of the most significant contrasts to diagnosis in that it offers a model that is neither biologically based nor exclusively focused on individual processes. Instead, it offers a map to guide and encourage systemic thinking. As we will discuss in the following chapter, systemic thinking is not predominantly the application of specific techniques but a way of thinking about problems and difficulties. One of the major developments of systemic therapy has been the extension of such thinking not only to different family problems and configurations but also to the relationships within and between organisations and agencies. The key feature of a systemic formulation is a view of problems as resulting from *interactional processes*. Systemic therapies also do not draw a simple division between assessment, formulation and treatment. Instead, these are seen as interrelated processes such that the process of exploring difficulties with a family is seen as one that fosters changes in understandings for the family and the therapists. Formulation becomes regarded as a more dynamic, ongoing and co-constructive process with families and individual members. This conceptualisation is important for the rest of this book since it raises the idea that in this dynamic, a co-constructive process of formulation and questions of blame, responsibility and accountability can be played out.

Before we pursue this further, a brief overview of the role of formulation in SFTs may be helpful. Though systemic theory always emphasises uncertainty in understanding how a system functions, the emphasis in the early models was on considering the family as an entity that was objectively distinct from the therapist – something outside oneself as the therapist that one was observing and could assess, something that could be predictably described (Dallos and Draper 2015). The purpose of formulation was seen to be to map the nature of the dysfunction, how individual problems were shaped by relational dynamics and how an understanding of this could lead to developing interventions. Included in the concept of formulation was the realisation that what one observes as a therapist is invariably influenced and coloured by one's assumptions, beliefs and prejudices. Hence, formulation was an active process of meaning-making that recognised the possibility of other ways of viewing the situation and family. Working in multidisciplinary teams, it can become apparent how our formulations are coloured by our personal experience and professional designations as formulations are discussed and shared.

Debates have raged about whether families are too complex for therapists to be able to develop causal explanations of their pathology. Historically, one approach – the *solution-focused* approach – was to develop a pragmatic stance and base interventions on what appeared to promote change, regardless of whether we understood the causes of the difficulties. Here, formulation focused not on factors within the family, but on how different interventions appeared to affect them. In effect, formulation became a *pragmatic* approach based on feedback about what effect an intervention had. If this was seen to facilitate change, it might be continued; if not, then something else could be tried. Some early approaches were not so strongly based on pragmatism as the solution-focused alternative, and a range of standardised tests measuring family function were developed. Among them were the Family Adaptability and Cohesiveness Evaluation Scale (FACES) and circumplex models of personality and emotions (Olson 1986). The aim was to assess 'dysfunctions' of family structure and process. For example, a family might be seen as lacking a clear hierarchy and decision-making capacity in the parental subsystem. Alternatively, they might be seen as caught up in a process whereby attempts by either parent to take control would be met by the other parent siding with the child. These formulations of dysfunctional structure and process would then guide the interventions specifically targeted to correct these. This early approach can be seen as a more retrospective process in which the therapist tries to develop general explanations about the family's functioning, including their connections with other systems such as education, work and social services. In contrast, a more dynamic approach was developed, which was initially referred to as 'progressive hypothesising' (Palazzoli et al. 1978: 3). This acknowledged that formulation about a family was a progressive process and that our formulations would change as new information emerged in our work with a family. The therapist aimed to maintain a stance of curiosity and openness rather than attain a definitive formulation (Cecchin 1987).

Systemic theory has evolved since its inception in the 1950s from a theory centred on a biological metaphor of families as homeostatic systems to one of families as problem-saturated linguistic systems. In short, symptoms are today seen as problems in interaction and communication between people rather than as existing within persons. Importantly, systemic approaches have increasingly come to regard all aspects of therapy as interactional and collaborative processes. Formulation, therefore, is not seen as something that the therapist does *to* the family but as something that they do *with* the family. The process of formulation is seen not as an *objective* process, but as a set of *perturbations* that start to change the family system. The questions that are asked, when and how they are asked, and ensuing conversations can prompt significant changes in families. SFTs thus make less of a distinction between assessment, formulation and intervention.

The construction of distress and deviance

Social constructionist theory and the therapies based on it also emphasise that meanings are jointly constructed in conversations. Exploring and documenting such processes has been a hallmark of family therapy, but arguably there has been little research looking at how this process happens and, importantly, how it is influenced by wider cultural discourses. There are various influential situations where families encounter and may be challenged by these discourses, or dominant constellations of beliefs and attitudes prevailing in their culture. One of these is the school situation where their child has to adapt to the expectations, rules and ideologies prevailing in the school. These in turn are shaped by what is deemed to be acceptable in any given culture: schools are prescribed the task of preparing children for entry into the wider world as acceptable citizens. There is considerable potential in this meeting between children, parents and schools for frictions and tensions. Families may adopt various strategies related to their needs and ideologies, including spending considerable sums of money to send their children to 'good' schools, which may be seen as a better fit for the needs and characteristics of their child.

Nevertheless, school (or even nursery) may be one of the first places where difference or deviance from expected norms is noticed. A child may start to be seen by some teachers as showing unusual behaviours, being too excitable, being unable to concentrate in lessons or falling behind. These signals then start to be perceived as potentially constituting a form of diagnosable illness – for example, ADHD. What should take place, I argue, is an exploration of a variety of possible causes outside of an illness or medical model, but this may be short-circuited given demands on schools, shortages of teaching staff and other pressures. Use of an accessible template or label, such as ADHD, may mean that a child is guided down a pathway towards such a diagnosis. Parents may quickly fall in line with this process, not least since one of the alternatives is that they may feel blamed as parents for failing to teach their children adequate self-control and discipline.

I have seen cases where a parent has experienced some encouragement by school to accept a diagnosis of ADHD for their child and to agree to the child going on a regime of methylphenidate. In some cases, the child becomes reluctant to take the medication because of side-effects, such as insomnia, irritability, proneness to crying, anxiousness, sadness/unhappiness and nightmares. In such instances, some parents decide not to continue with the medication but to not inform their school of this. However, on occasion, the schools report that the child's behaviour has continued to improve. This can be seen as a powerful example of a self-fulfilling prophecy process and placebo effects (Watzlawick, Weakland and Fisch 1974; Rosenthal and Jacobson 1968; Kirsch 2013). Kirsch (2013) has argued that a substantial proportion of the effects of drugs, such as methylphenidate and other medication used in psychiatry can be attributed to a placebo effect, or expectation that the drug will be helpful. It is not intended for this story to be critical of schools or to assume easy explanations, only to signal caution and encourage reflection on how unnecessary diagnostic processes and regimes of unnecessary medications may be set in place (Timimi 2002, 2005).

Pause for thought 2.1

- Consider for a few moments your own experience of use of medications to assist in relieving your physical or emotional symptoms.

Every day examples of this might be looking forward to a nice gin and tonic to help cheer us up or to wind down at the end of the day, or a coffee to help us relax. In fact, alcohol acts as depressant (increasing inhibitory neurotransmission and decreasing excitatory neurotransmission) and coffee as a stimulant. So, biochemically they should both encourage one's mood state in the opposite direction to what we are using them for. Also, their effects are influenced by where we are, perhaps a restaurant, bar or café, and who we are with. Similarly, psychotropic medications such as methylphenidate are subject to the influence of expectations of what effects they are predicted to have on the person taking them.

A second major influence on families is the medical profession. When encountering problems with one's child, it is likely that one of the first contacts will be with the family doctor or General Practitioner (GP). In the past, this may have constituted a long-lasting relationship where the family and GP knew each other. This could enable the GP to see a child's problems in the context of their knowledge of the family. For example, the GP might know that the family was generally in some state of distress due to other physical illness bereavements. They might even have ideas about the personality of the family as highly stoical and not given to a show of feelings or as anxious and frequently concerned about a wide variety of relatively minor ailments. This is less frequent in large health services where a family is less likely to see the same doctor on a regular basis. This is not to hark back to a golden age of Dr Finlay, but to suggest that a powerful and influential context exists for the formulation and more likely diagnosis of problems. In fact, intimate knowledge of a family can also be problematic. In a piece of research my colleague and I conducted, 'Pathways to Problems' (Dallos and Hamilton-Brown 2000), we heard an account from a mother where she described visiting her GP to whom she relayed her child's problems. In a friendly manner, the GP sympathetically empathised with her and said one of his children showed the same symptoms. He went on to reassure her that his child had been diagnosed with ADHD and he was pretty certain that her child had the same condition. At this point, the mother had not received a diagnosis for her child's condition and it was uncertain what the causes of the difficulties were. Given the reservations about diagnosis discussed earlier, the process of diagnosis needs to be thorough and conducted over a period of time in a variety of contexts, such as at school or in the home environment. It also needs to exclude the possibility that other factors, such as family dynamics, relationships at school, family losses and traumas, may be causal. Such apparently benevolent and benign advice can short-circuit this process and set the family on the path to the diagnosis becoming the main avenue of consideration.

Coulter and Rapley (2011) have explored the process whereby families attempt to construct meanings from their lives and distresses in interactions with professionals who may be regarded as experts in distress and problems. They suggest that parents may be caught in a trap whereby a significant body of government policy and legislation clearly imply that parents hold moral responsibility for the behaviour of their children. Contemporary legislation, like the use of parenting orders under the Crime and Disorder Act 1998, employed in cases where children act in unruly or in anti-social ways, can view parents as feckless, irresponsible, and as causing a variety of deviant and dangerous behaviours in the children. These political initiatives and policies clearly set a context whereby parents are made to feel responsible or blamed. Careful consideration is usually given in these cases, and evidence over an extended period of time is required to make such orders; however, they clearly hold a position that parents are responsible and that in some cases they are to blame and may incur punishments.[6] This diverges from the dominant therapeutic stance, which seeks not to ascribe responsibility to parents for causing conditions such as ADHD or anorexia. There are substantial debates about the extent to which parents have a role in causing these conditions. The extreme position is that they play no part in causing these conditions since they are purely manifestations of a psychiatric illness. In contrast, as in the case of anti-social behaviour, parents can be seen as having an influence and therefore *some* responsibility for such conditions. It is worth noting that Bowlby's (1969) initial work was with children who were displaying anti-social behaviours and he discovered that many experienced painful separations from their parents and a lack of attachment and care in their families. It is worth noting that therapeutic work in the context of children who engage in sexually

---

[6] Parents subject to such legislation may also be experiencing a variety of related factors, such as stress, poverty, illness and trauma from their own childhoods, all of which may contribute to their difficulties in controlling their children.

harmful behaviour is particularly likely to include consideration of the responsibility of parents, for example to comply with safeguarding measures (Dallos, Bord and McKenzie In press). Failure to do so could result in strong measures, such as removing a child into care.

Coulter and Rapley (2011) argue that there is a contradiction between common, everyday explanations of mental health problems and their causes and the reluctance of clinicians and psychotherapists to address the question of the role of families in the causation of problems, and that this adds an important layer of analysis to family therapy. In part, this can be understood in terms of a powerful backlash against research (as discussed in Chapter 1), which indicates that family dynamics have an important role in the genesis of madness and distress. Research psychologists and psychiatrists often have to tread a fine line to avoid lawsuits from family rights groups and arguably the support that these movements received from the pharmaceutical industry and mainstream medically oriented psychiatry.

At the core of the discussion about the role of family dynamics runs some important dilemmas and complexities, which unfortunately the emotions generated by the issues involved could easily obscure. One response to the concern that families may feel blamed was the move to a vulnerability–stress model. In the case of psychosis, this emphasised causation in terms of an individual's biogenetic vulnerability that could be triggered by stress and conflict (Boyle 1990; Timimi 2005; Coulter and Rapley 2011). As such, families were not implicated in *causing* the symptoms but merely as possibly *aggravating* the problems, in part because the problem (the 'illness') caused the family members so much tension and distress. Treatment consequently featured sympathising with the parents regarding the problem as a lifelong disability with which they were struggling to cope and supporting and educating them to be able to act in less critical and emotionally aroused ways. It has been suggested that this was a compromise that appeared to move away from a simple diagnostic model but on closer attention just relocated the cause of the problems as residing in the person's vulnerability (Boyle 1990; Timimi 2005; Timimi, Gardner and McCabe 2011). Given the same environment, some cope and those more vulnerable do not.

Discourses and families

Families can be seen to try to navigate forms of understanding to help guide their lives within competing accounts. Gergen (1999) argues that cultures hold shared but competing (and in some cases contradictory) discourses or sets of explanations including those regarding emotional problems and their causes. Some of these can be summarised as:

1. Focus on parents as responsible and culpable for the child's actions, especially where they contravene rules.
2. A medical discourse with a focus on individual vulnerability that is causal.
3. An emphasis on seeing the family, especially the parents, as not responsible for but instead responding to, for example, the child's biological conditions.

In relation to autism, the child's symptoms have been seen to cause high levels of mental ill health in the parents (McKenzie and Dallos 2017). This medical discourse (2), which frames the perceived problem as within the child, can shift responsibility dramatically when parents are seen to be engaging in physically or sexually abusive or irresponsible ways, producing anti-social children – the parents are then clearly seen as culpable.

Coulter and Rapley (2011) have examined conversations with families that indicate that the parents were fully aware of the dominant lay views of parental responsibility but employed a variety of strategies to soften the sense of self-blame that would apply. For example, they describe one key strategy directly connected to avoiding these views of parental responsibility that consists of a statement that since the parents are not experts, they do not know what caused their child's problems. In this, they avoid absorbing the lay moral positions of responsibility and potential blame for their child's psychosis and bow to professional knowledge, which is more unsure of the parent's role in causation and more likely to hold individualistic, 'illness' interpretations.

As always, there can be a danger in such discussions of the therapist appearing antagonistic to families. This is not intended in this book; on the contrary, it needs to be noted and applauded, given these dilemmas for families, how remarkable it is that, not only do they agree to participate in family therapy when directed to do so, but that many families voluntarily seek family therapy. This suggests that, despite the dominant professional clinical views, which favour a medical diagnosis, many parents are also willing to consider alternative explanations and may even show some resistance to the attendant labelling of their child (e.g. as 'autistic'). In my view, parents here show an impressive resistance to exclusively accepting the dominant medical discourse. They are often willing to consider that they may have some responsibility and to consider ways of changing their relationships with each other in the hope that it will help their child. This is not to be equated with a sense that parents, in doing this, are negligent or impervious to considering that their child may need assistance, for example in school, and that they may benefit from a robust assessment of their difficulties. What is at issue is this: the situation here is not equivalent to parents resisting medical explorations and explanations of their child possibly having a condition like diabetes – to resist a medical explanation *here* could be seen as negligent and dangerous. But a condition such as 'ADHD' is not of the same type as a condition such as diabetes, both in its evidence base and in the issues attendant to its labelling (e.g. how society interacts with someone with this label [see Timimi 2005]). There is no clear and uncontroversial evidence that ADHD or autism are medically based nor that medical treatments are to be preferred. Hence, what is required in clinical work is an openness to consider a range of explanations. Of course, the problems such as distress, agitation, restlessness and difficulties concentrating exist in relation to what may come to be diagnosed as ADHD and a family that refused to consider these could be regarded as negligent towards their child, but other options should remain on the table than a medical label and diagnosis. I frequently feel humbled by the openness of parents and their commitment to assisting their children by engaging in an enterprise in which they risk feeling blamed and criticised, despite the reassurance of therapists that family therapy does not involve blaming. In my experience, many parents in effect still have an open mind about causation and have turned towards possible medical explanations out of desperation, as a last ditch, because no one has been able to advise what else might be helpful.

> ### Research interview 2.1: Paediatrician–parent conversation regarding assessment and diagnosis
>
> McHoul and Rapley (2005) illustrated how in conversations with a paediatrician about their child's possible ADHD, the parents attempted at many points to introduce a consideration of non-medical explanations, such as social issues at school and family dynamics, but were directed back to a medical framework. They describe, for example, how parents' descriptions of normal sibling rivalries as potentially contributing to some aspects of difficult behaviours could be largely ignored and eventually the conversation steered towards a discourse of trying medication as a sort of trial or experiment. They also describe how in this extract the paediatrician and family were operating in different conceptual frameworks.
>
> **Mother:** 'Erm, that questionnaire I filled out – it's all based on school. What's he like in the classroom . . . I can't answer that as a parent because I'm not in the classroom . . .'
>
> **Father:** 'He idolises his brother and I think part of it, he may be trying to be like his brother.'
>
> **Paediatrician:** 'Mmhm.'
>
> **Father:** 'But he doesn't hav— hasn't got the guts to do a lot of the stuff his brother does.'
>
> **Paediatrician:** 'Mmhm.'
>
> **Father:** 'Chickens out . . .'
>
> **Paediatrician:** 'Well, I mean, I'd certainly make the diagnosis of ADHD based on the questionnaires plus, um, you know, observations in the class but— and give him a trial of medication and we'll see what happens.'
>
> *Source:* Adapted from McHoul and Rapley 2005: 426

Pause for thought 2.2

- What do you think about the role of the paediatrician in this research interview?
- How do you think she would explain and justify her actions with the family?

> - What factors influence the behaviour of the paediatrician and the parents?
> - Do you know of or have you experienced any similar processes?
>
> In my teaching, I have found medical practitioners, such as paediatricians and child psychiatrists, to be thoughtful and open about the nature of problems such as ADHD. I recently discussed with a group of trainee child psychiatrists how they felt constrained by the expectation that a central part of their role was to diagnose and prescribe medication. Also, in contrast to the example given, many parents actively seek a diagnosis and, for example in relation to autism, are frequently critical of services for delays in the process of diagnosis, which can take on average about two years. It is important, therefore, in thinking about encounters like this to consider how they are shaped by wider social and political factors. Paediatricians are typically *massively* overworked and do not have time to engage in therapeutic work. Unfortunately, the lack of resources to assist families in other ways than prescribing medication may mean that their problems persist and in fact the workload of medical staff increases rather than decreases.

As you can see, the paediatrician appeared to start from a position of gathering evidence to prove that the child had ADHD, understood as a disorder. Whereas the parents wanted to consider various possibilities, which included eliminating the notion that it is ADHD and that the condition might be alleviated by other methods. At various points, the mother, for example, offered some mild criticism of the diagnostic process, such as that the assessment forms she was asked to complete asked about her son's behaviour at school and, as she explained, she could not comment (first-hand) on this since she was not there. The assessment for ADHD is based on the Conners et al.'s (1998) assessment instrument, which has versions for parents and teachers. In this case, she had not been informed about whether an independent assessment had been made at school, nor had she been invited to discuss how this might have differed from her own ideas. Of course, parents can proactively attempt to gather information and talk to teachers at school about their children's behaviour, but this requires confidence. Many parents feel intimidated by 'experts' and concede to their status and opinions. This may be all the more likely when they already feel they are failing as parents and that it might be their fault. However, she appears to question the validity of using her speculations regarding the child's behaviour at school, despite this attempt to question the diagnostic process being ignored by the paediatrician.

We have to be careful not to slip too easily into blaming medical practitioners or parents. The paediatrician in this case was courageous and helpful in allowing his sessions with parents to be recorded for research. In my experience, practitioners are often wary of allowing such scrutiny of their work. Coulter and Rapley (2011) offer some criticism of the legitimacy of the process of diagnosis but medical professionals are not maliciously motivated, despite their research sometimes indicating concerning practices, not least the validity of some of the tests used and the claims made that these are objective and valid measures. Moncrieff and Timimi (2011) offer a view that the intentions of neither practitioners nor parents may be negative. They posit that part of the underlying drive for an overreliance on medical illness-based explanations may be anxiety about suggesting that parents are to be implicated and blamed for causing their children's problems. As in Research Interview 2.1, it might have been possible to pursue the parents' formulations about rivalries between the children; I see these as invitations or permissions from a family to pursue relational issues. One might have invited the parents in this case to consider what they do about such sibling rivalries or what experience they had of such things as children in their own families. Possibly, alongside time constraints, the reason many professionals do not do this is because they feel it is outside their area of competence and they lack training in family therapy. The paediatrician may not have felt competent exploring issues relating to family dynamics and therefore attempted to stay within their domain of medical expertise. Hence, clinical professionals typically use the knowledge base with which they feel familiar and competent rather than venturing into discussing other factors, such as family dynamics. This is an understandable anxiety since most clinical professionals do not receive training in how to talk with families or individual parents and most forms of therapy focus on conversations with individuals.

Summary and reflections

This chapter has drawn out some of the ways in which the question of responsibility and blame for parents relates to the question of assessment and diagnosis of children's difficulties. It has argued that a medical, illness or biological model of problems has dominated psychiatry and other caring professions. It has also argued that this is so prevalent in Western cultures that it tends to dominate the thinking of families. The chapter has offered a critical overview of some of the shortcomings of a medical diagnosis of problems such as ADHD, autism and anorexia. It has also attempted to convey that professionals and families are generally acting in what they regard as in the best interests of the child and their family. However, it has emphasised that when problems are present in families, parents are vulnerable to feelings of blame and may seek the reassurance of medical diagnosis and accompanying medication for their child. Further, it has described how families are often thoughtful about alternative explanations, such as family dynamics or social factors impacting on the family or that their child faces elsewhere. This is despite their recognition of the possibility that they might be seen as responsible for the problems or even blamed for them. The power of medical diagnosis can marginalise competing explanations and parents' anxieties and sense of blame, though temporarily relieved by a diagnosis, could in the long term trap them in an 'illness' view of the problems. A consequence of this may be that the impact and potential benefits or positive changes of other social and relational processes are missed. A child may become a silent voice in this process and subject to processes of labelling that they do not fully understand, and that may have long-term consequences for their sense of who they are. I have also seen that other family members, such as siblings, may be very confused about what, for example, their brother being diagnosed with autism means. In my current research on autism, I have heard some siblings talk about a sense of having 'lost' their brother or sister. One implication of this is that a suggested diagnosis needs to be carefully explained and discussed with everyone in a family – but alongside other possible explanations.

3 The development of problems in families: Attachment, narratives and systemic therapy

Introduction

> This chapter will explore attachment theory to illustrate how a sense of blame and responsibility are shaped by our early attachment experiences and come to shape family life, in particular our responses to perceived problems. This will include an overview of core concepts from attachment theory and systemic family therapy (SFT). Families will be discussed as dynamic systems engaged in communication at behavioural, emotional and cognitive levels that are shaped by wider social and cultural processes. This will be considered in terms of a mix of beliefs and narratives, including patterns of felt responsibilities and blame that shape family life. Finally, the chapter will discuss the power of medical models of distress in shaping the communicational process and ways of trying to manage distress.

Attachment, family systems and narratives

Bowlby's attachment 'theory' is not one theory but an eclectic mix of concepts from evolutionary biology, systems theory, cognitive neuroscience and object relations theory. The essential feature of attachment theory is that it is based on the observation that human infants, along with all mammals, seek the protection of their parents when they encounter danger. This is regarded as a hard-wired, evolution-based instinct that has evolved to ensure the protection of the species. Bowlby (1969) termed this the *attachment system*, a system triggered by actual or perceived dangers and threats. The triggering of the attachment system results in a flight–fight response with associated activation of physiological arousal. The parents' response of protection serves to remove the infant from the danger and to decrease the level of arousal so that the infant returns to a comfortable state. Bowlby (1973) described this as forming a 'secure base':

> For not only young children, it is now clear, but human beings of all ages are found to be at their happiest and to be able to deploy their talents to best advantage when they are confident that, standing behind them, are one or more trusted persons who will come to their aid should difficulties arise. The person trusted provides a *secure base* from which his (or her) companion can operate.
>
> (Bowlby 1973: 359; emphasis added)

This is analogous to a platform of security on which the child is able to explore, seek stimulation and experiment. The parent watches over the child and monitors potential dangers and the child's emotional state while being influenced by and monitoring their own feelings. This process embodies how tolerant the parent is to their child taking risks or experiencing some level of distress or discomfort before they intervene. Bowlby incorporated ideas from systems theory and cybernetics and suggested that the parent and child should be seen as an interacting homeostatic system that operates on the basis of feedback between parent and child. In this, he suggested that there was an optimal comfortable state for both parent and child to which they attempt to revert. He employed the classic analogy, also used in SFT, of a central heating system set to a comfortable temperature, which operates to maintain this state by either switching on turning off heat. He elaborated that the process was also analogous to a servo-mechanism in that over time, as the child developed and the parent grew older, the setting or calibration of what constituted comfort evolved and shifted and recalibrated itself. For example, a young infant would not be able to stray far from its parents while an older child might go off on a mountaineering holiday. Different tolerance for safety would clearly apply. In effect, the feedback system between the parent and child is continually being recalibrated by internal changes and external factors, such as socially shared expectations of what a child–parent relationship should be like.

This process has also been described by Powell et al. (2014: 10) as the 'circle of security'. In this, the parent is seen as holding a dual task of encouraging their child to *explore* and learn about the world but also to help them cope with the challenges, problems and distress that may result – a *return to safety*. The parent calibrates this process in terms of their own level of confidence, anxiety, expectations and beliefs about what is appropriate. For example, some parents may be extremely cautious about encouraging exploration if their own experience in their childhood was one of danger. Parents may also have beliefs about how safe (or otherwise) the environment is in which they live – for example, that the local play area is not safe or, in more extreme cases, they may live in situations of conflict or war. The concept of re-calibration is vital to add to the formulations that stem from attachment theory. It suggests that the attachment system, though based in basic evolutionary biological process, is also influenced by the cultural context in which families find themselves. So, for example, parents may be seen as overprotective if they appear to delay the freedom of their children to become independent, explore and move out of the family environment. In contrast, parents may be construed as neglectful if they appear to encourage too much independence and freedom too early on. The external systems that contribute to the regulation of the family attachment system include the extended family, friends, school and health systems, all of which may communicate evaluations of what is regarded as appropriate and acceptable. This process of monitoring the family attachment system – how safe the parents are keeping their children – is intimately connected to our discussion in the previous chapters regarding the perceived sense of blame and responsibility that parents may feel.

Development of attachment strategies

From this flux of interaction, a child is seen to develop their attachment strategies. The word 'strategy' is important as it indicates that these are adaptive patterns of responses that may change over time. In attachment theory, there is frequent reference to attachment styles and the idea that a person is 'secure' or 'insecure', 'avoidant' or 'anxious–ambivalent'. These can imply that this is a fixed feature of a person and a quality of their personality. Instead, these are better regarded as strategies that are developed in order to adapt to the environment in which a child or adult finds themselves and that may change according to whether they are adaptive and functional.

In attachment theory, the focus is specifically on how attachment strategies arise when a child seeks protection from their parents during times of anxiety, distress and anger. How the parents respond shapes the child's strategies. The concern has been to examine the 'primary' dyadic processes – that is, between a child and a parent or carer – though Bowlby (1988) stated that he was aware of the need to consider the whole family system. He felt this was a complex endeavour that needed to wait until he had been able to demonstrate clearly that insecurities could arise within dyadic relationships. His colleague, Mary Ainsworth, was instrumental in developing evidence, for example through the famous Strange Situation procedure, which consisted of a series of separations between infant and mother, illustrating how secure and insecure attachments operated. Ainsworth 1973; Ainsworth et al. 1978 discovered that children showed characteristic patterns of responses to the danger of being separated from their parent. In turn, the mothers' responses showed characteristic differences in how ready and able they were to offer comfort and reassurance to their child. For example, a mother who appeared to be uneasy with the child's request for emotional contact characteristically had infants whose behaviour in the reunion matched that of their mother's. Attachment was not just *in* either the parent or the child but was seen as a pattern *between* them and maintained by both. It was observed that children expressed their attachment needs in two ways: through *protest*, for example anger, and through *vulnerability*, for example sadness and distress. Expression of both emotions is important and necessary but there were found to be significant differences in which of these expressions parents encouraged or discouraged. Attachment always has two sides in responses to the non-availability of attachment figures. Depending on the responses of the parents, the child may develop in such a way that they learn to show one of these expressions more than another as requests to their parent to respond to their attachment needs. For example, she may learn that showing *vulnerability* activates the parents to respond positively. Alternatively, she may learn that distracted and unpredictable parents can only be activated by angry *protests*. In more complex cases, a child may find it difficult to work out a strategy that will elicit care from parents and they may alternate between patterns of protest and vulnerability. From these observations of mother–infant play and clinical work with children and parents, Bowlby and Ainsworth concluded that different attachment strategies develop. The three major behavioural patterns were:

1. children who seemed to feel safe to openly express both emotions and returned to a calm state fairly rapidly;
2. children who expressed neither protest nor vulnerability nor arousal but were in fact physiologically aroused; and
3. children who expressed both protest and vulnerability in alteration, were obviously aroused, and took a long time to settle down.

In these various patterns, conceptualisation of responsibility and blame are central:

Secure: Parents consistently available when needed, believe they're able to trust others, aware that parents will be available, able to show positive and negative feelings. Minimal and balanced BLAME of SELF and OTHER.

Avoidant: Parents consistently not available when needed, believe they have to rely on self, suppress negative/needy feelings, occasionally get needs met, especially by pleasing and caring for parents. Emphasised BLAME of SELF; minimised BLAME of OTHER.

Anxious/ambivalent: Parents inconsistently available, learn that exaggerating show of negative feelings and needs elicits care. Occasionally get needs met by coercing parents. Minimised BLAME of SELF; exaggerated BLAME of OTHER.

Extreme/disorganised: Parents inconsistent and unavailable, neither self-reliance nor coercion work to elicit care, may be frightening/frightened. Exaggerated and dysregulated BLAME of SELF and OTHER.

In all but the secure patterns, the process of developing explanations and narratives regarding difficulties that are emerging in the family may be more likely to become problematic. Blaming oneself or others may over time become increasingly extreme and untenable because it distorts the potential information that is available regarding problems. Blaming oneself may lead to an implosion of guilt and depressive processes in the family. In contrast, blaming others can promote the development of adversarial and conflictual relationships in school, with friends and with professional agencies, such as mental health and social care. One way of resolving these is to place responsibility on the child in the family, which is also problematic, but the easiest route may be seen as moving towards medically oriented diagnoses.

It was the intention of attachment theory that these patterns found in dyads could be extended to help explain the development of a variety of emotional problems and conditions. However, attachment theory-based research has tended to focus on dyads and there is a problem in attempting to generalise from the dynamics of dyads to families. An axiom of SFTs is that the whole is greater than the sum of the parts. This means that we cannot assemble an understanding of how a family will function based on attempting to piece together the functioning of individual members or separate dyads. Similarly, we cannot understand the operation of a dyadic relationship without also considering the wider context in which it is located. Family life can instead be regarded as attachment in interaction. Through their continuous processes of communication, family members both exemplify their attachment strategies and continually shape and re-shape these. Bowlby (1969, 1988) had suggested that attachments exist both as intra-psychic states and relational processes. Attachments exist through the dynamic process of interactions in families to constitute different states of security or insecurity in a family, which are represented as different attachment states held by the individuals within the system. Attachment theory has tended to emphasise the child as a recipient of the parents' attachment responses and care. But children also offer care and protection for their parents. This is obvious when we think about parents becoming older and more vulnerable, but the mutual process of care starts much earlier, even with young children who can be seen to be monitoring and responding to their parents' needs. A child is not a passive recipient of attachment responses from the parent but from the start is actively responding to the parents and responding to their attachment needs – both the parent and child are mutually responding to each other's attachment needs and requests. In my clinical experience, this has on occasion been expressed indirectly through the presentation of symptoms.

Clinical example 3.1: Cindy and her mother

Cindy, a 7-year-old girl, was reported by her mother to be extremely anxious and clingy to the point that she would cry and cling to her if she was out of her mother's sight. Cindy's parents were divorced and she was living with her mother with little contact with her father. As I explored their lives together, it became evident that Cindy and her mother were living in a threatening neighbourhood and that Cindy was worried about her mother's safety. As we discussed the anxieties her mother was experiencing and her concern to keep her mother safe, Cindy's anxiety and clinginess considerably decreased. In turn, her mother acknowledged that Cindy was a caring child and reassured her that she would take care to ensure her own safety. I often encourage children to draw pictures of their problems and Cindy drew a picture called her 'anxiety demon'. In our work together, as her anxiety gradually decreased, she painted us a picture of how her 'anxiety demon' had been driven away and she symbolically tore up the picture to show she was no longer under its influence.

> In some cases, this urge to protect the parent may mean a child decides to conceal some difficulties, such as bullying at school, with the potential negative consequence that there is an escalation of the distress into behaviours such as self-harming.
>
> Source: Adapted from author's personal clinical work and research.

Consider this example of a child feeling the need to protect and care for their parents while reading the next section, which moves to look at attachment in not just dyadic but triadic and larger systems. In particular, where children may be responding to and concerned not just about each of their parents but also their relationship with each other.

Attachment and family systems

Marvin and Stewart (1990) offer a framework that considers attachments as both intra-psychic states and relational processes. They suggest that the setting of the attachment system – the level of emotion, anxiety and comfort – will fluctuate in a dynamic way according to events that may impact on the family. A clinical example illustrating such a process of escalating insecurity in a system is given here alongside Figure 3.1.

Clinical example 3.2: Anita and her mother

A young girl, Anita, was referred to me because her mother, Manjeet, was becoming increasingly concerned that the girl was developing a morbid interest in death. Anita's father (a firefighter) had died unexpectedly, leaving behind his wife and 7-year-old. Both Manjeet and Anita were extremely distressed at this unexpected loss, but Manjeet decided it was best that she 'put a brave face' on things in order to protect her daughter. Subsequently, Manjeet's mother moved in temporarily to support her and help the pair to cope emotionally and with the practical arrangements such as organising the funeral. (This process of a de-stabilisation of the family attachment system following a bereavement of a parent, coupled with a grandmother's focus on the child, leading to an escalating process of increasing anxiety and problems is illustrated in Figure 3.1.)

Acting on good intentions, the mother was trying to protect her daughter by hiding her distress from her. Hence, they neither discussed their issues nor showed their emotions; they neither cried nor grieved regarding the father. Although the grandmother moved in to support Manjeet, she likewise held the belief that it would be best for Anita not to be exposed to the adult's distress.

THE DEVELOPMENT OF PROBLEMS IN FAMILIES **59**

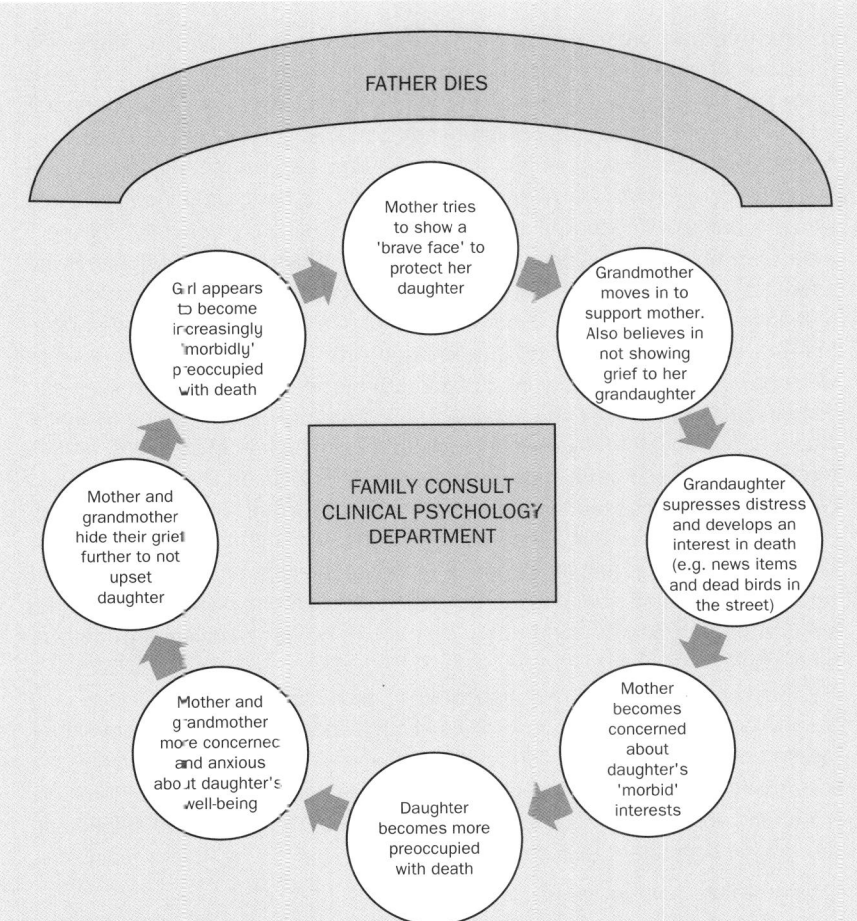

Figure 3.1 Escalating pattern of insecurity in a family

Unfortunately, this appeared to leave the little girl alone with her grief, thoughts and dilemmas about making sense of the death of her father. She seemed to express her distress indirectly, perhaps in turn not wanting to show her feelings in order to protect her mother, who she experienced at an embodied level as distressed. Children can pick up non-verbally and unconsciously distressing emotions that a parent is experiencing and if they are not helped to consciously understand this, they may experience confusion and distress (Crittenden 2006). The more Anita became preoccupied with death, the more the attention of the two adults focused on her and, in turn, the more they felt there was something wrong with her.

I met with the family in various combinations – the adults together, the mother on her own, the child and her mother together – in order for them *individually* to feel free to express themselves and *collectively* to be able to share and understand each other's experiences. Manjeet described her wish to protect Anita and we discussed what she felt her daughter understood and whether it might be helpful to be more open with her. She said she had wanted to do this but was not sure it was the right thing to do. She said her mother had advised her to be careful not to burden the little girl with her own grief. As she talked with me, she became tearful and apologised for losing control of her feelings. I reassured her that this was acceptable and she did not need to protect me as well. We discussed the ideas she had considered about ways of commemorating her husband and her uncertainty about sharing these with her daughter. Manjeet and I also discussed in a session with her grandmother how Anita was showing a normal curiosity about death for her age and that in such sad circumstances, children find their own ways of exploring the meaning of death. This 'normalising' and reassurance helped the adults and in sessions with all three, we discussed ways of celebrating the father's life and how brave he had been. We also discussed how being brave was important for them as a family but now was a time where they could also be sad and comfort each other. Manjeet and I asked Anita to describe what she thought her father might want for them to be doing now: she replied that he would probably understand them being a bit sad and thinking about him but he would have wanted them to be happy.

Manjeet and her mother appeared to appreciate the reassurance and acknowledgement of their efforts to be helpful. Their focus shifted from Anita's 'obsession' with death and, as they became more able to express and discuss their grief, the 'symptoms' rapidly subsided and Anita said she felt more confident and able to cope. The family decided that the sessions had helped and now all felt competent to cope.

Source: Adapted from author's personal clinical work and research.

From dyads to triads: Triangulation

This example offers an illustration of how attachment insecurity can be a dynamic and escalating process. It also suggests that attachment insecurity needs to be seen more broadly than in terms of dyadic processes. For example, the grandmother, in attempting a strategy of hiding feelings, appeared to contribute to the development of difficulties in the child. A central contribution of the SFTs has been the focus on triads and larger systems as the necessary units of analysis for family life (Bowen 1978; Minuchin 1974; Watzlawick, Beavin and Jackson 1967; Palazzoli et al. 1978), which has suggested that any dyad is potentially unstable and prone to escalating processes. The escalation is regulated by the presence of a third person (or in some cases, a pet). The classic example was of conflict detouring, as seen in Figure 3.2, showing how the child has an attachment relationship with the parents' relationship.

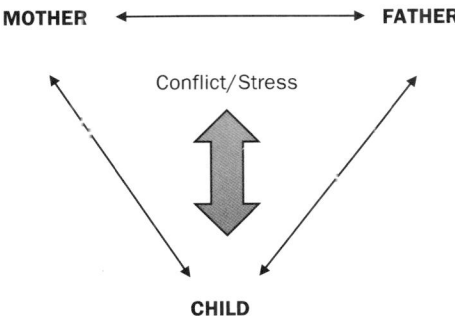

Figure 3.2 Attachment as a triadic process

For a child, the experience may be of trying to manage a relationship with each parent and feeling pulled in to take sides. Being exposed to the conflicts between the parents may make it difficult for the child to understand the relationship with each parent without this becoming confused by their view of the other parent. The child may struggle to differentiate between their parents because their thoughts about each one of them has become confused by their conflicts. Finally, attributing cause can become confusing. For example, the child might be confused about whether they are the cause of the conflicts between the parents and whether a parent is angry or distressed about something the child has done or is reacting to events in the *parents'* conflicts. More broadly, difficulties in developing understandings of other people and one's actions and feelings may be a longer-term consequence for the child.

To summarise, the concept of triangulation suggests that what is happening in a significant relationship between two people in a family can have a powerful influence on a third family member, and vice versa, in mutually reinforcing ways. Early SFT practitioners, such as Bowen (1978), Weakland (1976) and Minuchin 1974; Minuchin, Rosman and Baker 1978, observed that families may engage in a variety of triangular processes that could lead to stable coalitions or less stable and shifting alliances. This focus on triangles can both be an important bridge between systemic and attachment perspectives and a higher-order context marker for interconnected attachment relationships in a family system. It allows us to see a child as developing and functioning in both direct dyadic relationships with each parent and with the relationship between them (Palazzoli et al. 1989). The child can be seen as developing attachment strategies with each parent and, at the same time, having those strategies function to meet parents' emotional needs in their relationship, without the child's awareness. The situation for the child can become increasingly complex and confusing when there is no open or straightforward discussion in the family about what is going on between them all, what people are feeling, what their intentions and wishes are, and so on. In such situations, children and their parents may become increasingly confused by, or more unwilling to think about, the causes of events, what maintains relational patterns, and their own role in the developing problems.

The following clinical extract illustrates how a young person can experience being caught up in, or *triangulated* in, the conflict between their parents. The example also attempts to show how the parents were not to blame for constructing this process and both had experienced difficult childhood experiences of being parented themselves. They were attempting to be 'good parents' for their daughter. They had some awareness that their conflicts and arguments may have had an influence on precipitating her eating disorder. However, this insight could also serve to exacerbate their conflict as they not only blamed themselves but each other and their relationship for causing their daughter's problems. Unfortunately, this seemed only to aggravate their conflicts, which then further negatively impacted on their daughter.

Clinical example 3.3: Triangulation and the development of an eating disorder

Kate, aged 17, was living with her parents and attending school at the time of referral. She was the youngest child of four, with three older brothers, one of whom had recently moved back home. She had been suffering with an eating disorder for the past two years and had a number of paediatric ward admissions to assist with weight gain. Both her parents lived at home and were in full-time employment. Kate's mother acknowledged early in the family sessions that she was unhappy in her marriage and wanted to leave to find a more fulfilling relationship, whereas Kate's father claimed to want to save the marriage. Both Kate's parents had troubled attachment histories in their families of origin, having experienced emotional unavailability from their respective parents. The grandparents, in turn, were reported to have had troubled lives, including psychosomatic problems and attempted suicides.

I worked with Kate and her family in family therapy for 18 months. Therapy incorporated use of the Adult Attachment Interview (George, Kaplan and Main 1985), both individually with family members and parts of it as a family interview. The following quotes from Kate illustrate how a child may experience the tensions and conflicts between their parents as anxiety-provoking, which may result in expressing forms of distress. A child may feel that they are being drawn in to take sides in a battle between their parents, a battle they find highly distressing and confusing.

Kate: 'They used to really hurt me because they used to play each other off . . . And they would be like, "Go on, tell me all the bad stuff about the other one". And I used to sit there and think to myself, "I am made up of half of each of these people and they hate each other, and do they hate me?"'

Kate: 'They used to hate each other so much, I always used to be so scared that one of them would do something stupid and I would come home and . . . I used to hate coming home, just in case something happened. And they've both got the worst tempers, even Dad . . . Dad's rarely seen but it is really bad . . .'

Here Kate expresses very poignantly what the experience of being caught up in the conflicts between her parents feels like. There had not been any violence between the parents but considerable quarrelling, raised voices and threats of separation. One consequence of this was that Kate adopted a role of mediator and peacemaker between them. However, as this triadic process became entrenched, she found it hard to step out of this position – for example, when she went to university. It also had the consequence of her parents being less able to decide what to do about their relationship, partly because they were worried about Kate's health but also because she would intervene whenever she heard them discussing what she felt might be a provocative issue. Byng-Hall (1980: 355) has described this as a child becoming a 'distance-regulator' between their parents and that the symptoms become an increasingly central aspect of this. By this, he meant that the child's problems can serve to draw the parents together in order to care for them but can also serve to distance the parents as they might feel responsible and angry with each other. Kate expressed this poignantly in her understanding of the function of her anorexia:

Kate: 'The only thing I ever hear them talking about is me and, if I didn't have this [(anorexia)], it's kind of like, would everything fall apart? At least it's keeping them talking. And they won't argue while I've got this because it might make me worse. So um . . . that's kind of bought, sort of like, I'm not in control as such but I've got more control over the situation that way.'

It is tempting to see the responsibility as falling on the parents and, in fact, Kate's parents did blame themselves and each other. But once a triadic process like this becomes established, it is difficult for anyone to change or resolve it. For Kate's family, the picture was further complicated by the fact that her older brother was living at home and his formulation was that Kate was self-centred and 'putting her parents through a lot'. So the blame was seen by him to lay more on Kate's shoulders than her parents.

One important implication of this dynamic is that, in assisting clinically with conditions such as anorexia, it is important to consider how a child's symptoms may be related to triadic processes. This is a familiar and well-established idea for family therapists but it can imply that the parents' conflicts are to blame. This is not the intention of SFT or therapy that argues that family dynamics evolve jointly in families and no-one is to blame. Another way of seeing this is that there is a circular process so that, as the child becomes more 'ill', this may contribute to the distress and conflicts between the parents. They may feel they are failing and blame each other; consequently,

> solving their own problems and achieving intimacy becomes increasingly difficult. Likewise, children like Kate may come to fear that letting their symptoms reduce would pose a risk to the family. Helping the parents to feel less blamed is an important clinical step, but the danger is that this frequently involves seeing the child as having an 'illness' – and this risks them becoming trapped in an illness *identity*.
>
> Source: Adapted from author's personal clinical work and research.

Intergenerational consequences of triangulation processes

A wide range of intergenerational issues arise from the case of Kate. Not least, as we've just discussed, that the formulation presented here might appear to suggest a position of blaming the parents for having caused Kate's condition. There are many reasons, both in the present and in the past, why parents, separately and together, might feel distress, be insecure about each other, or engage in conflict and hostile interactions, and even why they might involve a child in such ways. Nor is it being suggested that this combination of apparent circumstances will invariably cause an eating disorder. Each family can be regarded to be unique but, at the same time, the consequences of being caught up in parental conflicts do invariably appear to be associated with some risk for children's well-being (Beuler and Welsh 2009; Dallos and Draper 2015; McKenzie and Dallos 2016). It can also be suggested, from a social constructionist position, that this is just Kate's narrative and represents her version of events, not the truth about the dynamics in this family. But in this family, Kate's parents supported her story when they reflected that they were concerned that their frequent arguments may have helped to cause Kate's 'illness' (i.e. anorexia). The parents described that they had been thinking of splitting up, which although was predominantly driven by Kate's mother, her father had reluctantly accepted that this might be inevitable. Minuchin, Rosman and Baker (1978) suggested that, although a child's problems might originally be connected to parental conflict, the child's problems and behaviours can serve to make it harder for parents to reconcile their difficulties, despite their best efforts. In a piece of research (McKenzie and Dallos 2016), I explored children's experience of parental conflict using photographs of triadic conflicts and my findings suggested that children *could* describe how such triadic situations could be very uncomfortable but they did not consider that they might have a significant negative impact on their mental well-being. Analysis of their responses also indicated a higher level of distressing and highly aroused, traumatic responses and imagery in relation to triadic conflict situations compared to the dyadic attachment scenarios, such as a separation or conflict with one parent.

A child may learn in difficult dyadic and triadic attachment conflicts to disguise their true feelings and develop what Crittenden (1997: 38) called 'false affect'. This is a display of positive emotions – smiles or even laughter – that serves to disguise emotional distress and pain. A typical example is when a clearly sad or dangerous event is described with instances of laughter (which are emotionally inconsistent). Some children who experience abuse within their families can become skilled at not just hiding their feelings but displaying a bright, happy, false emotional presence that they know is acceptable to their parents (Crittenden 1997). Over many years, such learning may result in the child becoming unclear about what they are feeling at any given time, as pointed out by Winnicott (1971: 109) with his notion of the 'false self'. The true self was seen as an experience of *authenticity* involving a sense of feeling real, a sense of trusting one's experiences and broadly that life is worth living. In contrast, the child could feel *inauthentic*, doubting their own experiences and grasp on reality. The child could feel compelled to comply with their parents' wishes about what they are allowed to think and feel and who they are, leading them to construct a false set of relationships including concealing what they are really feeling. For a child, this could become more confusing when the expectations and demands from their parents are contrasting and contradictory.

Considering attachment as a triadic (and wider) process contains a range of implications for how we think about the questions of blame and responsibility. In particular, a frequent criticism of attachment theory has been that it inordinately and unfairly focuses the question of responsibility predominantly on one parent – and this has typically been the mother. This has been widely criticised as potentially mother-blaming, especially by feminist theorists and clinicians (Birns 1999). It arguably still remains one of the major reasons that some clinicians are reluctant to incorporate attachment theory into their practice. To consider attachment as a triadic process shifts the emphasis so that parenting is always seen in the context of the relationship that one parent has with the other parent and, in turn, what relationship the other parent has with the child. As an example, if a mother is feeling anxious, distressed or even frightened in her relationship, this will influence her attachment responses to her child. If the child develops insecure patterns of attachment and other difficulties, it is clearly not simply or predominantly her responsibility.

Family narratives and working models

Attachment experiences become organised into what Bowlby (1969, 1988) termed 'internal working models' – an emotionally toned set of beliefs, understandings and expectations. The term 'dispositional representations' (Crittenden 1997, 2006) has also been used to capture the idea that the accumulation of these early experiences shapes the expectations we hold regarding the future. Bowlby drew on the emerging field of cognitive neuroscience to offer a model of the developmental pathway of how early experiences are stored (Tulving 1972). These may operate both consciously and unconsciously to shape our experiences and choices of action, sometimes outside of our conscious awareness. This concept has been elaborated by Crittenden (1997) to suggest that our memories, which are also the bases for our actions, feelings and choices, are stored in terms of five major levels. Two of these are forms of *non-verbal memories*: procedural and sensory and three are forms of *verbal memories*: semantic, episodic and integrative.

Five levels of representations

Non-verbal memories

Procedural memory is memory for how we do things, from remembering how to ride a bicycle to how we have arguments with family members. For example, when a baby cried, how soft or harsh the caregiver's response was or how calm, predictable, rapid, excitable and unpredictable the parents' actions were. The nature of the responses becomes held in the body so that we come to anticipate, at an embodied level, the responses and, for instance, unconsciously flinch or relax in later life when we are touched.

Sensory memory is our repository of memory for sensation, such as how things smell, what they look and taste like, how it feels to be touched in certain ways, and so on. An example might be holding a memory of Mum's smiley face or the smell of her perfume.

Verbal memories

Semantic memory is our verbal store of ideas, attitudes and beliefs. It is the words that we develop to label our relationships and attachment figures: 'funny', 'loving', 'kind', 'angry' and so on.

Episodic memory relates to memory for experiences and sequences of events over time. It is how we remember in terms of stories linking people, events and places to make sense of how events unfold over time. Embedded in episodes is also an indication of what we have learnt from an experience and what implications this holds for how we will act in the future.

Integrative memory is our ability to call on all our memory systems to narrate a full and detailed account of our experiences – our *procedural*, *sensory*, *semantic* and *episodic*. Integrative memory is sometimes called metacognition, metacommunication, mentalisation or reflective functioning (i.e. our capacity to reflect on how we think, feel and act and, importantly, to consider how others think and feel, why they act as they do, and to recognise that their motives and intentions may be different to ours).

All five of these levels constitute our narratives and we need to be able to employ all of them to develop coherent narratives that help us to view our past experiences, to anticipate future events, and to develop strategies to help us to keep ourselves and those close to us safe.

Attachment strategies and defensive processes

During our development in relational systems, such as family and kin networks, we learn to think about ourselves and others and to understand how relationships work. As children, if we are cared for in an attuned way that is sensitive and responsive to our needs for safety and protection, we develop ideas of ourselves as acceptable and loveable, and worthy and deserving of others' care and attention. If, while growing up, parents or carers have been emotionally unavailable or inconsistent and unpredictable in their care and nurturing, it can lead to the development of ideas about ourselves as unworthy of others' care, or that others are not interested in us. Attachment strategies for emotional survival and adaptation to family circumstances develop over time (Crittenden 1997; Crittenden et al. 2014). If they are not challenged with different, more responsive caregiving, they can lead to difficulties with establishing intimacy in adult relationships, lack of trust in others, difficulty with expressing and regulating certain emotions, and disappointment with self and others.

Attachment strategies, or styles of protective and defensive processes in relationships, can be seen on a continuum of attachment threat, both real and perceived. For example, if a child learns that expressing emotions cannot reliably elicit the comfort of caring, they may develop defensive strategies of distancing or excluding emotions. They come to rely on cognition, as this can be employed to help omit or distort emotional information, such as inhibiting affect and denying physiological discomfort and pain. This dismissing or deactivating style can lead to consequences of compulsive self-reliance, where the need for others is denied, or to idealising and compulsively caring for others. Similarly, at the other extreme, a preoccupied strategy or style can develop in circumstances where the child cannot predict the response from their carer, or where they cannot rely on promises of care that do not materialise. They may come to rely more on affective information and split off their feelings of vulnerability, instead focusing more on their angry responses to lack of care and disappointment. Constant blaming of others and avoiding their own responsibilities protects them from the complexity of their circumstances but leaves them vulnerable to unregulated feelings and their effect on others. Thus, the emotion of anger can become central in organising people's responses to one another in family relationships. With a more dismissing, deactivating style, where the expression of negative feelings is inhibited, anger can be experienced as an unwelcome intrusion. The expression of anger can become pathologised in the family and accompanied by a sense of shame and failure. Similarly, with a more anxious or ambivalent pattern, semantic understanding may be limited to managing unpredictability in responding, and the emotions of anger and felt vulnerability may be exaggerated. In these difficult interactional moments, strategies for processing negative feelings and understanding the impact of behaviour on others are limited.

Attachment and narratives styles: Same facts; different stories

In subsequent chapters, I will focus on how our attachment experiences shape the nature of the narratives that we develop. The stories that we develop to make sense of our experiences contain the five levels of attachment representations discussed earlier, while our experiences shape how we remember our experiences at these various levels. Especially when we feel anxious, distressed, frightened or confused, our working models can be seen to shape our narratives in various ways. Narratives are most effective in helping us to make sense, predict events and develop effective strategies for coping with difficulties when they are *coherent*. This is where our narratives use all of the five levels of representation so that we are able to recognise and remember emotions, to use cognition, and to put our experiences into words and stories. Importantly, we are also able to integrate the various levels of memories. Vital to this is that we are able to recognise contradictions between what we are thinking and feeling. In particular, two types of shaping of experience and our stories are likely to occur: attempts to downplay or minimise our emotions and the significance of dangers versus a process of escalating and exaggerating our feelings or anxieties. This is particularly relevant to thinking about blame in families – especially how families may differ in terms of experiencing guilt, such as blame about their parenting as opposed to minimising their responsibilities and angrily blaming others.

Our narratives not only depict our lives but also carry implications for how we anticipate the future. The stories we tell about our past are selective of what events we are able to remember and what meanings we ascribe to the events remembered. Our stories are our attempt to depict that past but they also have potential to anticipate and to replicate the past. An important study by Fonagy et al. (1991) demonstrated that pregnant mothers' stories of their childhood attachment experiences were predictive of the level of security or insecurity their infants demonstrated towards them in the Strange Situation procedure (Ainsworth 1973; Ainsworth et al. 1978). In short, the structure of the stories about their own childhoods predicted the relationship their infants subsequently had with them. The following case study offers an illustration of the style of the stories that can be told about events.

Case study 3.1: Narrative styles

A young woman I worked with in my clinical research project regarding families with a child with a diagnosis of autism told a story relating to her early childhood, which contained the following 'facts':

'My father was a rabbi; my parents offered me little guidance in my childhood; I engaged in some dangerous activities in my early adolescence; I had a child with a man who was violent to me; I left him; I ended up being bankrupt; my parents bought me a house but it was in a very poor condition; I had to pay some rent to them for it.'

In the first narrative style, feelings are downplayed and the parents are exonerated. In the second narrative style, feelings dominate and a sense of angry resentment permeates the story.

These styles reflect ways of interpreting events that have proved effective in some ways for the people telling these accounts. It is also possible that these styles of narrating may now be less helpful for them or become less

Dismissing strategy and narrative style	Preoccupied strategy and narrative style
'My parents were religious and held a view that prayer, rather than talking about problems was the best solution for difficulties. My father had a demanding job as a rabbi and his congregation put a lot of demands on him, so I think I was a bit of a handful. Talking about my problems was hard for them. Though they were not wealthy, they looked after me and bought me a house, which was a bit dilapidated <laugh>. They asked for a bit of rent because they could not really afford it.'	'My parents never offered me any guidance and said they would be supportive but actually, they didn't do anything to help. After the divorce, I had to go bankrupt, and my parents bought a house for me but with no hot water and we didn't have heating – it was absolutely shocking. It wasn't anything fit for habitation. They were taking the rent every month but not doing the repairs. My sister and I had absolutely no boundaries at any point. It was up to us to make our own mistakes and to learn from them … Never any advice or guidance.'

helpful in future relationships. The second, angrier preoccupied style of narrative comes from work with a mother who was concerned that her 5-year-old son might be showing signs of autism. She was angrily preoccupied about her childhood and described her parents as emotionally unavailable and uncaring. One potentially problematic consequence of her pattern was that she found it difficult to reflect on her child's needs to have a relationship with his grandparents or father. In contrast, the alternative story, which exonerates the parents, may shape a process of excessive self-blame and acceptance of inappropriate actions from others.

Source: Adapted from author's personal clinical work and research.

Summary and reflections

This chapter has offered an overview of concepts from attachment theory and how these can be incorporated with SFT to offer some helpful ways of assisting families. It has been argued that attachment theory has essentially been a dyadic theory and that there is a need to consider, in addition to these dyadic relationships, that a child has a relationship with their parents' (or carers') relationship. These triadic processes are powerful in shaping current dynamics and problems in a family. They also influence a child's ability to develop coherent and effective stories to make sense of their experiences and to provide a map to help plan their future. Under-awareness of triadic processes and their effects may not only be an aspect of family dynamics but part of a wider cultural phenomenon. Research (Ugazio et al. 2012; McKenzie and Dallos 2016) suggests that this may be, in part, because European cultures do not foster triadic views of relational causality. The chapter has also explored attachment narrative therapy, which offers an integration of attachment and systemic ideas and attempts to offer a way of working with families that feels safe for them and limits the risk of them feeling blamed while allowing an exploration of responsibility. Finally, the chapter has argued that most families act on the basis of good intentions and want to do their best for each other. What they hope for appears to be shaped by their own attachment experiences.

In the following chapters, we will focus on the interaction between (i) how parents acquire patterns of attachment that appear to be unconscious and scripted and (ii) the role parents' conscious intentions to do things better or repeat good aspects of their own childhoods play in familial interactional processes.

4 Attachment and family scripts

Introduction

> This chapter will offer an overview of the concept of the attachment internal working model (IWM) as composed of multiple levels of *implicit* and *explicit* representations of attachment experiences. The explicit representations will be discussed to suggest that they allow attachment theory to include the idea of choice and autonomy of actions in families. How IWMs are transmitted across generations and how they function in dyadic and larger family configurations will then be described. The first part of the chapter will elaborate on the concept of the IWM as guided by attachment scripts as implicit and largely unconscious plans that shape actions. The second part will focus on how IWMs contain explicit and conscious intentions relating to attachment and parenting. The discussion of IWMs will later be extended from a dyadic focus to consider wider family configurations, especially the challenges faced by children in developing attachment scripts in conflictual triadic family processes. The chapter will conclude with an integration of the concepts of scripts and conscious intentions to suggest that this offers a way of considering the development of problems in families, together with a discussion of the dilemmas and conflicts resulting from contradictions between implicit and explicit representations.

The internal working model

Bowlby's (1969) notion of the child as developing an IWM set the scene for attachment theory as an approach that could offer a valuable developmental perspective of how the child's internal world evolves in the social context of their family life. From the outset, Bowlby emphasised that attachment is essentially an instinctual, biologically driven survival system that connects the child to its parents for its own safety and protection. But it also incorporates a system of meanings that develops

72 ATTACHMENT AND FAMILY SCRIPTS

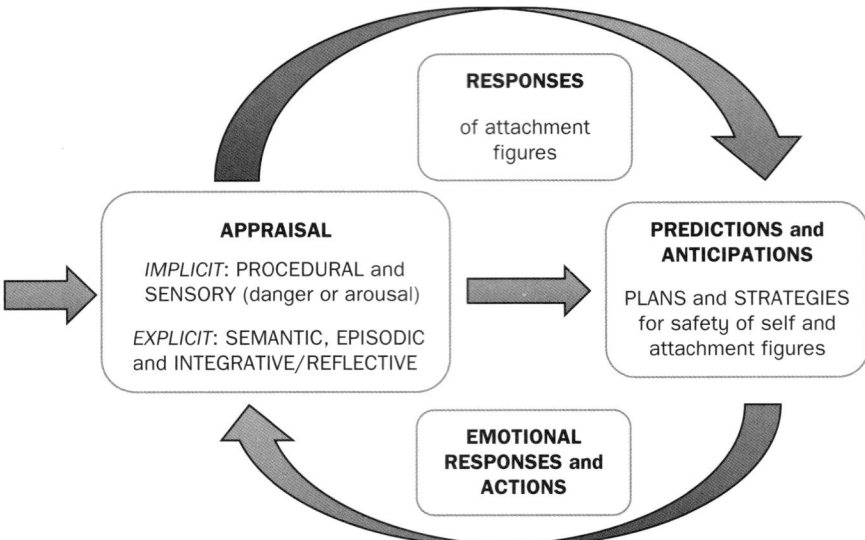

Figure 4.1 Internal working model of attachment

in sophistication as the child matures. He drew on the emerging field of cognitive psychology to suggest that attachment could be regarded as the development of an IWM. Such models influence memory, expectations and response availability in subsequent social interactions (Schank and Abelson 1977; Schank 1982, 1999). Craik (1943), meanwhile, had developed the concept of *mind* as constituting an IWM. He regarded this to be an active and dynamic model of the world that not only constituted a representation of past events but offered the possibility of contemplating future choices of actions and evaluating their consequences. For example, we can imagine interactions and conversations we might have with others and, from predictions about how these might progress, plan different strategies to deal with various possible consequences. We act on the basis of plans we derive from the model and the consequences feedback to confirm, re-appraise and update the model as necessary. In order to be effective, it has to be amenable to revision or we risk repeating mistakes and compromising our safety and that of our family members. Figure 4.1 is a schematic representation of the attachment working model.

The attachment working model implies a dynamic process that allows prediction to occur and suggests that the person is involved in a constructive process – actively making sense of reality. It also suggests that, once established, the IWM may operate outside conscious awareness and, though needing to be revised with new information, has a stability. New information and events are likely to be assimilated into the model and dramatic change may be disturbing and painful. Importantly, this model could also include re-experiencing how we, and others involved in interacting with us, felt in the past and how we might feel in the future. It is therefore not simply a cognitive model but one that integrates logical and emotional processes. In generating this model, it can be argued that Bowlby anticipated later empirical research that demonstrated the centrality of emotional processes in decision-making (Oatley and Johnson-Laird 2011).

Representational systems

The IWM is a multi-layered system in which memories are represented at verbal/explicit as well as non-verbal/implicit levels (Crittenden 1997, 2006). This corresponds to developmental processes in that an infant initially interacts with parents at an embodied sensory level and later, as language emerges, also comes to represent the relationship verbally. The *implicit* memory systems comprise:

1. *Procedural memory*, an everyday example being the embodied memory of how to ride a bicycle. For an infant, this might be an embodied sense of how calm as opposed to frightening, exciting or rapid the responses are from the parents. In adults, procedural aspects of memory can also be seen in 'how' we speak – for example, fast and animated as opposed to slow and deliberate ways of describing an event that has occurred.
2. *Sensory memory* whereby, as the infant's brain develops, she is able to develop images of the parent and hold memories, for example of the mother's face, how she smiles, her smell, the sound of her voice, and so on. These memories are established in the first few years of life and are regarded as emotionally toned such that, as we remember our mother's face or her smell, this may arouse powerful emotional states.

With the emergence of language, the representational systems become *explicit* and consist of semantic, episodic and integrative memory systems:

1. *Semantic memory*. This includes descriptions such as my mother being kind, caring, affectionate and so on. The development of these memories requires assistance from parents to develop a language to describe relationship, actions and feelings. For example, a parent might help a child to identify and name their own emotions – 'I think you are a bit upset' – as well as helping them to represent those of other people. Semantic memory can also contain emotional content, especially when we use 'strong' language, evocative words, swearing and so on. However, it is predominantly related to cognition rather than emotional states.
2. *Episodic memory*. This arises as children develop language abilities and it includes the stories that link people, events and actions over time. Again, the child is assisted in developing these as parents help the child to construct stories, for example what we did at the seaside last week, as well as helping them to recount events where the parent was not present. This process becomes established towards the end of the second year of a child's life. At first, the child may have difficulty and the parent's close involvement in supporting the emergence of episodic memory can mean that it may at

times be difficult for a child to differentiate her own from her parents' memories. Looking back at their childhoods, people may comment that they are not sure if a story is their own or something they have been told by a parent. Episodic memory combines the other representational systems in that the stories we tell contain, words, images and how we tell the story, whether in an animated or flat manner.

3. Finally, *integrative memory* comprises an overarching online reflective system that includes reflection on what we have learnt from our experience, reflection on how we are telling a story, and importantly an appraisal of possible discrepancies between our representational system. As an example, I might notice myself laughing when I have described an incident that was frightening and upsetting.

Crittenden (1997, 2006) suggests that the processing in the cortical area of the brain occurs in two parts: the first is a process whereby information from the various memory systems is held and compared with distracting information filtered out; the second process involves making connections with other information held to forge meanings and new connections. Our experiences, through development, are encoded into these various systems and their integration occurs with assistance from our attachment figures. Children are regarded to be developing narrative skills, which involve being able to integrate these various representational memories and to articulate them in stories – to *communicate*. A number of researchers (Baerger and McAdams 1999; Habermas and Bluck 2000) indicate that the ability to author our lives in terms of a coherent story is a highly complex 'skill'. Initially, it seems that stories of young children around the age of seven are relatively concrete, immediate and episodic. Developmentally, it appears that the ability to develop sophisticated narratives starts around adolescence (Habermas and Bluck 2000).

Scripts and intentions

A criticism of attachment theory has been that it is essentially a deterministic model in that early attachment experiences are regarded as shaping the child's attachments and these continue into adulthood to shape their lives. This also assumes a transgenerational process whereby, more or less faithfully, attachment strategies are passed on from parent to child (Bowlby 1969, 1988; van IJzendoorn 1995). However, it is apparent from the earlier summary of the IWM that it contains the capacity for conscious autonomous choices of actions as well as the view that early experiences are held implicitly and shape our actions unconsciously. I want to distinguish between the aspects of the IWM and emphasise that implicit representations shape our actions as 'scripts' while the explicit system is driving our conscious intentions. The two sets of representations influence each other and in clinical practice are not so clearly easy to separate. Nonetheless, this idea is core to the rest of the book in that it offers a way of thinking about how parents may unintentionally cause experiences for their children that they are not aware of and their explicit intentions may collide with these implicit processes. Hence, parents in a sense have some *responsibility* for what happens in their families but are not to *blame*.

First, I will offer an overview of research and models regarding attachments and the IWM as comprised of scripts; second, I will explore the idea of conscious intentions that interact with scripts.

Attachment scripts

As noted, the attachment system has been viewed as analogous to the concept of a *script* (Byng-Hall 1995; Waters and Waters 2006). In many everyday situations, our interactions can be seen to have a script-like quality. For example, when I go to a shop there are culturally shared rules about what is likely to happen: I enter the shop; I am asked by an assistant what I want or how they can help me; I state what I need; the assistant tries to find the item; if it is available, I buy it and leave; if it is unavailable, I find a substitute item to purchase or I immediately leave. Of course, there are variations of this, such as pleasantries about the weather, how far I have travelled and the like – but veering into politics or my relationships and sex life is not usually within the script! Scripts are also linked to the idea of goals, the processes whereby we achieve what we need, and how these are based on feedback processes such that we may adopt different pathways to achieve our goals.

The concept of a script has been developed more specifically by Schank and Abelson (1975, 1977) to provide a model for such aspects of human action. They suggest that scripts are enduring mental structures and that they include a set of propositions that shape how we interpret events, what courses of action we see as viable and our predictions of the outcomes of these choices. These are also described as conditional ('if, then') propositions (e.g. '*if* the shop stocks what I desire, *then* I will purchase the item').[7] Scripts can be seen to develop through the repeated experience of interactions from which we are able to build up a generalised picture of what is likely to happen. For instance, a child may come to develop a script of what happens at bedtime: 'bedtime: bath time – story – kiss – light off – leave to sleep'. More broadly, we can be seen to operate on the basis of basic scripts in everyday life, for example the sequences of behaviour in a restaurant, shop or lecture hall. These are rather formal scripts; however, there are scripts that are more flexible and propositional. Harre and Secord (1972) has offered the concept of *enigmatic* scripts where participants in an interaction are engaged in improvisation analogous to music. For example, we might not be sure that we are entering a script of developing casual chat or a friendship. Even young children at age three can provide a simple script, such as the customs they adopt while eating dinner (e.g. washing their hands, which hand they use to hold their fork or when to leave the table). Initially, the scripts are likely to be local and specific and consist essentially of generalisations of episodic memories (e.g. a generalised dinner-time script). Cognitively, it makes

---

[7] Conditional propositions like these form the basis of computer programming and AI systems.

sense to reduce mundane events in this way rather than carry unnecessary detail of every event; we would find it difficult to remember a mass of specific detail and without developing this into summarised plans, we could not make general predictions. It helps to know that most restaurants, for example, operate with a similar set of procedures otherwise I would need to study the protocols of any establishment before I could venture in. Of course, there will be local variations and more major cultural ones such as sitting on the floor, eating with chopsticks, self-service, set-menus and so on; generally, however, I will be asked initially what I want to eat and expected to pay at the end. Interestingly, children are unlikely to recall specific details of episodes unless they were somehow unusual or dramatic.

In relation to attachment, it is suggested that children similarly develop a set of expectations based on implicit propositions regarding relationships with their parents or other attachment figures. Waters and Waters (2006) suggest that children can develop a secure attachment script that contains three key propositions:

1. **P1:** *If* I encounter a difficulty or distress, *then* I can approach an attachment figure for help.
2. **P2:** An attachment figure will be willing and available to help.
3. **P3:** Relief and comfort will result from this support seeking.

These propositions initially develop at a non-verbal level.[8] A child cannot articulate these steps in their decision-making but they can be seen to act *as if* following such a script. Waters and Waters described their three propositions as embodying the *secure base* attachment script.[9] For example, infants in the Strange Situation procedure (Ainsworth et al. 1978) can be seen to respond in a similarly predictable way. In this experimental procedure, a child and mother engage in a number of separations and observations are made of how the child responds to the parent's absence and their return (or the reunion). Research using the Strange Situation procedure has revealed that infants show characteristic patterns such as minimisation of feelings of distress (avoidant); exaggerated displays of distress and anger (anxious–ambivalent); or a balanced (secure) pattern. Waters and Waters (2006) argue that the development of a script is an accumulative process and, with repetition, the script becomes established and can accommodate exceptions – for example, the parents may not be available invariably. They suggest that once the secure base script is established, regardless of whether family members always respond consistently with the script, it will continue as a set of generalised expectations about intimate relationships – the script will be used to develop and organise narratives about attachment. It will also be used selectively to remember events that are consistent with it. In contrast, people who have not experienced support consistent with a secure base will not organise and consolidate a secure base script; instead, they will have different or less consistent expectations in secure base interactions. As the child develops, the bid for help may be asked in different ways

---

[8] See Chapter 3 for more on non-verbal memories.
[9] See Bowlby's (1973: 359) quote in Chapter 3 for more on the secure base.

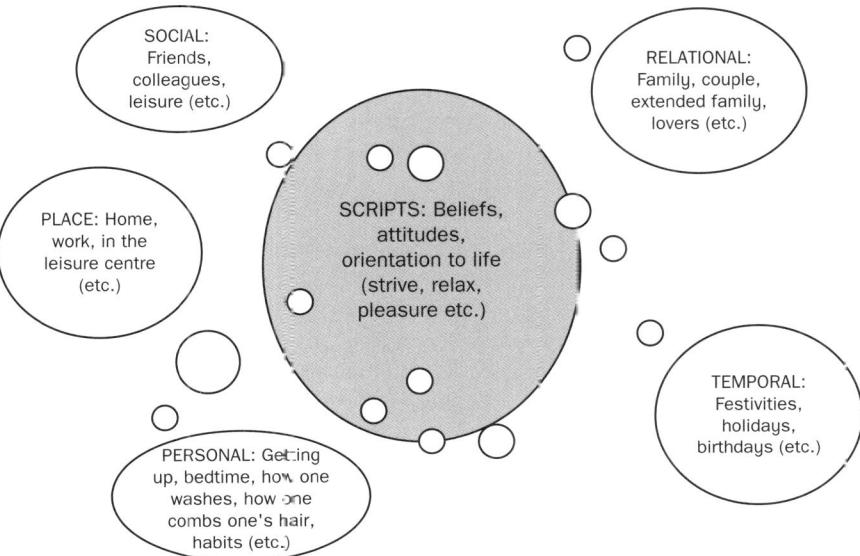

Figure 4.2 Types of scripts

or repeated, or the child develops understandings about when the best or most appropriate time is from the parents' perspectives. For example, a child might see that a parent is exhausted or distressed and wait until later in the day when they can see that the parent is more relaxed.

Scripts are seen to be organised in hierarchical levels from general abstract overviews to scripts that are specific to particular settings or times. They also include personal and private scripts and social and relational ones (see Figure 4.1). They consist of implicit plans that can become activated in different settings, at different times, occasions and with different people. Initially, they are learnt by infants in implicit and unconscious ways – for example, a child will 'know' to act differently at school, in the park and at home. As they mature, they become more conscious and may experiment with elaborating or deliberately contravening them. Schank and Abelson's (1975) model emphasises flexibility and the dynamic nature of scripts in including and organising new information obtained from direct personal experience. This includes recognising and appraising variations from what is expected and revising the script to be able to accommodate new information restructuring to take account of new information. This is consistent with the central concept of *feedback* from systems theory. This is the concept that information about the effects or consequences of an action is 'fed back' and employed to alter the subsequent action.[10] Without the possibility of change and revision, scripts would be inflexible and potentially counter to a child's survival and development.

---

[10] The concept of feedback from systems theory formed the basis of 'intelligent' mechanical systems, such as missile guidance to be able to continually correct the direction of a missile if it was veering away from its target.

Adult attachment representations and the secure base script

Waters and Waters (2006) have conducted extensive research to explore the nature of the *secure base* script (see also Waters and Cummings 2000 and Waters et al. 2000). One of their research protocols is the prompt–word outline method consisting of a basic prompt of an attachment scenario – for example: 'Baby's morning' and 'Trip to the doctors'. In this task, mothers are provided with: a set of words depicting people and objects such as mother, baby, teddy bear and blanket; and a set of words for actions and emotions such as play, smile, story, found, lost, hug, pretend and nap. The task is to weave the words into a story that includes the people, objects and events. The task is not framed as selecting a good or best story but rather as the same set of words being able to elicit any number of equally valid stories. Waters and Waters' studies indicated that the stories that people developed could be analysed in terms of corresponding to their prototype of a secure base script. The stories could be rated according to the extent to which they contained, in an integrated way, the key components, experience of distress, seeking of support and effective resolution of the distress with the help of others. In a *secure base* story, the baby's feelings and those of the mother were woven into a story and some emotional shifts, such as losing a teddy, were indicated with a positive but realistic story about these being resolved. In stories from mothers who employed *dismissing* attachment patterns, the story tended to be a matter of fact description of events with a rather dry, factual and emotionless tone to the story. There was also an absence of emotional issues arising or how they were resolved.

In a second series of studies, instead of using words as prompts, they employed picture prompts. For example, in one sequence – 'hospital' – the first picture showed a young adult who had been injured lying in a hospital bed with a sad facial expression. The second picture showed them being cheered up by someone else, and the third picture showed them still in hospital but now with a happy expression. The participants were asked to use the three pictures to construct a story that could build on and elaborate the three outline pictures in any way they wished. The ratings of the stories elicited by these protocols demonstrated a significantly high correlation with measures of attachment security and insecurity. Their research suggested that the scripts that originally developed at a non-verbal level become elaborated into our IWMs, which then influence the nature of the attachment relationships that we develop (Waters and Waters 2006).

Connecting their findings with the discussion of memory systems,[11] scripts can be seen as initially formed at the level of implicit representations – procedural and sensory memory or knowledge systems. Infants are not consciously aware of their scripts; however, a child employs feedback to alter her attachment behaviour according to the circumstances at a particular time. An important question is how this concept of a script can be integrated with the notion of conscious choice of action. Not only do we act out such scripts like sequences, but we may become consciously aware that we are acting out a script. This is evident when we experience a sense

---

[11] See Chapter 3 for more on these memory systems.

of, 'Oh, here I go again', or in a family a relational script, 'Here we go again'.[12] A further question is whether the concept of a secure base script adequately covers the variety of attachment patterns. For example, in Waters and Waters' (2006) model, children who appear to demonstrate avoidant attachment patterns are seen as indicating a depleted or incomplete secure base script. However, it could be argued that they have developed an avoidant script that has a different set of propositions. Given that the children in insecure family systems lack the experience of the secure base script, it is perhaps more likely that they have developed a well-established insecure script along the lines of the scripts indicated in Table 4.1.

Table 4.1 Insecure attachment scripts

	Avoidant Script	Anxious–Ambivalent Script
1	A child (or infant) and mother are minimally occupied.	A child (or infant) and mother are ambivalently occupied; the parent may be ignoring or interrupting the child's play and autonomy.
2	They are interrupted by an event or another actor. The infant is distressed.	They are interrupted by an event or another actor. The infant is distressed.
3	There is a bid for help.	There is a bid for help.
4	The bid for help is not detected or is ignored and help is not offered, but a communication may be sent that activity-based interaction is acceptable.	The bid for help is detected, but the response may be to escalate, ignore or focus on the attachment figure's needs.
5	The offer to engage in activity (as opposed to a request for emotional reassurance) is accepted.	The offer of help is ambivalently accepted, with escalation of the distress, anger and the like.
6	The activity offers a distraction that is marginally effective in overcoming the difficulty.	The help is not effective in overcoming the difficulty and may exacerbate the distress.
7	The help does not include effective comforting and affect regulation.	The help does not include effective comforting and affect regulation.
8	The child attempts to self-soothe or suppress their attachment need and pair return to minimal interaction or activity.	The pair are both likely to be emotionally aroused and may attempt to separate and/or continue to escalate.

---

[12] In the next chapter, this question will be explored in more detail, especially the issue of how we may select to overwrite our scripts and attempt to abandon or resist them as opposed to continue with and even emphasise them. This is a central issue for attachment theory in that the attachment system can be seen as combining both unconscious scripted sequences that are triggered by attachment stresses but also conscious intentions and choices.

Rather than these patterns representing degrees of deviation from a secure base script, it may be more appropriate to consider that children develop different types of scripts that carry an expectation that a parent will either be unavailable or inconsistently available.

> ### Pause for thought 4.1
>
> Consider the following 'facts' regarding aspects of a person's life and attachment experiences. These are fictional but typical of many families with whom I have worked clinically.
>
> > John's dad hit him sometimes. He worked nights as a security guard and drank sometimes. John occasionally got into trouble at school.
>
> First, how would you connect these into a brief story? What first comes to your mind?
>
> Second, think about how these might be told by someone using dismissing, preoccupied attachment and balanced secure attachment orientations. When you have done so, read the remainder of this box for how in research and clinical practice I have found them to be told.
>
> **Dismissing Attachment Narrative:** This would typically feature minimisation of the father's abuse, exoneration of his actions and overall self-blame rather than blame of the father. There is no balanced resolution but instead an over-emphasis on dismissing the events and assuming self-responsibility.
>
> > I was hit a few times by my dad <laugh>but I was a bit of a handful as a child. Dad worked nights as a security guard and used to drink a bit to cope with the stress of his job. He must have got a bit fed up with me and clipped me one now and again <laugh>.
>
> **Preoccupied Attachment Narrative:** This is typically driven by emotion and anger and tends to place most of the blame on the other. There is typically no sense of resolution but a lingering sense of injustice.
>
> > The drunken old bastard used to whack me all the time for no f'ing reason – black and blue. He was such a useless prat and could only get a job as a security guard. He practised his hard man Rocky stuff on me, the sod, when he was drunk all the time . . .
>
> **Balanced Secure:** This might contain a balance of blame towards the parent as well as acceptance of some self-responsibility and indication of resolution.
>
> > I was hit by my father sometimes and I did not like it. He worked hard and must have got tired, but he could still have controlled his temper a bit better than he did. I was frightened at the time and sometimes hated him for it. I reacted a bit and got into some trouble and that must have wound him up a bit, and I can understand that. We get on a bit better now and have talked about things, but I have promised myself not to hit my kids.

Waters and Waters' (2006) research suggests that our core attachment scripts come into play as we start to connect the facts of such events. How did you start to connect these? As you can see from the example accounts, they give different meanings to the facts, prioritise certain aspects of them and imbue them with different emotional content. In my clinical and research experience, these dismissing and preoccupied patterns are common and, as will be the focus of the next chapter, they contain limited resolution and integration, especially in terms of implications for parenting one's children. The lack of emotional awareness in the dismissing patterns and the exaggerated emotional arousal in the preoccupying patterns might leave the parent less able to develop effective strategies to manage difficult or painful emotions in their children and other relationships.

A further complication occurs when a parent acts in highly inconsistent ways with a child – for example, being affectionate at one time and cold and rejecting at another. This has been observed in the more problematic, so-called 'disorganised' attachment patterns. It has been suggested (Bowlby 1973; Main, Kaplan and Cassidy 1985; Crittenden 1997) that in this situation, the child may develop multiple models of the attachment figure. One representation the child holds may be that the mother is loving, but at the same time a competing sensory memory may be that she is frightening and unavailable. It was suggested that the multiple models may differ in terms of how they originated and which of them serves a dominant role (Bowlby 1973; Main 1991). Generally, though, the models that develop in infancy were seen to be more influential because they developed in terms of more primitive non-verbal, procedural and sensory representations and were less open to conscious awareness and reinterpretation. It was also argued that such incompatibility is managed by a process termed *defensive exclusion* – since, for example, the perceptions of the parent are so painfully incompatible, one of them is excluded or dissociated. Being out of awareness, the assumptions are not subject to conscious reappraisal, discussion or testing to explore whether the perceptions are still true. As a result, there is little opportunity for change and elaboration (Bowlby 1973). Bowlby emphasised that problems arise when a child needs to hold multiple models of her attachment figure and cannot find a way of resolving these into a coherent model.

Internal working modes, scripts and triangles

Attachment theory has predominantly held a dyadic focus of exploring the child's relationship with one parent at a time. But children have a more complex task in developing an IWM when there is inconsistency between the parents. We saw an example of this in the case of Kathy and her family (Chapter 1, Therapy extract 1.2) where her father, George, employed a predominantly dismissing strategy and her mother, Mandy, a preoccupied one. This makes it difficult for a child to develop a consistent attachment script since what is acceptable with one parent is not so with the other. In terms of the child's IWM, it requires the child to supress expression of emotion with one parent and exaggerate it with the other. Figure 4.3 illustrates how the child faces a complex task in developing a strategy in such a situation.

82 ATTACHMENT AND FAMILY SCRIPTS

The child can assimilate such a configuration into their IWM, especially if the parents, though different in their responses to the child, do not attack each other's approach or employ the child to get at each other. It is even possible for a child to hold a coherent IWM if the parents separate. For example, that 'Mum and Dad are not married any longer and, though they do not like each other anymore, they still each like me; both are still good parents to me and both love me, though they do not love each other'.

However, in cases where there is substantial marital conflict that disrupts the parenting roles, it becomes more difficult for children to distinguish between the roles (i.e. confusion exists in the family dynamics), as seen in Figure 4.4.

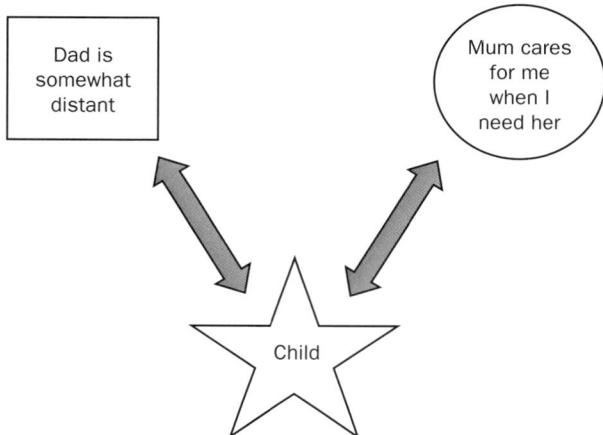

Figure 4.3   Different attachment patterns shown by parents towards a child

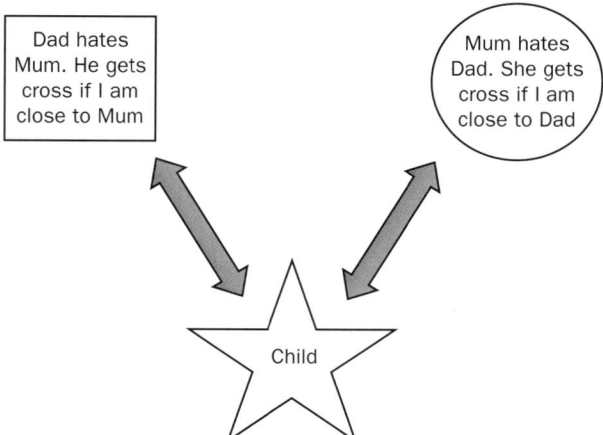

Figure 4.4   The child caught up in parental conflicts: Attachment triangulation

The child is caught in a no-win situation in such a triadic process. Again, we saw an example of this in Kathy's case in Chapter 1 (Therapy extract 1.2) and the combination of having to try to adjust to both conflicting attachment orientations of the parents with conflicts between, and pressure to take sides can amount to a highly challenging and potentially problematic process. A child may *appropriately* conclude that it is impossible to maintain positive emotional connections with both parents. The child, therefore, has difficulty in constructing coherence in terms of the relationship with each parent and any overarching schema to help resolve the incongruities. A consequence can be that developing an IWM is impeded, which has negative implications for the development of friendships. Problems can particularly surface at adolescence, when children are more in need of developing peer friendships and moving towards independence from their parents (McGoldrick and Carter 2011; Dallos and Draper 2015). Possibilities may also include attempting to side with one parent, intervening to resolve conflict or withdrawing altogether. Any of these solutions can help clarify the IWM. The inconsistencies decrease if the child completely rejects one parent or both. Alternatively, intervening to resolve the conflict gives the child a higher-order self-schema of 'my role is to resolve their conflict'. Nevertheless, all of these solutions, well-known to family therapists, result in the child losing important attachment relationships or becoming a carer who *provides* rather than *receives* attachment security.

Choice, autonomy and reflective functioning

The IWM develops initially through *implicit* representations and later through *explicit* or conscious ones. This allows the IWM to permit autonomous action and conscious choice and helps to extend attachment theory to include a social constructionist perspective.[13] This is the view that core to human experience is to understand and give meaning to events in our lives through social or relational frameworks, and the meanings we develop are seen to be unique and based on our personal experiences. A central point is that our understandings of the world do not just describe events, but we actively shape our world through the meanings we ascribe to these events, which we ascribe in accordance with certain socially produced 'constructs'. In essence, our constructs define the boundaries of what we perceive to be our possible choices.

This view of the IWM resonates with George Kelly's (1955) idea of a *dynamic personal construct system*. Kelly employed the metaphor of 'man the scientist' to capture the idea that people are continually making choices of actions based on their understanding and predictions about the world. He emphasises that our choices are based on bipolar constructions: safe versus unsafe, rejected versus accepted, good child versus naughty (etc.). In a similar way, our attachment experiences can be seen to lead to such constructs about the world and our self. A child

---

[13] See Chapter 2 for more on social constructivism.

learns not only that a parent may be rejecting but that they are not worthy of love and comfort. Here, the child is learning both sides of the constructs in that they learn the role of being *rejecting* as well as *rejected*. This reciprocal role may later be employed to guide their constructions and actions towards themselves and others. Similarly, a child who experiences a relationship of trust and support from its parents learns about receiving emotional support as well as giving it to others and their actions in later life may reflect this.

The IWM needs to be able to not only adapt to and integrate new information but to be open to revision and elaboration. It needs to be susceptible to the possibility of reflection and the development of understanding to help manage the confusion and contradictions in family dynamics. Main (1991) has suggested that an important feature of a child's development and a way of resolving contradictions and incongruity in or between parents is to be able to develop *metacognitions*. This involves one's ability to stand outside or to take a 'bird's-eye view' on one's thinking processes – to think about one's thinking. In relation to conflictual family situations, between parents or where the child experiences the parents as inconsistent, the child may be able to resolve this by recognising that they have mixed feelings and that these result from the contradictory ways the parents behave. Main (1991) traces the development of metacommunicational abilities to the core mental development of the child and how this may be impeded by the nature of the attachment context. She argues that the capacity for metacognition is linked to the basic ability of the child to understand that the world can be perceived in different ways by different people and one's view and understanding of it can change. Main suggested that children under four tend not to be able yet to understand that the world can be perceived in different ways and so are not able to reflect on and question their own or their attachment figures' views. Piaget (1955) also described metacognition in terms of a young child's views of their parents as omnipotent and omniscient, as being infallible and not to be questioned. He described how this can change dramatically in adolescence where children delight in challenging their parents and demonstrating their own critical powers. Main (1991) also clarifies that young children have difficulty with *dual-coding* (i.e. the idea that something can be seen in two different ways) – for example, that mother can be both 'nice' and 'mean'. She argues that older children are therefore less vulnerable to difficult attachment experiences because they are able to form metacognitions. For example, a response from a mother that 'You are a bad child' is more easily dealt with by an older child who is able to reason, 'I *may* be a bad person because Mum seems to think so but, on the other hand, she has been wrong about other things – she is not always right'. For a younger child, it is harder to resist the parents' perception. Moreover, the young child may be in a particularly vulnerable situation with a parent who is highly unpredictable and incongruous – as in the case of parents who display preoccupied, mixed or disorganised attachment patterns.

Particularly problematic may be situations where the parents engage in distortions or deceptions regarding experience. This may be motivated by a wish to protect the child. Bowlby (1988) had described how in some complex and distressing family circumstances, such as a suicide of a parent, there may be attempts by one parent to protect themselves and the child from distress by engaging in a distortion of the facts surrounding the circumstances, such as a death.[14] Main (1991) links such findings to the question of children's ability to mark the source of information in their lives. Children under three are less able to do this and are not easily able to tell if their memory of an event comes from their own experiences or what was told to them by a parent. Because older children are more aware of the source of information and place greater value in what they have experienced, they are less prone to develop contradictory multi-models. This cognitive developmental perspective is important because it adds to explanations that emphasise mental suffering as the key explanation of why we hold multiple models and do not process or resolve the contradictions between them.

Fonagy et al. (1991, 1994) have similarly emphasised that a central feature of the child's IWM is the ability to engage in metacognition. They offer a broader concept that includes the ability to think about others' internal thoughts and feelings and suggest that this is the fundamental ingredient of attachment processes. As in Main's (1991) formulation, they identify the mother's ability to be able to reflect on the child's internal state as central and argued that the child experiences security in the sense that they can feel safe that their mental state will be accurately understood and responded to by their parents. The parent's ability to be reflective is in turn acquired through their childhood experiences with their parents, and it is argued that this *reflective ability* is the core feature of the transmission of attachment patterns across the generations (Slade et al. 2005). The parents transmit to the child a sense of whether it is safe to engage in an exploration of people's feelings, intentions and beliefs. Fonagy et al. (1991) demonstrated a close link between reflective functioning and attachment patterns by developing a measure of parents' reflective ability and the attachment style classification of their infants in the Strange Situation. The ability to understand one's child, it is argued, is based on the parent's attachment history, especially their own parents' ability to understand their thoughts and feelings (Fonagy, Steele and Steele 1991). Likewise, Bion's (1962) concept of *containment* proposes that the parent is seen as both understanding what has caused the child to be distressed and being able to experience what the distress feels like. The mother also needs to communicate that she does not feel overwhelmed by the distress herself and a reassurance that, together, they will be able to cope. Fonagy et al. (1996) suggests that mothers who tends to employ dismissing patterns are likely to emphasise a practical sense of an ability to cope but an inability to convey an emotional empathy so that the child feels that their mother understands how they are feeling. Conversely, preoccupied parents may be able to communicate that they understand the feeling but are less able to communicate a sense of coping. West (1997) suggests that reflective functioning is both biologically

---

[14] In studies of children who had lost a parent due to suicide, Cain (2002) found that a quarter of them reported having been subjected to pressure from the remaining parent to believe that they had been mistaken in what they had seen or heard. In one case, a girl discovered her father's body hanging in a closet but was told later that he had died in a road accident (Cain and Fast 1972).

based and will develop naturally in humans unless impeded. Reflective functioning and metacognition abilities are central to our ability to change. An important phenomenon is that some people, despite extremely adverse childhood experiences, appear able to create coherent IWMs. This suggests that reflective ability is available as a potential resource to aid us in this, though at the same time it may be impeded in various ways. It is also suggested (as will be discussed in Chapter 5) that the utilisation and promotion of metacognition is one of the core features of most forms of psychotherapy.

In summary, Fonagy et al. (1991) argue that reflective functioning involves us in a variety of sophisticated mental activities. These include being able to:

- reflect on our own thoughts;
- see contradictions in our own views;
- contemplate alternatives;
- recognise where our beliefs and memories arise;
- hold the view that it is possible to see things in different ways;
- recognise that we may have become stuck in a particular way of thinking;
- recognise the consequences of our thinking in particular ways; and
- recognise how we may be influenced by other's opinions.

Some of the most severe psychological disorders appear to be linked to the breakdown of these abilities. For example, personality disorders appear to include a deficit in reflective functioning, which is seen as resulting from relationships in childhood where the child experiences negative and possibly abusive behaviour from a parent. This means the child is punished for showing attachment behaviours, and any attempts to reflect on this punishment may be further met with discipline. At the same time, the child may inhibit their attempts to be reflective and think about why the parent may be acting in this way, since the conclusion may be negative and produce further anxiety: 'she hates me', 'she cannot be trusted', 'she is dangerous' and so on. A solution is to block out these thoughts and not to engage in reflective processes regarding the parent. While it has been suggested that this leads to a 'disorganised' attachment style (Fonagy et al. 1991; Main 1991), it might instead be possible to see this as organised and appropriate given the dysfunctional context occupied by the child (Crittenden 1997).

Summary and reflections

This chapter has described the IWM and how it encapsulates the concept of attachment as constituting a multilayered set of representations. These are initially implicit and non-verbal and form the basis of attachment security acquired in infancy. Since they are non-verbal and unconscious, they may be less easily amenable for revision and instead more entrenched. The IWM has also been described as consisting of explicit, conscious and verbal representations. The (implicit) former has been considered in terms of attachment scripts and the (explicit) latter in terms of conscious cognitions and intentions. In secure patterns, information from all of the levels is available for developing self-protective strategies, as opposed to insecure patterns where it is unavailable. Blame and responsibility for one's actions and those of others was considered and research was summarised to suggest that people using dismissing patterns are more likely to blame themselves for problems and those with preoccupied patterns tend to blame others. The chapter reviewed how reflection is necessary to assist in integrating the levels of representation and to resolve inconsistencies. However, children need the assistance of their attachment figures to help them to develop reflective capacities and it is necessary to extend the dyadic focus of attachment theory to consider triadic and wider family systems. Parents may employ contrasting attachment strategies with a child or draw a child in to take sides against the other parent in marital conflicts, which can pose a considerable challenge for children and their attempts to use reflective thought to try and resolve difficulties, not least due to their parents' unavailability to help them reflect. An important theme of the chapter has been that the implicit and explicit representations may be in conflict with each other.

The following chapters will discuss how experiences of danger, trauma and loss may impede resolution and instead aggravate familial conflicts. In particular, Chapter 5 discusses how conscious intentions regarding parenting – how a parent wants to parent their child – may conflict with implicit attachment scripts, which may leave parents not only confused about why their intentions do not seem to be realised, but also inflicted with a sense of failure and self-blame.

5 Autonomy and attachment: Corrective and replicative scripts

Introduction

> This chapter elaborates on the concept of attachment scripts and develops the central theme of this book, which is that our narratives and attachment representations can simultaneously embody *unconsciously* determined, scripted actions and the potential for engaging in *conscious* choice.[15] Scripts and internal working models (IWMs) contain not only representations of past events but our anticipations of the future and strategies for coping. A key feature of this combination is the intention to repeat or change aspects of our childhood experiences of how we were parented – this combination shapes how we act as parents towards our children and contains ideas regarding intimate relationships with our partners and other family relationships, such as grandparenthood and step-parenthood. There will be an emphasis on how scripts can be seen to contain *positive intentions* – either to do things better or to repeat what we experienced as positive. This allows a consideration of parental responsibility over how a child develops without necessarily implying *blame*.

Continuity, change and conscious intentions

The concept of attachment scripts, discussed in the previous chapter, offers an understanding of how attachment experiences in childhood combine to form patterns of actions that are transmitted across generations. There have been extensive debates in attachment theory regarding whether there is continuity of attachment across generations and how much change occurs. One of the important ways that this transmission has been studied is to compare parents' narratives in the Adult

---

[15] This chapter is inspired by the concept of *family scripts* from John Byng-Hall (1995), and attempts to build on his ideas in exploring how the influence of scripts can operate at conscious or unconscious levels.

Attachment Interview (AAI) with their child's responses in the Strange Situation procedure. To illustrate:

- Fonagy, Steele and Steele (1991) found that the AAIs of pregnant women predicted how secure or insecure their child was with them in the Strange Situation procedure;
- studies using the AAI suggest that the style of narrating and the extent to which we have been able to develop a coherent narrative about our early experience appear to influence how securely attached our child will be to us; and
- while estimates across studies vary, broadly the attachment strategy of parents as shown in AAIs has been found to predict their child's attachment response in the Strange Situation procedure between 50–70 per cent, and this may be higher for clinical samples where the parents have experienced substantial traumas in their childhoods (van IJzendoorn et al. 1992; Hautumäki et al. 2010; Crittenden and Landini 2011; Ensink et al. 2015).

On the other hand, in general, findings indicate that there is considerable continuity as well as change between the parenting patterns and attachment responses revealed by the AAI and Strange Situation procedure (van IJzendoorn et al.1992; van IJzendoorn 1995; Crittenden et al. 2014). Crittenden and Landini (2011) have therefore argued that the findings can offer support for continuity and for variation and change across the generations; arguably, both are true and there is a need to explain both how we parent in ways that seem to reproduce our attachment patterns and ways that exhibit change or divergence. Without the possibility of change, families would be hostages to a relentless transgenerational cycle – this is evidently not the case, with parenting patterns constantly changing.

These studies rely on the use of correlations, which can only show that the AAI and the Strange Situation procedure classifications are associated with each other; they arguably cannot satisfactorily establish a causal relation (van IJzendoorn et al. 1992). So, a question remains: how do continuity and change occur in attachment patterns across the generations?

The AAI ends with an invitation for parents to reflect on what they have learnt from their childhood experiences of being parented, and what aspects of these they wish to repeat or change. This part of the AAI is generally just employed as part of the overall classification of attachment security. In my research and clinical practice, I have focused on this section since it indicates parents' conscious intentions regarding parenting their own children. I have found that most parents, when asked, express some conscious intentions to either do some things differently from their parents or repeat aspects of their parenting. Possibly, these conscious intentions help explain both the continuity and some of the changes that occur over the generations. One of the key themes in this chapter will be that both the variation in and the continuity of attachment patterns is explained by the extent of coherence or division between *conscious* and *unconscious* representational systems. Hence, change and continuity may be significantly shaped by conscious intentions to repeat patterns acquired in childhood and by unconscious attachment scripts similarly acquired. Where these are consistent, the continuity is very likely and relatively unproblematic. But continuity may also occur when, despite our intentions to do things differently, we find ourselves repeating unconsciously acquired patterns. The conscious intention to do things differently (e.g. to allow our child greater freedom) may be influenced by unconscious scripts so that, if our child experiences distress or problems, our anxiety may trigger our unconscious scripts so that we react by overly restricting them, imposing strict curfews and monitoring our child closely in order to keep them safe. Here, despite our intentions, our child might develop an anxious–ambivalent attachment pattern, perhaps angrily resisting what they might perceive as our interference but also becoming increasingly unsure and anxious. Changes in patterns across the generations might also be prompted by the child. For example, where parents predominantly employ a dismissing attachment strategy, a child can develop a more preoccupying strategy to arouse attachment care from the parents. This can be understood particularly in larger families where the siblings may develop distinct strategies to gain the parents' attention (Crittenden et al. 2014). We need to explore the nature of unconscious scripts and conscious intentions carefully.

Positive intentions

Many parents intend to do things differently, at least in part, to how they experienced being parented. In my clinical experience, this is possibly one of the most significant patterns in that a parent may feel at a loss, desperate and unable to understand why their conscious attempts to do things differently, and sometimes much better, than their parents appear not to be working. This may be accompanied by a sense of despair when they find themselves repeating the same negative behaviours. The following quote is from someone who was part of my clinical and research work with families who had a child diagnosed with autism. It illustrates an intention, and a sense of desperation, to do things differently to, in this case, one's mother:

> I wanted to be more of a friend and we [(them and their children)] could laugh and joke together and they could come to me and say whatever they needed to say and not feel uncomfortable and have an opinion and be able to express an opinion.

I have seen over 40 families with such a diagnosis and the quote is typical. Every parent articulates some intention to repeat or alter aspects of the parenting that they experienced. Likewise, parents of children presenting with other conditions or problems, such as anorexia, self-harming, depression or attention deficit hyperactivity disorder (ADHD), also typically express a variety of positive corrective intentions derived from their childhood experiences. This fits with the general orientation of most forms of therapy in assuming that parents and other family members are generally acting on the basis of positive intentions – they want the best for their child. This has become a cornerstone of systemic family therapy (SFT) – for example, Tomm's (1988) approach of positively connoting intention and Palazzoli et al.'s (1980) technique of positive connotation. More broadly, it is central to most individual-oriented therapies – for example, Rogers and Truax's (1965) unconditional positive regard and Kelly's (1955) concept of validation of a person's construing as a key ingredient of change.

Of course, we can think of circumstances where parents appear to hurt, attack, neglect and abuse their children and it can be difficult in these circumstances to see any positive intentions behind their actions. This poses some fundamental dilemmas for therapists and professionals working with families, children and couples. It is always important to protect people and help ensure their physical and emotional safety. It also offers some moral dilemmas regarding whether holding a view of positive intentions can serve to excuse or exonerate actions that need to be controlled or to incur punishment. A considerable debate has raged concerning these issues in the practice of family therapy. An important concept is that of *neutrality* – that no one has unilateral control over events and that all contribute to relational patterns that have developed. Palazzoli et al. (1980: 11) stated this as 'the therapist is allied with everyone and no one at the same time'. However, the work of Stratton (2003) highlights the tension between therapists' attempts to achieve a non-blaming context and the family members' desires to have their own accounts validated. Even when, as therapists, we are trying hard not to appear to be blaming of parents, they do not necessarily experience it this way.

Scripts and narratives

As we saw in Chapters 1 and 2, this position of validating intentions poses dilemmas and contradictions. How is it that if parents' intentions are positive, they often appear to do things that are counter to their intentions and, from the outside, do not look positive? We might be drawn into formulating that they are deliberately being deceptive and masking their actions by claims of good intentions. The clinical and research evidence suggests otherwise, however. Intentions are conscious plans for action based on what we have learnt from our accumulated experiences through our childhood and subsequent intimate relationships. It has been suggested that the fundamental way that we make sense of our experiences and cope with the demands of life is through *narratives* (Bruner 1990; White and Epston 1990). The concept of a script can be understood within the framework of a narrative in that narratives can be seen as having both a conscious and unconscious component. The unconscious part of a narrative constitutes the way we tell our story.[16] This is similar to the idea of a script – that our story has an unconscious pattern of anxiety, anger or security. One definition of a narrative is that it consists of the *facts* of a story

---

[16] As we saw in Chapter 3, the same set of facts can be told in an angry and exaggerated way or in a flat and minimising way.

(i.e. the setting, participants and key events), the *manner of telling* the story and a reflective conscious component called the *resolution*, which is about what we have learnt from the events, what they add up to and what lessons we can take from them for the future (Labov and Waletzky 1967).

> ### Therapy extract 5.1
>
> The following is an extract of a session with an adoptive mother (Rita) who was struggling and asked for help with her adopted daughter (Marcia). Marcia had been previously placed into care and her birthparents refused to take her back, despite taking back her two siblings. Rita described her childhood as featuring an emotionally distant and formal relationship with her parents. Her father, of African-Caribbean heritage, had been a police officer and Rita described how as a child she had felt compelled to keep up appearances and not display negative emotions. The following are two sections from her AAI, which was employed to guide the therapeutic work with Rita and Marcia.
>
> **RD:** *'Can you remember when you were hurt physically as a child? What did you do, what happened?'*
>
> **Rita:** 'Oh you had to be brave. I broke my leg, it took them three days <laugh>to take me to the doctors . . . well, I say I broke it, I tore the ligaments in my knee, I kept having baths. They [(her parents)] said that it would get better; it didn't get better. I had to be six weeks in hospital, you had to be brave <laugh>, so it's a standing joke in our family: *don't* break your leg! <laugh>'
>
> **RD:** *'What about if you were upset emotionally, what would you do? Can you remember a specific time?'*
>
> **Rita:** 'I can't, I didn't really show much emotion, I tended to put myself away. In a way, I didn't like the comfort back. Problems at school, I took myself away and dealt with it myself.'
>
> **RD:** *'Can you remember why you thought that?'*
>
> **Rita:** 'I just felt that she [(her mother)] wouldn't understand. I was the only one who went through these things, so I needed to deal with it . . .'
>
> Source: Adapted from author's personal clinical work and research.

Rita was locating her responses to Marcia within a life-story narrative of a strict, religious, African-Caribbean family environment in which self-reliance and minimising emotional outbursts was expected. In terms of the secure base script[17] suggested by Waters and Waters (2006), we can see that Rita did not use any of the three

---

[17] See Bowlby's [1973: 359] quote in Chapter 3 for more on the secure base.

core premises: she suppressed her attachment needs – for example, the pain with her broken leg; she did not expect her attachment figure to respond; and she did not experience her needs being resolved. The component called *resolution* constitutes what we have learnt from our experiences and shapes what we take forward from these experiences. The resolution part of a narrative is what can be called the point of a story, what it adds up to. When this resolution is missing, the story can have a sort of 'so what' quality, in that we cannot see what the story adds up to, what the person telling the story has learnt from their experiences, and what it is that they are wanting to share with us or lead us to understand about their experience. In attachment terms, this translates to the concept of what strategies we have developed to keep ourselves and the people we care about safe This involves sets of contrasts in terms of what we perceive as having been useful, what should be replicated, and what has been ineffective or dangerous and should be abandoned or corrected. Corrective scripts can be seen as encapsulating the part of the narrative that constitutes parents' intentions to be better than their own parents – for example, to be more emotionally available to their children or to have a more affectionate relationship with them (Dallos and Draper 2015).

Byng-Hall on script: Corrective and replicative, autonomous choice, and conscious intention

Byng-Hall (1985) developed the concept of corrective and replicative scripts to further explain the central premise of attachment theory: that emotional patterns are transferred across the generations.[18] In the first way in which Byng-Hall employed the concept of scripts, scripts can be seen as relatively automatic and, by analogy, as pre-programmed patterns of actions, beliefs and emotions. These can appear to be *replicative* whereby we repeat ways of dealing with our attachment demands in ways that appear similar to what had been our experience. For example, I may have learnt not to bother my parents when I was upset as a child and to instead turn to myself by way of distraction, play or other activities. I may then repeat this pattern in my current relationships – for example, with my children or partner. Alternatively, I employ a *corrective* script and try to act differently. For instance, in not being so impatient with my children or, in more extreme cases, I am determined to act in opposite ways to what had been my childhood experience. Setting a course to act differently to our parents often seems to be associated with strong unresolved feelings towards them. A balanced approach is recognising that there might have been some positive aspects of their actions but also some things that we want to do differently. Related to this is the extent to which we can also think about our parents' intentions and what forces drove them. I have heard parents talk about how they recognise that their parents meant well but unfortunately it did not work out as

---

[18] This has also been discussed in terms of a *pendulum swing* (Crittenden et al. 2014) in relation to intentions to employ different attachment strategies when parenting or engaging in romantic and other intimate relationships.

they may have hoped. It is also common to hear parents describe how they recognise that their parents were from a different era and influenced by different values and circumstances. In my experience, parents who struggle to develop ideas about their parents' intentions and demonstrate either strong emotional reactions, such as preoccupying resentment or a shutting down of feelings and reflection about this, also have difficulty in relation to their own children.

> **Pause for thought 5.1**
>
> In the appendix, there are some examples of parents' attempts to contemplate their actions and intentions. The inability to think about our parents' thoughts, feelings and intentions has been linked to difficulties in reflecting about our own children (Fonagy et al. 1991). You may wish to look at some of these examples now.
>
> - How do the examples of parents' intentions in the appendix serve as guides for their parenting?
> - Do they seem helpful in setting our ideas about how they will parent their own children?
> - How might we start to have a conversation with the parents about their parenting?
> - How might we try to positively frame their intentions?
>
> Research has suggested that some parents have low reflective functioning, and this is associated with insecure attachment and the development of problems in their children (Fonagy et al. 1991). Unfortunately, this can be regarded as a form of deficit and one that requires considerable time and therapeutic input to improve. We might consider instead that the parents are trying their best and have positive intentions and share this thought with them. This might permit a more positive framework for our work with them and allow and encourage them to be able to develop their abilities to reflect. In my experience, this is more productive, in part because it feels less blaming to start with an exploration of how they understand their parents' intentions before progressing to an exploration of their understanding of and intentions regarding their children. Once parents sense they will not be blamed, I have been surprised at how quickly their reflective functioning can improve (Stedmon and Dallos 2009).

Corrective scripts are more typically associated with the second manner in which Byng-Hall employed the concept of scripts: as *a form of autonomous choice*. This connects with the discussions in the previous chapter concerning secure base scripts as sets of implicitly held propositions and orientations to action intended to reduce attachment needs. It also connects with the basic conceptualisation of the attachment system as evolution-based, something triggered by dangers and that needs to respond rapidly and automatically when one is faced by potentially dangerous situations. It is possible that replicative scripts operate most clearly at the unconscious and implicit level. In contrast, corrective scripts may more accurately be regarded as *corrective intentions* that operate at a conscious level. Their purpose is to override what we may have experienced as unhelpful actions from our parents. Though it is possible that this correcting happens in part at an unconscious level, it may nevertheless be vulnerable to break down at times when we are highly emotionally aroused and experiencing danger. We frequently hear parents remark, for example, that despite their intentions to do things differently to their parents, they find themselves repeating what their parents did, as seen here:

> We were turning the page and I was like 'be careful, don't turn the page too hard or you'll tear it, you'll tear it' and I don't know how many times I'd said this . . . I said, 'and you need to be really careful because, you'll tear it' and then he just . . . he . . . was pushing boundaries . . . and he tore it. So, I just grabbed his hand and I smacked it and he looked at me, horrified . . . and I just cried. Weirdly, I can't remember things in my childhood. But I can remember what I did to my son. (Adapted from author's personal clinical work and research.)

This leakage or intrusion of a replicative script into a corrective script is a very frequent phenomenon in all forms of therapy and has been variously referred to, for example, as 'negative automatic' thoughts in cognitive behavioural therapy (CBT) and 'transference' or 'projection' in psychodynamic therapies. Though not *exactly* the same conceptualisations they point to the sense of inevitable replay of past experiences despite conscious awareness or insights.

The third usage of scripts by Byng-Hall was as *conscious intentional processes*. Here, we can hear people describe how their experiences have led them to consciously choose to follow and replicate aspects of the parenting they experienced as opposed to forming deliberate choices to avoid or even reject most aspects of what their parents had done with or to them. In therapy, we typically find that most parents can consciously articulate what they have chosen to replicate or correct from their childhoods. When invited to think about their parenting intentions, sometimes parents describe that it is not something that they had previously thought about. A typical response is something like, 'But you are making me think and yes, I do want to do things differently'. For some parents, it is expressed as a strong emotional reaction – that they 'hated' much of what their parents did and that they want to try to do things differently, in explicit condemnation of their parents.[19]

This concept of conscious intention is vital for attachment theory. Without this concept, it risks remaining essentially a deterministic account of human action, as if we are relatively blindly driven by the attachment programming that we experienced in our childhoods. This is a narrow-sighted critique of Bowlby's formulation

---

[19] Later, we will discuss this in relation to unresolved states of trauma and loss, which can lead to strongly reactive scripts.

of attachment theory, since he was also very interested in and committed to the idea that positive change and resolution of attachment difficulties was possible. In addition to seeing therapy as a vehicle for promoting positive change, he promoted changes in social policy – for example, careful exploration of the potentially negative effects of institutional care. Unfortunately, this critique is still frequently articulated by social constructionist theorists and therapists (Birns 1999) and leads to an unhelpful lack of cross-fertilisation of ideas.

Unconscious scripts and conscious intentions: Becoming aware of contradictions

The rest of this chapter will focus on exploring the important interaction between consciously and unconsciously driven action.

As with psychodynamic theory, it is apparent that we do not simply act on the basis of logical choice but that we are driven by forces that shape our actions, sometimes despite our best intentions. Attachment script theory indicates some important and highly prevalent ways that this occurs in families. Reconciling the idea of scripts and conscious intentions has been a major debate for the social sciences, and the debates have been widely articulated (Gergen 1999). I suggest a view of people as *both* driven by unconscious forces *and* as capable of forming conscious intentions. It is possible that conscious intent 'trumps' our unconscious attachment scripts, though this is not predominantly the case. At times, we may be unaware of the extent to which, despite our intentions, our actions are being shaped by unconscious scrips based in early procedural and sensory memories. Even when we are aware of attempting to do things differently, this does not always work, and we find ourselves repeating patterns we want to avoid.

> **Pause for thought 5.2**
>
> Suppose you are a parent or care-giver. Reflect for a few minutes on what you might want to repeat or change from the parenting you experienced in your childhood. This might be in relation to how you wish to be a parent to your children; in terms of your romantic relationships; or as a grandparent, social carer or member of another close relationship. As you reflect, try to identify times when you feel a sense of 'Oh dear, I am acting, talking, feeling (etc.) just like my mother, father, carer (etc.)' to notice that, despite your intentions, you may be repeating some patterns.

In the following extract, we return to the characters we encountered in Therapy extract 5.1. This time, we will see how Rita articulates a moment of awareness of repeating emotional responses towards Marcia that she consciously does not want to. In therapy, such moments of insight can be experienced as powerful instances of positive change, especially if they occur spontaneously from the person rather than from being offered by the therapist. When the insights are internally generated, they are compatible with the person's narrative of the world and make sense for them. In contrast to when they are offered as interpretations by a therapist, there is the possibility that they are less compatible with the person and less easy for them to assimilate.

> **Therapy extract 5.2**
>
> In this extract, Rita articulates a typical dilemma when she is asked specifically about her conscious intentions regarding parenting. Rita makes a connection between her *heart* – the implicit script from her childhood – and her *head* – the conscious intention she has to allow Marcia to express her emotions. An interesting feature of this extract is that Rita does not explicitly blame or criticise her parents but just remarks that, 'I am never going to do that as a parent'.
>
> **RD:** *'What thoughts have you had about, as a parent, how you want to do things differently?'*
>
> **Rita:** 'I'm in complete conflict. As you're growing up you say, "I am never going to do that as a parent" but, I find myself doing it [(feeling cross with Marcia for her temper)] anyway – so that's my heart. But my head is saying, "Marcia is not capable of that, so I can't expect her to do that" – so I'm in complete conflict.'
>
> **RD:** *'So, do you see that in contrast to how your parents were with you?'*
>
> **Rita:** 'Yeah, I have those thoughts, "it doesn't matter if she is throwing a tantrum in the middle of the street, she needs to do that", but inside me I think, "Ohhh, if Mum and Dad knew . . ." It's that sort of conflict.'
>
> **RD:** *'So you try to be not so bothered by the image?'*
>
> **Rita:** 'Try not to, but still am.'
>
> Source: Adapted from author's personal clinical work and research.

The three types of scripts

Scripts can be seen to lie at an important cross-road between unconscious actions and conscious intentional choice, but it is important to disentangle these two uses of the concept. The first use of scripts as implicit, programmed patterns of actions connects to the early conceptualisations of attachment theory, which were based on research with infants (Ainsworth 1973; Waters et al. 2000; Waters and Waters 2006). The second use may perhaps be better conceptualised as conscious or sematic intentions (Critterden et al. 2014). To simply call these 'scripts' is perhaps confusing, unless we add that they serve as conscious attempts by people to re-author their lives, in effect to re-write their scripts (Anderson, Goolishan and Windermand 1986; White and Epston 1990). In the rest of the book, I will be differentiating between employing the concept of a script to refer to repetitive patterns and to refer to conscious intentions leading to a repetitive pattern *or* circularity.

There is also a third use of the concept of scripts. This relates to the *relational* aspects of scripts. This is central to attachment theory in that attachment is both the accumulative effect of the experiences that we had in our childhoods and an active, 'live' and ongoing process. It can appear that there are transgenerational patterns of attachment dynamics in families over generations in the repetitive patterns that seem to emerge. This is an idea that is very widely used in the repertoire of SFTs and is seen in examples like families where there is an evident pattern of coping with distress by turning to alcohol or other drugs. A typical example might be a family script running across generations where families turn to professional systems such as social services or mental health services. This might also involve children being removed from the family and taken into care. Importantly, we should distinguish scripts like these from conscious family values, such as educational or artistic achievement being important.

Pause for thought 5.3

Consider what might be some scripts in your family. In particular, there may be characteristic ways that people cope with distresses, setbacks, losses and illness. Also consider what differences there might be on the different sides of your family. For example, on your mother and father's side of the family and between you and your partner.

One of the most frequent examples of scripts in family therapy is parents describing how the traditions in each of their families are different – for example, in relation to dealing with illness, emotions or discipline. This can be a source of creative difference for families; it can also come to form the basis of conflicts and arguments. It is salient to note that parents may accuse each other of carrying negative aspects of the scripts from their family. Often, they have forgotten that the main way that their partner knows about this history is because they have told them! Rather than being seen as stories that have been told by their partner, they can assume the status of *facts* about each other's families. Revisiting these stories in therapy of their ancestry can be helpful – for example, in considering what positive as opposed to negative scripts they may have gained. We can also see an overlap between this idea of family scripts and biological concepts such as heredity or genetics. For example, food may have been employed as a source of comfort and connection across generations in a family. But it may be argued that certain difficulties, for example difficulties with obesity, are predominantly biologically based rather than related to a family script (Holland, Dallos and Olver 2012). Similarly, there may be a transgenerational script regarding the importance of logical and rational thinking as a way of dealing with distress and difficulties. This has also been regarded as the influence of autistic genes shaping the actions of various members of the family. Often, the family scripts are unconscious and not readily apparent. Byng-Hall (1988) described how he grew up to perceive his family script as encompassing a sense of anxiety across the generations and having a theme of not facing up to challenges. He traced his family tree back to discover that his great-grandfather was the famous British admiral, Byng, who had been shot, allegedly for cowardice in the face of the French navy. He described how this script pervaded his family and his own experience but without a recognition of how this shaped attachment processes in the family over generations.

Scripts, intentions and improvisation

A further important consideration, which has been central to SFT, is that repetition over the generations may be more apparent than real. As an example, we typically hear parents stating that they experienced their parents as using harsh discipline and frequent physical punishments, but they go on to explain that their parents were a product of their times and that's 'how parenting was done back then'. This can function as a form of exoneration and idealisation of parents in not wanting to blame them – but it also has an important grain of truth in it. Historically, there have been important changes in family life, including expectations of family roles, how parenting occurs and how childhood is played out. As an obvious example, currently children are almost born with smartphones and spend a considerable amount of time engaged in social media. This is something I have little knowledge of and it was not a significant influence on parenting my own children; it is, however, influential for parents of young children today, especially around remaining safe online. Young children of four and five may be using digital camcorders to record their actions in ways that would have been science fiction for movie-makers 50 years ago. In addition, there are cultural variations. I am Hungarian and have an English wife. How I enact replicative scripts is influenced by British culture and how aspects of this have been absorbed by my partner. As Heraclitus (~535–475 BCE, Fragment XXI) wrote, 'You cannot step twice into the same river'. Analogously, replicative scripts may be illusory in that we cannot repeat what had happened to us as children because history has changed, the members of our family are different and so on. Hence, in order to replicate, we have to consciously modify what we have learnt in order to produce similar effects. What parents tell us is that they experience the same or similar emotional processes or reactions but realise that these may not fit the situation or in fact produce the contrary to what they intended.

Byng-Hall (1995) refers to the concept of improvisation in relation to scripts, which connects to the idea of *adaptability*. In applying scripts, we need to be flexible and realise that the context may not simply fit, as the following mother with a son who was diagnosed with psychosis explained:

> What they would do is show you that they are angry with you, whatever you have done. They cut off the communication and you feel isolated, so that's something that I tried. I did it, but I felt after some time— I reflected,

and I said, 'okay, this is not the right approach. I didn't like it when it happened to me, I don't want it to happen towards my children'.

(Adapted from author's personal clinical work and research.)

The extent to which parents are able to be flexible and adjust the application of both the implicit and explicit aspects of scripts appears to be related more broadly to their attachment styles or working models.

Attachment styles and scripts

In this section, we will look at how self-protective attachment strategies vary according to the way scripts are employed. I will present evidence from my research studies exploring scripts and clinical evidence. Broadly, this suggests that both the implicit and explicit components of scripts are substantively influenced by attachment strategies and that strong corrective scripts are associated with preoccupied attachment patterns in adults and, in contrast, replicative scripts with the dismissing patterns. People who have experienced secure attachment experiences in their childhood appear able to flexibly utilise both types of scripts in an integrated and balanced way. In people who have experienced consistent and secure attachment experiences in their childhood, there is a consistency between these implicit and explicit aspects of the working model or attachment scripts. However, approximately half of the general UK population have insecure attachment patterns, despite there being degrees of inconsistency between these implicit and explicit intentions (van IJzendoorn 1995).

People approach parenting with a combination of implicit scripts that are based on procedural and sensory memory systems. These scripts, as Waters and Waters (2006) have argued, constitute an important part of their core attachment strategy. In addition, their approach to parenting is shaped by conscious, semantically based intentions. The two combine to shape how the parent responds to their child and intimate partner's attachment requests, as seen in Figure 5.1.

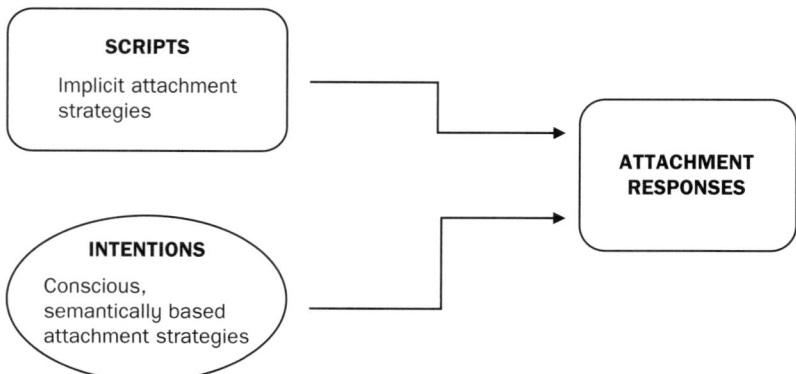

Figure 5.1 Attachment styles and intentions: A triadic process (the structure)

The division of implicit and explicit may be useful but there are also subtle variations on this. Most parents do not come to therapy explicitly stating what their corrective or replicative intentions are; however, when asked about these intentions, most parents are able to understand this concept and to offer illustrations of how it has influenced their parenting.

Attachment style, typically described as the 'working model', can be seen as a subtle and complex interplay between implicit attachment scripts and conscious intentions. These two facets of the attachment system may be congruent or conflictual. Specifically, the balance between a conscious and explicit intention to apply *corrective* intentions as opposed to *replicative* ones varies in line with people's fundamental implicit attachment script. I have explored the expression of parenting intentions through my research and clinical practice in the contexts of psychosis, ADHD and autism. This has utilised AAIs, Parent Development Interviews (PDIs) and qualitative interviews to explore how parents in these contexts express intentions. Broadly, my findings so far suggest that parents whose AAIs indicate an overall balanced and secure attachment orientation are able to articulate a balance of corrective and replicative intentions. They appear to feel safe and emotionally balanced in articulating some of the positive aspects of what they experienced as children but also to offer some criticisms:

> I think I try and do some things similarly, because they were always there when I needed them. So I try to be there. Like, if they need something, like a cuddle, I sort of try to give them what they need. And I try and teach them responsibility, that they can't always have exactly what they want, right now this minute. And I try and sort of teach them to do things themselves rather than doing it for them. And . . . those are the kind of similar things. But I do try and make sure that they each get that attention; that if they need any help with something, then I'll fight for each and every one of them. Not just kind of focused on one. I feel a bit like that's how it was when I was a child. I don't feel like it was intentional. But . . . it's just . . . that's how it felt.
> (Adapted from author's personal clinical work and research.)

In my research, such accounts were rare and most of the parents demonstrated essentially dismissing attachment patterns. For example, in work with families with a child with a diagnosis of high-functioning autism, I found extensive evidence of extremely dangerous and potentially traumatic events having occurred in their childhoods; in work with parents of such children, the predominant attachment pattern shown seemed to be a dismissing one; and a similar pattern emerged in my studies of parents with a child with a diagnosis of psychosis. Each time, I was initially surprised to find that, despite the severe experiences that had been stated, the parents generally did not articulate strongly worded corrective scripts. The following is an adapted quote from a mother of a child with a diagnosis of autism:

> Umm . . . well I guess I really want to stay calm, that's the most important thing. But the thing is, I don't always— umm, sometimes I am just driven to distraction. Yeah, so I think that's the main thing: to stay— to try and stay

> really calm and not— and I was blamed a lot, so I wouldn't want to do any sort of blaming. Umm . . . but unfortunately you do sort of find yourself slipping into these sorts of patterns with your children.
>
> (Adapted from author's personal clinical work and research.)

This mother described in her AAI that her father had severe mental health problems when he was a child and could act in physically abusive ways towards her. However, in the section where she was asked what she has learnt from those experiences with her father, rather than expressing a strong corrective intention, she describes, rather mildly, that she did not want to engage in any sort of blaming of her own children. She went on to describe, apologetically, that despite these intentions, she found herself slipping into some of the same patterns. This was consistent with her overall defensive style, which featured a strong wish to be self-reliant and not to burden others. In her AAI, she tended to minimise her difficult experiences and described them in a matter of fact, non-complaining manner. She also tended to emphasise small events where her father had been available for her and tried to see things from her father's perspective.

The findings from this mother and other parent indicated an important connection between how such intentions were articulated and attachment patterns. We discovered that parents like this, parents who predominantly were employing dismissing attachment strategies, found it uncomfortable to articulate any indication of criticism towards their parents. Their attachment strategy through their childhood had been to try to please their parents, to comply with their wishes and suppress negative feelings towards them, so the expression of criticism was difficult. Clinically, this is significant, since it alerts us to the fact that it is important to pay close attention to the language that people employ and realise that corrective intentions will be expressed in a mild form. In the previous case, this almost implies that her experiences were not that problematic or destructive. Likewise, in an account from another parent:

> I can remember feeling alone, emotionally, and confused. And I think it makes me more— and I think just like talking about stuff, having space to just chat about that and acknowledging emotions more helps.
>
> (Adapted from author's personal clinical work and research.)

This parent does not explicitly blame or criticise their parents but suggests, by both a reference to their own unhappiness as a child and a wish to acknowledge emotions more, that they wish to do things differently with their child, that there was a failing in the parenting they experienced. Again, this parent indicated an overall dismissing strategy and described earlier in their AAI, in a calm non-accusatory manner, various traumatic events in their childhood, including sexual abuse and emotionally distant parents, but was reluctant to explicitly identify the issues with the parenting they had. A pattern of muted expression of corrective intentions was very evident in this research and related clinical work. However, the factual details of the parents' childhoods frequently indicated that they had experienced many events about which they could have chosen to be extremely critical. This was consistent with the rest of their narrative in that expression of intense anger or derogation of their parents' actions was relatively absent. These findings were striking and may have important implications since the corrective and replicative intentions that parents develop and how intensely they apply these encapsulates what the parents have learnt to guide their strategies with their children. Frequently, the parents also indicated either some attempt to focus on replicative intentions in terms of picking out some aspects of what they considered their parents to have done well or to indicate, as the first parent did, that they find themselves slipping into certain sorts of patterns. Parents also described how these patterns that they felt a reaction against and wanted to correct could also appear as reminders of how their parents acted with the grandchildren.

Similar patterns emerged in the context of research I supervised in relation to parents with a child with a diagnosis of psychosis. One parent described how as a child her parents had made unfavourable comparisons between her and her siblings and expressed mild criticism that she didn't think that was a good idea. However, she quickly turned her account into an exoneration of her parents in terms of the adversities they had suffered:

> They would compare us unfavourably to one of the others and they now do this with the grandchildren. I can see them doing exactly what they used to do to us, which created ill feeling between us and wasn't a good thing to do. I don't think they realised that it was a bad idea, but I know with both of their upbringings that— that my dad was one of about 9, so I expect that he had lots of competition and also his mum died when he was 2 and he got shunted around between different people. So— and umm yeah, my mum, yeah there were only 3 but I don't think there was much money so umm— I don't think it was that they were trying to undo something that had been done to them. I just think they had perhaps not had consistent parenting maybe, I don't know.
> (Adapted from author's personal clinical work and research.)

The process of slipping into replicative scripts is a very potent one for parents but, importantly, many reflected that they developed some awareness of this process and consciously attempted to make adjustments. For example, the following parent describes inadvertently slipping back into replicative scripts but with an awareness starting to compensate for this:

> With the first two, initially I found that I automatically became firm and strict, and I wasn't aware then that maybe I don't need to be this firm with them, I can be softer with them. So it eased off, it did ease off, so yeah initially I think I fell into that mould, 'this is how you are a parent, this is what you do' and then realise actually no, you don't have to be like that. I became more my own person with them.
> (Adapted from author's personal clinical work and research.)

Preoccupied patterns

In contrast, some people articulate a strong sense of blame and condemnation towards their parents. I found this was typically consistent with attachment styles where there was a general sense of criticism of the parents, anger at the injustices that they had experienced as children and frequent derogations of parents. In the most striking cases, this was of both parents:

> To be more— umm, just to be more open and honest. I think I just felt like they were never— because they, they didn't, umm, show any emotion one way or the other. Umm . . . so yeah, to just be, just to be a bit more emotional, I guess.
> (Adapted from author's personal clinical work and research.)

For this parent, this explicit blaming of their parents and a clear expression of a wish to do things differently connected to a broader preoccupied relationship with them. They generated three words to describe their relationship with their mother: superficial, distant and unemotional:

> I would say it was just a general— a general pattern. So, for example, she never ever came to sports day or took me to school or picked me up from school. Umm . . . she would never talk about anything emotional or you could tell her the most horrific story in the world and there's no reaction.
> (Adapted from author's personal clinical work and research.)

Combining these two extracts, the parent emphasises 'never ever' to indicate a strong emotional negative reaction to their mother, and their AAI was peppered with criticism of their mother. Their corrective intentions, however, are rather vague. So, although the emotional reactivity against their mother is strong, they suggest that they want to be 'a bit more emotional, I guess'. Again, this was a characteristic pattern that, although now there was a strong expression of a corrective intention and a dismissal of any replicative intentions, this appeared to be driven by an emotive process leading to the intention lacking specificity and detail.

Triadic processes and multiple script models

In previous chapters, I have discussed the dyad focus of attachment theory in some detail and outlined processes in triadic family patterns. A triadic focus is also salient for considering attachment scripts and intentions. There may be significant differences between parents and they may disagree with and criticise each other's approaches to parenting. Where differences are accepted and valued, this can provide a richness for the chid and greater choice in their strategies. In contrast, where differences are undermined and the parents criticise each other, this may make choosing strategies all the more complex. In the following example, a parent

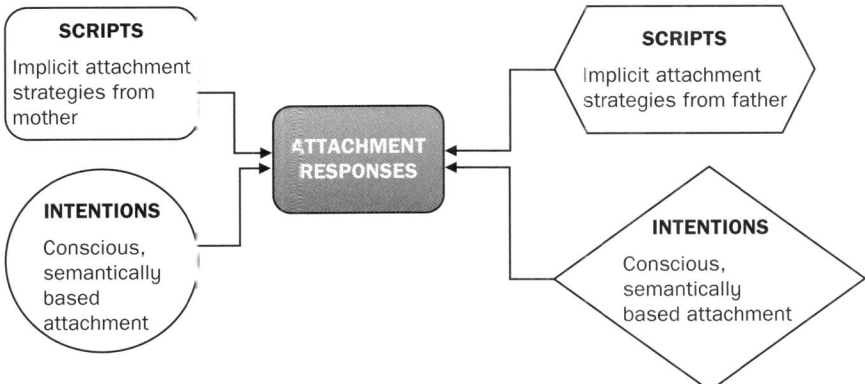

Figure 5.2 Attachment styles and intentions: A triadic process (the split)

describes differences between their parents and how they experience themselves in a corrective script in relation to their mother and a replicative one in relation to their father:

> My mum most probably doesn't show good affection. She loves everybody, she loves the kids, she wants to spoil them, all the usual sort of stuff. My dad was a little bit more umm— I think he was more emotional. He's quite, you know, he cares— my mum cares, but if my mum gave you a birthday card, it's a birthday card because it says 'birthday card' or 'birthday'. But my dad gets you a card, he's read it 10 times. If I buy a card for anybody, I read it, sometimes I go to five or six shops.
> (Adapted from author's personal clinical work and research.)

In this example, the differential pull of their corrective and replicative scripts is apparent but is not expressed in an extreme manner. It reveals that there is considerable potential for this to become problematic as the split can become not just between the replicative and corrective scripts and corrective and replicative intention in relation to one parent – but between them, as seen in Figure 5.2.

The influence of fathers

Though attachment theory has predominantly focused on mother–infant relationships, both my clinical and research experience indicates that fathers also have an extremely important role in the construction of both the implicit scripts and explicit intentional aspects of attachment responses. Fathers are often referred to as important attachment figures and, in some cases, as offering an intimacy that the mother did not. Sometimes, as in the previous extract and despite stereotypes, fathers are more emotionally expressive and available than mothers. It is also apparent that the role of fathers alters as children develop. Typically, fathers are less involved with very young babies, and the father's role in the early stages has been seen in attachment theory as supporting the mother (Ainsworth 1973; Crittenden et al. 2014). Arguably, cultural expectations in Western cultures regarding the involvement of fathers (e.g. the EU directive on paternal leave in 1996 [Hardy and Adnett 2002]) has changed to regard them as central attachment figures (Radin 1982; Grossman et al. 2002; Bretherton 2010), though the extent to which rights to paternal leave are accessible is mixed across EU countries (Hardy and Adnett 2002).

I suggest that it may be an important direction for future research using attachment theory to explore how both parents work together as attachment figures (McHale and Rasmussen 1998). For example, very few studies have been conducted looking at how parents work together in the Strange Situation procedure to manage the child's separation from one or both of them. The few studies available, however, suggest that when parents co-ordinate and co-operate effectively, a child may experience only minimal distress (Marvin and Stewart 1990; Dallos and Vetere 2012).

Changing the mode of expression

A striking feature of my research and clinical work has been that conscious corrective intentions are typically mildly or implicitly stated in clinical and research interviews. I supervised research in which we explored whether other ways of exploring intentions, such as using scaling questions, might be able to reveal their intensity more clearly. People were asked to rate on a scale from 1 to 10 how they saw their parents, themselves and their ideal view of themselves as parents. A range of dimensions were employed that were drawn from their AAIs, interviews and prior clinical experience. For example, parents were asked to place each of the following on the following scales:

- P – me as a parent.
- MP – my parents.
- IP – how I would ideally like to be as a parent

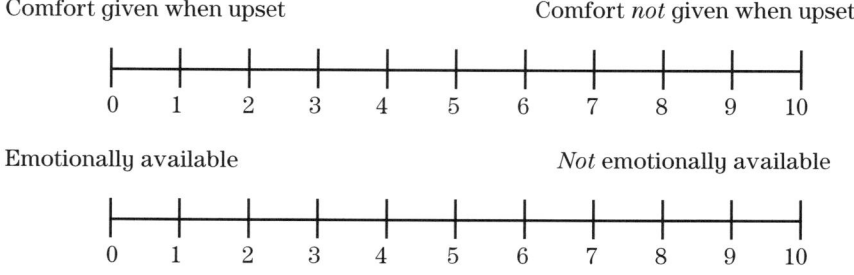

Large differences between P and MP indicate corrective intentions, small differences indicate replicative ones. Further large differences between these, but also between IP, could be seen to indicate intrusions of replicative scripts. Unexpectedly, in this and previous uses of this scale with a population of parents with a child with a diagnosis of psychosis, we found some extreme differences in ratings between P and MP. This was surprising given that these were not so evident in their AAIs or interviews. It appeared that placing indicators on a line was less threatening for many people than explicitly stating that they intended to do things differently to their parents, since this implied some disloyalty and overt criticism or blame. It was also an interesting finding that most parents saw their parenting as consistent with their ideal intention. But they articulated that they could not always achieve this and that replicative scripts could intrude.

Returning to our main theme, an interesting finding has emerged from these studies: parents frequently appear to attribute some failures in their intentions as not predominantly due to the intrusions of replicative scripts – repeating their learnt patterns in unhelpful ways – but, as in the case of one father of a child with a diagnosis of autism, as due to the lack of fit between one's intentions to repeat good aspects of one's childhood and the condition (i.e. autism). This father felt he was less able to be honest, to speak openly or show his feelings within his family than his parents were when he was a child, because of his child's autism. Being emotionally expressive, open and so on could be confusing for his son and trigger problematic behaviours.

Cultural values and intentions

Parental intentions are not only based on the experience parents have had in their own families but located within wider cultural discourses. These include a mountain of advice and instruction on parenting. Especially when parents have experienced difficulties in their own childhoods, they can become vulnerable to becoming confused by this advice. In particular, the parents in the examples I have offered wanted to do things differently as parents but were reluctant to express explicitly what they felt was unsatisfactory. This could leave them in a vacuum of mistrusting their experience, with a sense of inadequacy and a reluctance to adopt different strategies out of a sense of disloyalty. As in the case of the father with a child diagnosed with autism, one solution may be to capitulate to a medical model and see the failures as inherent in the child's diagnosis. This is tempting in relation to autism, which is described in terms of neuroatypical characteristics of these children. Sometimes parents explain this further by suggesting that their strategies work with other children. However, this may be insufficient as an argument, since differences between children are seen in all families and parents need to develop flexible strategies to adapt. Parents not only need to be able to reconcile the unconscious scripts from their childhood experiences with their conscious intentions but, further, to try to reconcile the contradictions within the cultural ideas, theories and values to which they are exposed. This can involve competing theories, for example, about the causes of ADHD and how to parent a child with symptoms of such a condition. As we have discussed in earlier chapters, parents may be wary of explanations that appear to blame them. Further, there are cultural differences in ideas about parenting that also shape parents' conscious intentions. For example, corrective intentions may be informed by ideas, such as how to be a 'good' Christian, Islamic, Jewish (etc.) parent.

Summary and reflections

The chapter has described attachment scripts and intentions and how these relate to different attachment orientations. It has also explored how attachment scripts function largely as unconscious patterns established in early attachment relationships and how conscious intentions intersect with each other. Where there is consistency between these unconscious scripts and conscious intentions, we are able to respond to attachment requests from others and to clearly articulate our needs. The chapter has also discussed how in a variety of clinical conditions there may be a mismatch between these two. Further, when we are unaware of this mismatch and where the unconscious scripts may operate outside of awareness, this may be associated with a range of clinical problems.

The next chapters will examine the clinical implications of these ideas. Note that some approaches, such as the Circle of Security (Powell et al. 2014), emphasise the therapeutic value of assisting parents to become consciously aware of how their implicit scripts operate to construct types of problematic interactions with their children. Chapter 6 will explore more complex and potentially problematic patterns, where aspects of a relationship show a repetition and a reversal of patterning across the generations. It will consider cases where parents have experienced severe dangers and losses leading to unresolved states of trauma and loss (the nature of these splits may be a significant component of what is described more broadly as *dissociated states*). For example, a script whereby a parent who has experienced being frightened or abused by their parents may attempt to correct this with their child but inadvertently appear to produce a mirror inversion of this script and experience being bullied and abused by their child. Parents in these situations have typically described having childhood experiences that were frightening and dangerous and left them with unresolved states of trauma or loss. The intersection of attachment scripts, intentions and unresolved states will be considered in relation to a range of clinical presentations. Solomon and George (2011) describe how the experience of trauma can result in parents feeling helpless and hopeless in the face of problems in their families. Finally, we will explore how such experiences can be understood in terms of collisions between their implicit scripts and their corrective and replicative intentions.

6 Trauma and scripts

Introduction

> This chapter will consider the influence on scripts of unresolved traumas and losses. It will develop the idea that the split between the replicative implicit scripts and one's conscious intentions as a result of unresolved traumas and losses may expand and result in dissociative states and that this can lead to scripts becoming inflexible and non-adaptive, which may in part explain the concept of *failed attempted solutions* – a key concept in systemic family therapy. Examples will be offered from research and clinical practice of how dissociative processes underlie such rigid scripts such that people are not aware of what drives their commitment to correct or repeat aspects of their experiences. The chapter will discuss the painful consequences of the failure of corrective scripts, which will be illustrated by clinical and research examples of such escalating cycles, for instance of parents desperately wishing to do things better for their own child and believing that they have worked hard to overcome their own negative experiences. When their positive intentions appear to be failing, it can be tempting to do more of the same and apply the scripts more strongly and rigidly. This pattern of repeated failure, however, increases negative arousal and a sense of failure, making it harder for the parent to reflect on the failure of the script and to apply modifications.

The road to Hell is paved with good intentions: Cause of problems and a non-blaming stance

This chapter has an ambitious aim, which is to draw together what may appear to be contradictory positions of (1) seeing family dynamics as causally related to the development and maintenance of problems in families while at the same time holding the view that (2) parents are not to blame. We saw in earlier chapters that this has presented such a challenging task that a predominant path has been to avoid research that appears in any way to hold families responsible for the problems that have developed. The vehicle for this is typically through the use of medical and illness analogies such that problems like anorexia, psychosis, autism and attentional difficulties are seen to be located within individuals and not in family dynamics. More specifically, this serves to avoid consideration of the possible influence that parenting and other inrerpersonal processes may hold. The central suggestion in this book is that it is possible to hold both a compassionate view of parenting and to consider it as having a causal role in the aetiology of problems. Parents' intentions can be positive and part of deeply held attempts to repeat what they consider to be good aspects of their experience as children or to alter what they perceived to be unsatisfactory. But these conscious intentions may conflict with the implicit scripts that can be activated by attachment demands and conflicts. My research and clinical experience have also indicated that even though many parents appear to have experienced extremely negative, dangerous, rejecting and even abusive early childhood relationships, their criticism of their parents is often quite mild. Strongly voiced and conscious corrective intentions appear to be rare and restricted to people whose overall attachment orientations are characteristically hyperactivating and preoccupied.

> **Running case study: Maria and her family (background)**
>
> Maria and her family will be referred to at various points in this chapter since she vividly exemplifies someone who has experienced a troubled childhood, one characterised by both traumatic loss and a highly dangerous and confusing experience of parenting. She took part in my research project exploring the lives of parents with a child with a diagnosis of autism and in my clinical feasibility study of SAFE – a family/attachment-based intervention for families with autism (McKenzie et al. In press). Maria described a childhood in which her mother had become increasingly emotionally volatile and frightening. As an adult, Maria came to the view that her mother had developed a form of undiagnosed psychosis that involved her being extremely angry towards her, threatening her and locking her in her room.
>
> *Source:* Adapted from author's personal clinical work and research.

Conflict between implicit scripts and explicit corrective intentions is a common experience and, though related to some difficulties, may be relatively unproblematic. However, the situation may be more problematic when this is driven by an experience of severe dangers and losses resulting in unresolved traumatic states, as in the case of Maria:

> When my son starts screaming, it triggers those feelings of stress that I had when my mother used to scream [at me] . . . that kind of brings it all

> back, it's sort of like triggering, which is why I think that I find it particu-
> larly stressful . . . you know there's a link between the past and the present.
> (Adapted from author's personal clinical work and research.)

She went on to describe how when she became a mother, she wanted to be different with her own children:

> My mother was getting all sorts of religious delusions. Everything was a sin, you know? She was hearing voices from God and, you know, appari-tions and— that was quite a disturbing thing, so . . . I've learnt to I, I umm . . . <clears throat>I would not bring David [(her son)] up with any sort of religious notion at all. I see that very sort of strict religious upbringing as a form of abuse.
> (Adapted from author's personal clinical work and research.)

Maria indicated in her interview, in an apparently calm manner, that there were aspects of her experience with her mother that she wished to correct, and she used the term 'abuse' in relation to an excessively strong religious ethos imposed on her. However, she articulated this criticism in a general manner rather than explicitly blaming her mother:

> The main thing is to stay— try and stay really calm and not— and I was blamed a lot, so I wouldn't want to do any sort of blaming, umm . . . but unfortunately you do sort of find yourself slipping into these sorts of pat-terns with your children.
> (Adapted from author's personal clinical work and research.)

Maria appeared to articulate a sense of futility in that she seemed aware that her intentions to do things differently to her mother may be frustrated, enforced by the fact that she found herself repeating certain patterns. An important feature here is that Maria appeared to be aware that she was replicating some of the negative aspects of her childhood experiences, but this *did not* free her of the repetition.

This conflict between conscious awareness and intentions and repetitive actions fuelled by unconscious attachment scripts is central to this book. I suggest that an important aspect of understanding this dilemma is to understand how con-scious intentions may be overridden by traumatic states resulting from childhood and, in some cases, from more recent experiences.

Unresolved states: Trauma and loss

The term 'trauma' is now widely used both in professional practice and everyday language. Both the major psychiatric systems (DSM-5: 309.81 [F43.10] and ICD-11 [WHO 2016: 6P40/41] include the following in their definitions of states that are described as indicating trauma:

- First, they require that there has been some *triggering event* – this includes experiencing first-hand or witnessing severe, life-threatening events; prolonged exposure to stressful events; or details of traumatic events. Hence, the events may not have happened to the person but there has been the act of witnessing some harmful or highly dangerous actions towards others.
- Second, they are described in terms of *reactions*, which includes states such as flashbacks and intrusions of disturbing memories or a sense of numbing and frozen states. Table 6.1 is a summary of the core reactions, which have been framed in terms that connect with attachment theory.

Overall, the symptoms are required to have lasted for some period of time (over a month) and to be causing significant impairment in social and occupational activities. A critical point that is often misunderstood is that trauma is a *reaction to* an event and does not *reside in* the event itself (i.e. a 'traumatic event' is an event that an individual has reacted to in a certain way, either at the time of the event or in later reflection on the event). The outcome of dangerous events cannot be predicted directly from the events themselves. To illustrate: in a piece of research I supervised (Freh, Chung and Dallos 2013) on young people's experience of having been in a car bomb attack in Iraq, we discovered major variations in whether they were in a state of post-event trauma or post-traumatic stress disorder (PTSD). One of the most significant variables determining whether trauma resulted was how the young person's family system reacted. Where the events could be openly discussed and emotional support was provided, the likelihood of long-term PTSD appeared to be significantly reduced. Within an attachment and relational framework, trauma can be seen as a

Table 6.1 Summary of core reactions

Preoccupying	The person may experience recurring memories of the event, dreams and nightmares, flashbacks, or intense reactions to a wide variety of cues associated with the events.
Dismissing	Continued efforts to avoid thinking about the events, avoid activities associated with the events, inability to remember important aspects, withdrawal and general diminishing of activity, or a shutdown of feelings.
Negative cognitions and mood	A persistent and distorted sense of blame of self or others, to estrangement from others or markedly diminished interest in activities.
Embodied state	The criteria include aggression or irritability, heightened startle – reactions, reckless or self-destructive behaviour, sleep disturbances, hypervigilance or related problems. These encapsulate the flight–fight reactions that are seen as part of attachment responses to danger.

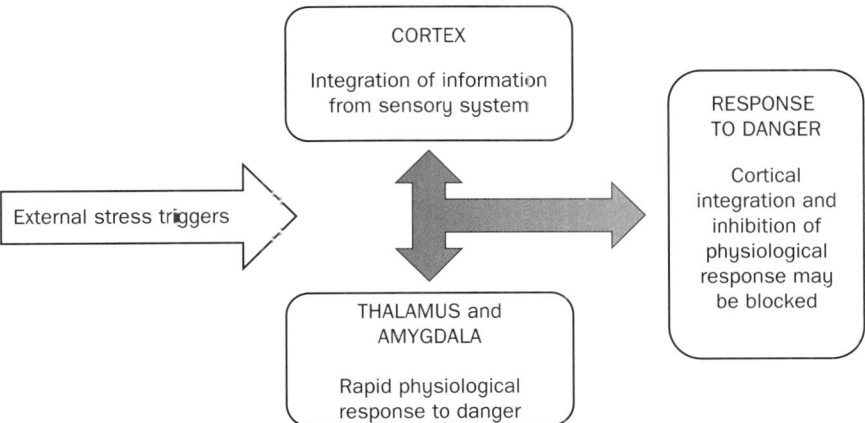

Figure 6.1 Trauma: Stress and cortical integration

process of how the attachment system responds to high levels of danger. For children, the response is to turn to their attachment figures for support and assistance to attempt to gain safety and to manage their fear and distress. Where parents are able to provide this, it seems that the consequences are likely to be less destructive.

All of our thoughts and actions can be traced to sensations that are transmitted, decoded and organised within the brain. Internal and external stimuli are processed to enable us to regulate and organise appropriate responses. Exposure to high levels of danger alters the way the infant's brain develops and how they organise sensory experiences. Repeated exposure to stress sensitises the developing infant so that an intense neurological response can become activated by relatively minor triggers. This ultimately leads to difficulties with regulation of arousal and physiological states, which in turn impacts on sensory processing and the capacity for learning self-calming techniques and emotional responsivity (Perry et al. 1995; de Gangi 2000). When children or adults operate in a heightened state of anxiety, lower-level processing networks take the lead in the learning and storage of information. Information about external stimuli reaches the amygdala via the thalamus to allow a speedy response to danger, but it only provides a crude archetypal representation of the stimuli as it bypasses the cortex (LeDoux 1998) (see Figure 6.1).

The cortex integrates information from the different sensory systems and provides an elaborated and relatively accurate representation of situations we are in. It guides interpretations about what is dangerous (and what isn't) and the degree of danger. For survival, the brain must be able to operate rapidly and below consciousness in order to generate appropriate flight–fight reactions to help ensure safety. One of the roles of the cortex is to inhibit this automatic responding when it might be inappropriate – for example, so that a relatively minor expression of anger, or an argument, does not immediately activate a massive physiological arousal and flight–fight response, like physical altercation. In other words, one role of the cortex is to inhibit or prevent an inappropriate or disproportionate response. A lack of

114 TRAUMA AND SCRIPTS

ability to inhibit such responses has been described as central to a number of clinical conditions, such as personality and affective disorders (Fonagy et al. 1991, 1994).

Trauma and attachment strategies

Children and adults in a variety of clinical populations have been seen to exist in a persistent state of hypervigilance (Fonagy, Steele and Steele 1991; Siegel 2012; Crittenden 2018). A persistent state like this suggests that these persons have been exposed to a variety of dangerous and potentially traumatic events in their childhoods or a particularly negative experience of severe and enduring danger, such as abuse, neglect and disintegration in their families. When this occurs for children, and especially when the source of the danger lies within the family, their experience is likely to be one of helplessness and a sense of failure of their self-protective strategies. I therefore want to consider how the basic attachment strategies are activated as the first response to danger but may be compromised and challenged by extreme, continuous dangers, resulting in states like hypervigilance. Particularly difficult may be when the danger emanates from one's attachment figures – for example, abuse by one's parents.

Developmentally, a child learns by how their parents respond to them and, more generally, to stressful or dangerous events. An important part of this is whether the child learns to *inhibit* or *exaggerate* expressions of fear, anxiety, and fight or anger responses. These two patterns relate to attempts to deactivate or hyperactivate arousal of the autonomic (flight–fight), para-sympathetic nervous system. Mikulincer et al. (2009) describe two processes at work: *deactivation* (avoidant–attachment) strategies involve attempts to reduce physiological arousal associated with the flight–fight system by attempting to deny or ignore danger and to rely on oneself to cope. *Hyperactivating* (anxious–ambivalent) strategies involve an extreme response to and a preoccupation with the danger and a sense of fear towards coping without the availability of the attachment figure. As we have discussed in earlier chapters, these two strategies are *functional* and *adaptive*. Use of deactivating strategies allows a child not to be rejected by their attachment figure, from which they will gain some protection and occasional comfort. Likewise, in hyperactivating strategies,

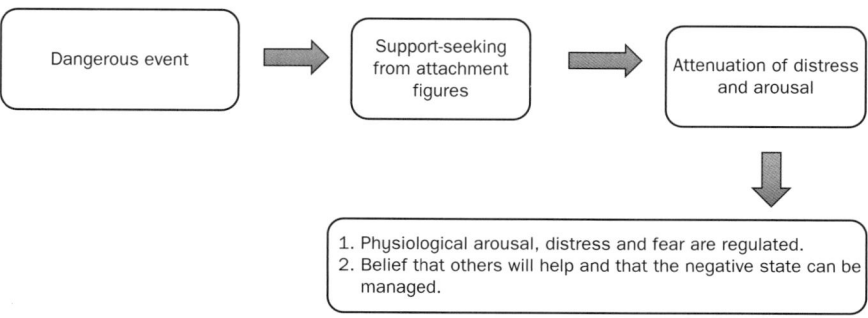

Figure 6.2 Trauma: A relational response to danger

though the relationships with the attachment figure may be conflictual, again some positive protection and comfort will result. However, for children who experience high levels of continual danger, these strategies may be less effective.

As you can see (Figure 6.2), the responses of attachment figures to trauma function at two primary levels: danger leads to an activation of the flight–fight response system via (1) activation by the amygdala and (2) regulation by the sympathetic nervous system. Assistance from attachment figures can mean that this system does not stay activated for long and physiological arousal may quickly subside.

Returning to the idea of the internal working model as composed of a set of representations at implicit and explicit levels, the response to danger can be summarised as:

1. **Implicit memory systems**: In deactivation, there is an attempt to suppress the physiological arousal and associated sensory material; in hyperactivation, there is a continual preoccupation with sensory material.
2. **Explicit memory systems**: This includes the conscious semantic representations, cognitions, understanding and future expectations regarding the events that have occurred. Importantly, this includes whether we can expect others to support us and the extent to which we should rely on ourself.

The relation here is that the pre-frontal cortical integration interacts with the arousal that is evoked at the implicit memory-processing level. However, when we have experienced a highly dangerous event, the level of arousal may be so extreme that there is a breakdown in our ability to use conscious cognition and to manage our fear and distress. This can lead to cognitions such as: 'I cannot, and will not be able to, cope', 'there is something wrong with me' or 'I should be stronger'. We need the assistance of our attachment figures to help us cope with these waves of intense and potentially overwhelming emotional reactions.

Facing the future: Self-protective strategies

Crittenden (2014) has suggested that to ensure the survival of ourselves and others we care about, we need to be able to use information from dangerous events to develop anticipations about the future and effective self-protective strategies. In other words, the key function of the attachment system is to help us cope with dangerous events and to ensure that we are able to extract information from dangers that will help to keep us safe in the future; resolving the experience of dangers is intended to enable the individual to take into the future information that is relevant to future protection and comfort and keep in the past what was unique to the specific event. In this, the definition of *trauma* or lack of resolution has three main forms, which relate to the characteristic attachment strategies that we have developed: *dismissing*, *preoccupying* and *secure–balanced*. Due to the continued intense arousal (i.e. flight–fight response) the child is likely to stay physiologically aroused and may become less flexible and more extreme in the use of these strategies.

In a study of children of looked-after children who had experienced long-term and severe dangers, Bhreathnach (2009) found that they all displayed aspects of trauma and a constant state of being in flight–fight mode. Further, children with the avoidant patterns displayed more fear and those with preoccupying patterns showed more anger than those with deactivating–avoidant patterns. Some displayed a combination of both, especially when they had contrasting attachment patterns with each of their parents. This is important because none of these patterns were effective in using available information to help the children to remain safe in the future. Later, we will look at how these patterns developed in childhood prepare us to be able to assist with keeping our children safe. First, let's look in more detail at the role dismissing (deactivating) and anxious–ambivalent (hyperactivating) attachment strategies have in response to high levels of danger.

Dismissing (deactivating) strategies and danger

People who typically employ dismissing strategies are likely to react as the first response to danger by suppressing, minimising, or pushing away information about the events that have occurred. A consequence of this is that information that we need to keep us safe in the future – for example, places or people to avoid or precautions we need to take – is missed. We may even tell ourselves that this was a one-off event, that there was nothing we could have done about it and so on. This unfortunately leaves people vulnerable to repeating the events. On the other hand, the short-term positive value of this strategy is that it pushes out of conscious appraisal thoughts and potential triggers that might reactivate the highly unpleasant state of arousal. The continuing problem may be that because the memories, imagery and so on are suppressed, their power to re-evoke high levels of emotional or physiological arousal does not diminish or become attenuated. This leaves the person vulnerable to intrusive memories or the so-called *flashbacks* that can be highly distressing for the person and their family. They can also be associated with a sense of loss of control and feeling at the mercy of the memories, which may be triggered by unforeseen circumstances, rather like standing on a land mine.

Dismissing strategies are associated with a range of indicators or trauma markers. Crittenden and Landini (2011) summarise these as indicated in the Adult Attachment Interview (AAI) but they can be seen as strategies that are employed to cope with highly dangerous events or extreme losses. These include:

- **Dismissed** – severity of events minimised and apparently relegated to be almost out of consciousness.
- **Blocked** – the distressing events are not consciously remembered and no explicit account is given, though there may be some hints in unusual imagery.
- **Displaced** – the distressing and dangerous events are minimised or dismissed for the person but are described as having severely affected someone else, such as a sibling.

Preoccupying (hyperactivating) strategies and danger

People who employ preoccupying strategies are likely to respond to traumatic events by maintaining the state of anxiety and distress and focusing on all aspects of the experience. This can lead to a highly generalised sense of anxiety and fear such that a wide range of stimuli have the potential to produce arousal, anxiety and distress. The consequence is that too much information is assumed to be relevant and there is a lack of ability to discriminate what is relevant information for future self-protection and what is not. The world consequently becomes experienced as unsafe, with the potential to lead to withdrawal and attempts to avoid any potential reminders. There may also be a constant concern to share the anxiety and stress with others, potentially leading to a sense of exhaustion in family members. The short-term benefits may appear to be a belief that by remaining alert, the chances of repetition are reduced. High states of arousal are likely to thus be maintained. It is as if fuel is being poured on to the fire – the power of the memories to evoke negative emotions is enhanced rather than diminished. Also, it is likely that over-generalisation takes place such that other places, people and events not part of the original dangerous event(s) develop the power to evoke negative emotions *as if* they were present. Consequently, attenuation of the arousal is reduced and the arousal spreads like a forest fire. The strategies associated with preoccupying responses include the following:

- **Preoccupying** – there is a pervasive conscious awareness of the events and emotional re-enactment as if the person were experiencing the event again.
- **Vicarious** – this is a concern with events that have occurred to others and can represent a pervasive fear of the world as a dangerous and overly hostile place.
- **Anticipated and imagined** – these consist of concerns that have a basis in reality, for example family conflicts, but an anticipation or imagination that these might turn to become extreme, such as severe violence or murder.

Secure–balanced (balanced activation) strategies and danger

In many ways the concept of secure versus insecure attachment is confusing and unhelpful. Hyperactivating and deactivating strategies are not simply or predominantly insecure. Instead, they are what the attachment system is composed of and both are necessary. They can become problematic when we in effect become hostages to one strategy and lose flexibility to alternate freely, in a balanced way, between them. Some suppression and dismissing of the memories and effect may help us to maintain our activities and confer a sense of coping. On the other hand, expressing feelings can allow the processing of the sensory memories and imagery to diminish. The flexibility to be able to use both strategies means that the potency of the emotional arousal may eventually be diminished and that this arousal is less likely to operate in a dysregulated way that interferes with cognition and the reflective thought required to deal with future events.

Trauma as relational

Trauma theories have predominantly focused on explanations at the individual level. Attachment theory offers a significant development by clarifying that it is a relational process. Children, and adults, turn to their attachment figures to assist them in managing dangerous events. This is not just in terms of protection but also to help in the process of integration and resolution. Specifically, as we are in the flight–fight state of arousal or prone to this being re-triggered, we need our attachment figures to assist us in regulating our affect and in extracting the information that we need to help keep us safe in the future.[20] To support this: in work with young people who were engaging in self-harm or suffering with eating disorders, I frequently heard that they felt unable to turn to their attachment figures, for example because they felt that their parents were already overwhelmed with their own problems and would therefore be unavailable (Dallos 2006; Crittenden et al. 2014). Similarly, a programme of research conducted by Harvey et al. (1991) found that positive prognosis for recovery from sexual abuse in young women was associated with a close confiding relationship in which the women were validated, believed and supported. In contrast, they described many scenarios where the opposite had occurred and there was a sense of never being believe.

Pause for thought 6.1

'I waited until I was 19 to tell my mother about the priest (*sexual assault as a small child*). She said it never happened. I waited until my middle 30s to bring it up again in a letter to my parents . . . My parents never engaged in a conversation about it until last summer (*she is now 41*) when my mother asked for information about the priest. My father refuses to discuss it' (Harvey et al. 1991: 526).

- What were your first reactions to this?
- What are your thoughts about the reasons why this woman's parents appeared to be reluctant to discuss her experiences?
- If you were able to talk with her parents, what explanations do you think they would offer?
- Why do you think this woman waited years before telling her parents?
- Do you know of similar examples from your own experience of parents struggling to believe or talk about similar events in their children's lives? How common do you think this is?

---

[20] Unfortunately, this is precisely what often does not occur in many clinical circumstances.

> In clinical work with abuse, it is common to encounter feelings of blame: 'were you angry, disappointed at the parents?' 'Were you angry towards the priest?' It is also possible that parents might have feelings of injustice and wanting punishment to be administered, a desire for revenge. Such feelings can similarly arise for therapists. I have had experiences of working with cases such as this where I have felt disappointed and even anger with the parents. But this may become a therapeutic dead-end. Instead, seeking information from parents and inviting and acknowledging their fears and concerns is usually more productive. I have been fortunate to work in teams where the other members have been able to act as attachment figures for me and help me to regulate such feelings so as to be helpful for the family.

Attachment theory emphasises that we need to understand traumatic states as a *relational* process. This includes a consideration of how (based on the core response to danger described previously) the person seeks help, avoids it or stays highly aroused and perhaps angrily blames others for what has happened to them. It is significant in the previous extract that the young woman did not tell her parents about the sexual abuse for over 10 years. This suggests that she was anticipating, correctly as it seems that they would not be supportive and help her to manage her feelings or to develop strategies for keeping herself safe in future. We can also note that she describes more of a response from her mother who eventually asks her for information about the priest. Children can experience themselves as being in a trap in such situations. For example, because she did not continually mention the abuse, it might lead her parents to think that it could not have been *that* important or even that she was exaggerating the event.[21] On the other hand, continually talking about the event can also be seen as part of an overreaction and even, in this case, risk the woman being rejected by her parents. It is also possible, as has been my clinical experience, that parents may feel helpless and do not know what to do. It is vital to be cautious and consider whether parents' attempts to assist were understood and acknowledged. We can also return to our discussion in Chapters 3 and 4 that it is not simply the facts of what people tell us but how this is done. For example, the woman in this case describes her parents' lack of response in a relatively matter-of fact manner, suggesting she is not attempting to exaggerate.

Interactions between corrective scripts and trauma

The desire of parents to correct and do things better than their parents did may mean that attachment requests from children become distorted or misinterpreted

---

[21] One might relate this to the #MeToo movement.

by the parent. For example, in the following extract, in discussing interaction with her daughter diagnosed with autism, this woman describes an apparently minor incident with her daughter that led her to feel some anger:

> I think once I was so angry with Jenny [(her daughter)] that I went into the kitchen . . . and I . . . it was probably only a dishcloth or something but I threw something and banged on the kitchen surface! And I was like 'Argh!' I mean, it wasn't in front of her [(Jenny)] – but she would have heard it. And I was like, 'Oh . . . that's what my mum did' and I hated it!
> (Adapted from author's personal clinical work and research.)

This woman describes an incident where, rather than being able to offer support and protection to her child, she reacted with fear or anger. In her case, she became concerned that her daughter had witnessed her anger. She appeared to have been less aware that her daughter may have also witnessed her anxiety and confusion

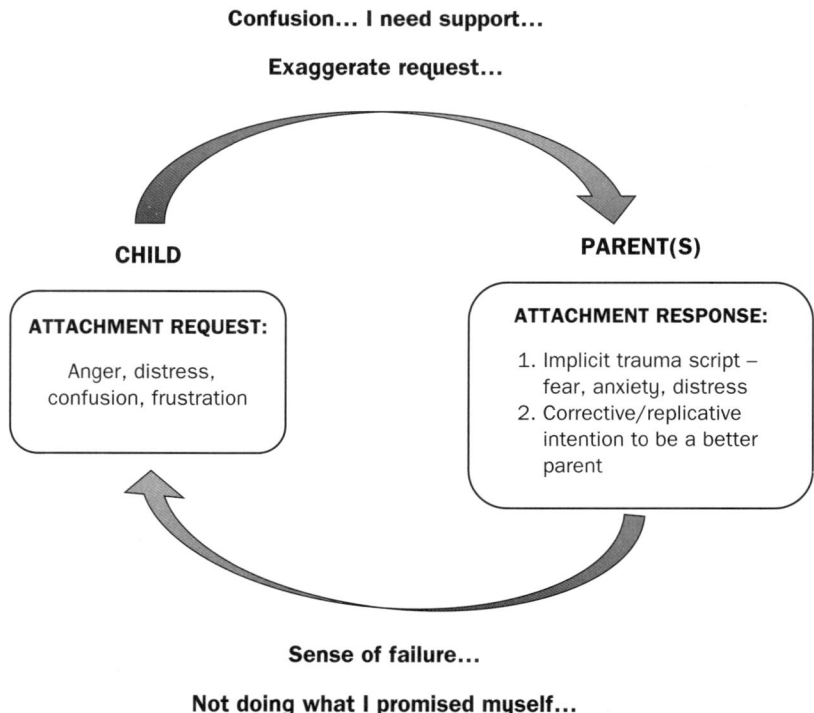

Figure 6.3 Interaction between trauma and scripts

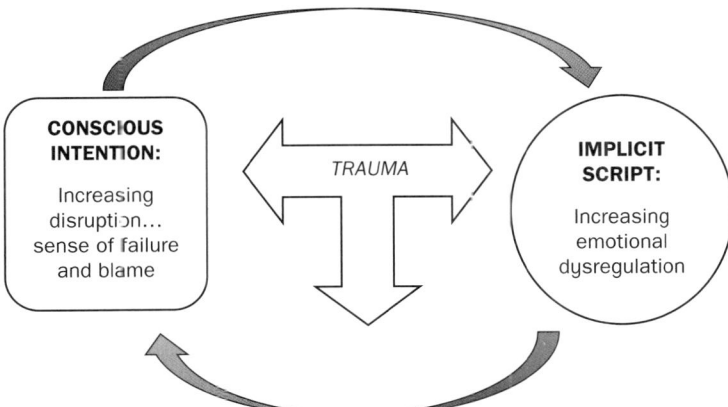

Figure 6.4 Scripts, intentions and trauma

that she had over-reacted. Not only expressions of anger by a parent but the desperation and fear of repeating what they so much want to avoid can be confusing and even distressing for a child. Unfortunately, negative cycles can become established even when they are triggered by positive corrective intentions. A schematic of this can be seen in Figure 6.3.

Young children may find it especially difficult to untangle the cause of a parent's distress, anger or confusion. As in the previous extract, the parent is critical and disappointed with herself for repeating what she promised to herself she would not do – express the anger she experienced from her mother. But for her child, this is not clear, and she can easily misunderstand her mother's distress as being her fault. Even if the woman tried to explain to her child why she was upset, this might be hard for her to understand and risks criticism of her grandparents.

The next figure, Figure 6.4, offers a summary of a recursive process between a child's actions and the response from the parent.

It is suggested that the parent responds in two ways:

1. at an implicit embodied level, activating their attachment scripts; and
2. in terms of conscious intentions. For example, for Maria, who we encountered at the outset of this chapter (Running case study), her intentions were to not shout and frighten her children as her mother had done to her.

The emotional arousal activated for people who have experienced traumatic events may result in a conflict between these two levels, which may cause the parent to feel out of control and likewise the child to feel confused and frightened. I have found this conflictual process to be frequent for parents who are carrying traumatic states from their childhood as these potentially lead to a number of dysfunctional strategies, for example:

i. Increasingly rigidly applied corrective intention.
ii. Employing a replicative intention that denies trauma and loss.
iii. Disorientation – attempts to apply but then abandonment of the corrective intention.

Let's consider these three dysfunctional strategies in turn.

i. Increasingly rigidly applied corrective intention

When the implicit scripts are embedded within a childhood history of trauma and loss, the conscious intentions may become driven or captured by powerful emotional memories. For example, where there has been a history of violence in the family, indications of anger and frustration, which are ordinary features of their attachment response (protest alongside vulnerability) in the children, may trigger powerful memories and an emotional reaction from the parent. This can unfortunately lead to a process whereby a child's attachment requests are misread as indicating aggression, which may result in the child becoming confused and attempting to suppress expression of their attachment needs and anxieties. Case study 6.1 is an example of a piece of clinical work with a family in a child and adolescent mental health services (CAMHS) setting. It was part of the family therapy service that I conducted with a colleague as the joint lead therapist (Figure 6.5).

Case study 6.1: Dan and his family (Part 1: Background)

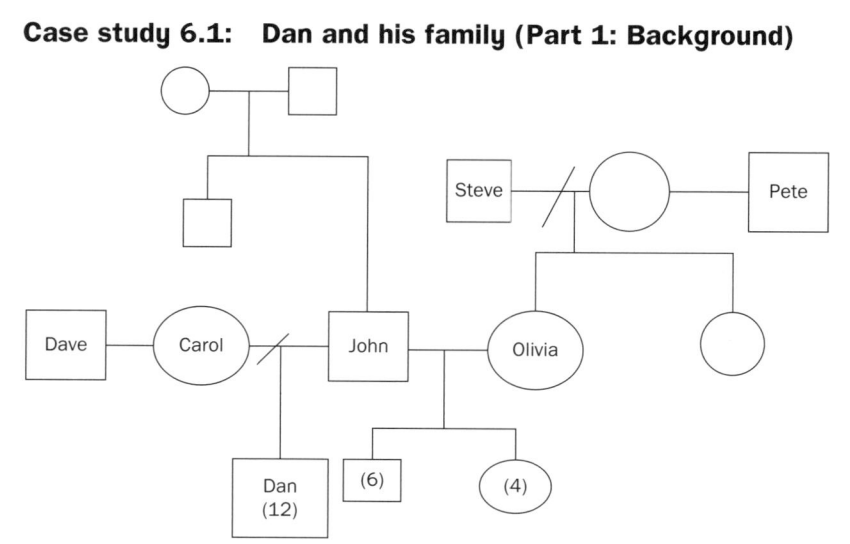

Figure 6.5 Genogram: Dan and his family

Dan attended therapy at a CAMHS setting with his step-mother, Olivia. She was becoming increasingly concerned and distressed at his 'angry and abusive' behaviour, which she saw as mostly directed towards her but feared for the well-being of her two younger children. Dan was described as, at times, very angry, smashing objects, locking himself in the bathroom and setting pieces of paper alight. Social services had arranged for Dan to live with his father's family because of concerns that his birth mother had started a liaison with a man with a previous conviction of a paedophile offence. Olivia said she was sympathetic to the difficult experiences that Dan had suffered. She and Dan's father were both critical of Dan's mother and described how she frequently let him down. Olivia described that she had tried hard to help and get close to Dan, including studying books on parenting that included the application of a time-out or 'naughty step' technique from the TV programme, *Supernanny*. Dan's father worked away a lot and left the brunt of the parenting to his new wife. Olivia displayed a deep sense of frustration and fear surfaced; she repeatedly cried and asked us for help.

On meeting Dan, he struck me in the sessions as slight, quiet and polite and did not contradict his step-mother; on the contrary, he was very deferential towards her. We were therefore somewhat puzzled by the extent of Olivia's distress and fear. She asked if we could spend some time with Dan to try and 'improve his behaviour' and we agreed that we could try some 'anger management' work with him. We also offered some time for her to discuss her own needs and sense of exhaustion.

Source: Adapted from author's personal clinical work and research.

Pause for thought 6.2

In a preliminary session with a family, I attempt to develop formulations about their concerns, what might have shaped the development of the problems and what might be maintaining these problems. This includes thinking about each person's attachment needs and orientations and the family's relational dynamics.

Think about some of the following in terms of your reactions to the information offered so far in Case study 6.1. Part of the purpose of this formulation activity is to help think about which avenues to explore further. It is essential in work with families to be able to focus one's attention, otherwise one can feel swamped by irrelevant information and risk missing helpful information:

- What attachment challenges do you think Dan has had, both in his history and currently?
- What thoughts do you have about Olivia's fears and reactions? Do you think they are predominantly related to Dan or might there be aspects of her history that may be influencing her actions, thoughts and feelings?
- Supposing Dan's behaviour is generally good, what do you imagine might have occurred in Olivia's childhood to influence her accounts?

Case study 6.1: Dan and his family (Part 2: Individual sessions)

We saw the family together, and most meetings were with Dan and Olivia. Olivia, however, was keen for us to see Dan on his own to help 'correct his anger'. Our formulation was that anger was a symptom of his difficulties and that he had a lot in his life to be angry about. However, we felt it important to be seen to take Olivia's concerns seriously and to offer individual as well as family sessions to assist them and gain further information.

Dan

In the individual session with Dan, he stated that he was not angry with Olivia and, in contrast, appreciated what she had tried to do for him. He minimised any negative feelings towards his birth mother and the main sense of loss he expressed was losing contact with his friends, since he had moved to another part of town away from them and had to change schools.

Olivia

In the individual session with Olivia, she expressed that she realised that Dan had suffered a range of negative experiences and, though she was sympathetic towards him, she also frequently found herself feeling anxious, fearful and resentful. When invited to describe her childhood, she revealed that she had experienced trauma and abuse in relation to her stepfather, who had been an alcoholic and violent towards her and her mother. She went on to describe how she vowed to herself never to express that kind of anger and violence in any way in her own family. It was discussed how this conscious intention might have made her especially sensitive to indications of anger in Dan. It appeared that she was being emotionally driven and selectively attending to indications of anger in Dan, which was blocking her conscious awareness that he was a vulnerable child who had much to be upset and angry about. When she was able to make this connection, it appeared to help her significantly and she said she now felt less fearful and helpless regarding Dan's emotions.

Joint session

In the subsequent joint session between them, we repeated the many positive things that Dan had said about her and likewise what she had said about him.

Source: Adapted from author's personal clinical work and research.

ii. Employing a replicative intention that denies trauma and loss

Some parents develop a strategy that involves a severe dismissal of the traumatic events in their childhood, almost to the point of blocking out their influence completely.

The conscious intention consists of a sense of portraying the childhood as happy and nurturing and using this perception as a guide to their parenting. For example, the following parent described in his AAI a childhood in which he had witnessed his father routinely physically abuse his adopted brother:

> I remember when we lived in the woods and my brother was really young, he [(his father)] made him stand outside with no clothes on, in the freezing cold – that wasn't nice either, umm . . . my brother was looking in through the window <laugh>it was cruel, umm . . .
> (Adapted from author's personal clinical work and research.)

This parent also described, in a matter of fact manner, that the husband of one of his father's mistresses had set their house on fire so that only his room was left. Further, he stated calmly that his father had engaged in '80 affairs'. Despite these facts, he described his childhood as happy:

> So, no sorry, I don't have a messed-up childhood <laughs>.
> (Adapted from author's personal clinical work and research.)

This parent's story indicated a remarkable dismissal of the difficult events in his childhood and a delusional replicative intention that, since he did not have a 'messed-up childhood', he was able to draw on this to replicate effective parenting. There is also a strong hint in his quote that he was wary of the formulation that he *did* have a difficult childhood, since this might imply that he was responsible for some of the difficulties that his child was experiencing.

Pause for thought 6.3

- What were your responses (i.e. thoughts and feelings) to reading these quotes?
- What thoughts do you have about why this father laughs when describing his adopted brother looking through the window, naked and freezing?
- The passage indicates some very distressing events. What type of attachment strategy does this father appear to be employing as he recounts these episodes?

When we read these episodes, powerful feelings may be invoked in us. For example, I felt angry about the grandfather's actions and I felt a sense of distress at his laughter. It seemed to me that the laughter represented a sad form of whistling in the dark. Use of humour has been described as a key component of resilience but in cases such as, this may also appear as a powerful way of turning away from unbearable feelings (Crittenden and Landini 2011; Kanai 2019). This father demonstrated in his AAI a strong dismissing attachment pattern in relation to his father and a somewhat angrier preoccupied one towards his mother. It appeared that it might have felt safer for him to be able to acknowledge some anger towards his mother, whereas his father continued to represent a more deeply frightening experience, which he attempted to minimise and deny.

When parents have learnt to use extreme dismissing attachment strategies in their childhoods, they sometimes demonstrate a remarkable need not to blame their parents. Part of this may be that the father remembers *some* positive times with his father as well as these distressing memories – but the relatively rare positive examples are exaggerated and selectively focused on in contrast to the more distressing ones. When, for example, he laughs as he remembers his adopted brother watching in through the window, this was not callous or uncaring but an attempt to manage his painful feelings as he recalls this event. Such laughter accompanying highly distressing memories is one indicator of the use of dismissing patterns in the analysis of the AAI (Crittenden and Landini 2011).[22]

iii. Disorientation – attempts to apply but then abandonment of the corrective intention

A third process appears to be a sense of disorientation, or loss of a compass to guide one's parenting, accompanied by sadness and, in some cases, a sense of despair. One may abandon explicitly trying to understand or utilise corrective or replicative intentions.

The following parent, a father with a child with a diagnosis of autism, explained that he had not been able to enact his replicative intentions from his childhood because they were not appropriate for his son with autism:

> I just assumed that they'd [(his two sons with a diagnosis of autism)] be interested in all the sports I would be interested in and want to do them – the same way I was desperate to do them with my dad. I think parenthood is like a vacuum: you make it up as you go, especially so with our two boys, we have to make it up as we go.
> (Adapted from author's personal clinical work and research.)

This example highlights the reciprocal nature of scripts and the effects of diagnosis. For this parent, having two of his children diagnosed appeared to have resulted in a profound experience of loss at missing out on the kind of relationships that he hoped he would be able to have with his sons, in this case to be able to replicate some of what he saw as positive aspects of his relationship with his father. For this parent, the theme preoccupied the narrative in his AAI to the extent that it was consistent with a pattern of unresolved loss. Despite this wish to replicate the relationship

---

[22] See the appendix for examples of laughter and humour in illustrative AAI extracts.

he had with his father, his AAI indicated that his father was largely emotionally absent from his life and, when he had been involved, had only chosen activities for himself such as going to a football match where his child 'could see bugger all'. It seems more that this parent wanted to replicate the *wished-for* closeness with his father than the *actual* relationship he had with him. So he wanted to repeat contact through sporting events, which he construed as repeating his relationship with his father but was in fact correcting for the emotional closeness that was largely absent yet defensively excluded in his account.

Multiple scripts: Triadic and family processes

The *implicit* scripts and the *explicit* intentions to correct or replicate do not simply arise from our experience with one parent. Attachment theory emphasises how our working models may be predominantly shaped by our primary attachment figure, typically our mother, but as we have seen in the examples throughout this book, the process is more complex. We may be drawn to develop our explicit intentions more in relation to one parent than another but may also hold combinations that include features of both parents.

Byng-Hall (1995) described how one's conscious intentions relate to wider family scripts spanning generations. We can consider this multiplicity of scripts as composed of the following:

- Parents may develop different implicit scripts from each of their parents or attachment figures. For example, a child may develop an avoidant and deactivating pattern towards one parent where they have realised that they will not be emotionally available and that, rather than asking for comfort and attention, they should inhibit this or even take on a reversed role of providing it for their parent.
- Children may hold a hyper-activating script towards one parent and maintain a preoccupying, hyper-activating emotional, angry and blaming stance with them.

Either of these scripts may be activated independently or together when interacting with one's child or partner. These may also become more exaggerated as a consequence of triadic processes. So, for example, where a child is developing an avoidant relationship with their father, this may escalate as they become more intensely involved with their mother, who also withdraws from her husband. This pattern has been identified as significant in cases of substance abuse in teenagers where a child regulates the intense emotional involvement with their mother by escaping temporarily into a drug-induced separation (Schindler et al. 2007). Furthermore, parents may develop different explicit corrective and replicative intentions towards their children or partner.

The running case of Maria will now be used to illustrate some of the complexities in corrective intentions and replicative scripts in relation to parents who offer different attachment strategies in relation to their children.

Running case study: Maria and her family (complexities)

Dismissing attachment with father and replicative scripts

Maria related that her father was very ill throughout her childhood with cancer and died when she was 9 years old. She described having to be very careful not to upset him. She also described her relationship with him as 'loving' and his death appeared to have been a traumatic loss for her, promoting a strong replicative script of trying not to upset others:

> But it was fairly distant 'cause he was so ill, and I'd say 'hands off' 'cause I had to. I was always told to keep away from him 'cause he was ill, so it was always 'stay away from daddy', you know?

Preoccupied attachment and corrective intentions

In contrast, she described her relationship with her mother as 'erratic' and it appeared to be suffused with emotion, anger and, at times, was very frightening and unpredictable:

> She became very ill, yeah, she became very paranoid. She thought everyone in the town was after her . . . I, you only had to look at her sideways and there could be screams, screamed at for days on end and, you know . . .

Transgenerational family scripts

Maria explained that she was influenced by a wider norm of putting up a false show of normality and respectability:

> The complete secrets and lies, the lack of communication, you know? My mother's family just wanted to put a gloss on everything to show what this fantastic perfect family they were, and their way of dealing with my mother was to pretend she didn't exist.

It appeared that the combination of the family script and the relationship with her mother led Maria to develop a powerful corrective intention that was in opposition to this transgenerational family script:

> I think umm . . . it's just made . . . I suppose there's a healthy amount of . . . it's that just kind of hypocritical repressive sort of attitude is what caused all the problems, why she never got treatment, you know? It was just something you didn't talk about.

Balancing competing replicative scripts and corrective intentions

Interestingly, it also seems apparent from the last quote that both Maria's corrective intentions and her dismissing replicative script in regard to her father come into play for her, in that she partly exonerates her mother by her anger towards the wider family's 'hypocrisy', positioning this as responsible for why her mother was not helped. Further to this, she went on to articulate more specifically how it has led her to develop a set of corrective intentions regarding mental health problems, parenting and how she discusses her own child diagnosed with autism:

> I don't hide the fact that my mother was schizophrenic, I don't hide anything. Umm . . . I'm very open about his condition. I don't want to just shove—shove things under the carpet.

Source: Adapted from author's personal clinical work and research.

Maria's example captures some important aspects of multiple scripts where different attachment scripts developed for her with each of her parents and related to differing corrective and replicative intentions (see Figure 6.6). This was fuelled by a transgenerational pattern whereby she felt that her mother's family were deceptive and covered up important emotional issues that needed to be explicitly discussed.

One of the clinical implications for Maria was that this combination left her vulnerable to the demands of her own autistic child. She had developed some explicit corrective intentions but, without the experience of secure attachment experiences, she was vulnerable to becoming emotionally hyperactivated in interactions with her child. She tried to find assistance in parenting books and courses but concluded that these left her even more confused and unsure what to do, feeling that 'nothing

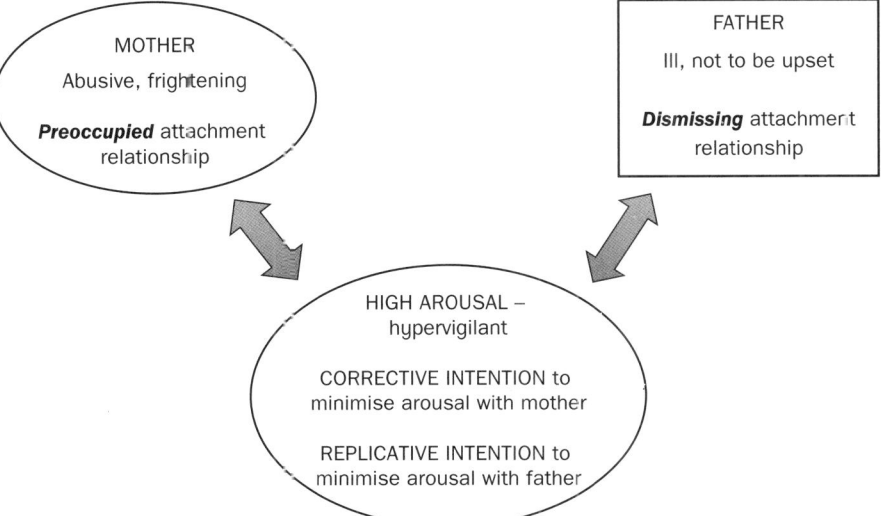

Figure 6.6 Competing and contradictory attachment scripts

worked'. Eventually, she concluded that there was nothing she could do but accept her child screaming at her. In effect, this was a replicative pattern with her as a victim of emotions but now the abuse was coming from her own child towards her rather than from her mother towards her. This mirrored inversion of parent–child roles across the generations has appeared to typify some patterns in families where the parents have experienced dangerous events leading them to hold traumatic states that trigger feelings of being powerlessness and becoming victims to their own children. Some similar findings have been reported by Solomon and George (2011) who describe parents who feel helpless and hopeless as parents and, in some cases, cannot prevent their children from emotionally or even physically abusing them. As in Maria's case, they describe how a parent with unresolved trauma may feel helpless to control a child who is angry with them and how the parent's fear and anxiety distresses, confuses and, in some cases, fuels the anger in the child. A dangerous and escalating process arises, which may underpin some of the problematic sequences – for example, those termed 'meltdowns', in autism (Montague, Dallos and McKenzie 2018).

An interactive model

We discussed in Chapter 2 how attachment needs and dilemmas are not predominantly the fallout from the *history* of attachment experiences but are *currently* re-created and maintained in family interactions. Figure 6.7 is a schematic summary of how scripts and interactional dynamics can be mapped.

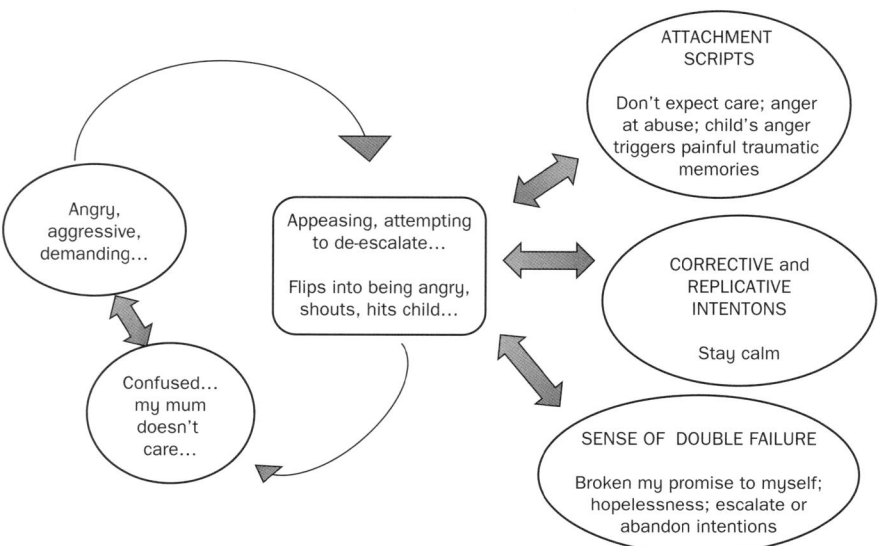

Figure 6.7 Trauma and scripts and the interactive model

This figure summarises how a parent's attempts to apply corrective intentions may become subverted by the intrusions of powerful feelings triggered in their interaction with their child. It is exemplified by the case of Maria in how she was attempting to apply corrective intentions of staying calm and not 'screaming at' her children, while feeling anxious and frightened. She also mentioned how the powerful traumatic memories and scripts would break through so that she 'lost it'. She relayed how this resulted in a sense of failure and eventually hopelessness – she felt that she could not parent appropriately, she felt she was getting things wrong and was turning into being like her mother. (Remembering this also appeared to trigger memories of feeling frightened and angry with her mother.) This can be a difficult mixture, and some parents may feel angry with their child for not acknowledging their good intentions by responding with positive behaviour. Presumably, if the child were to do so, the parent could feel proud that their corrective intentions had paid off. Unfortunately, this misses to some extent the child's experience, resting on the idea that they may pick up something inexplicable to them, somehow understanding why the parent is acting in an extreme way when all they are asking for is an attachment response. Of course, young children cannot articulate this in words but only actions such as shouting, crying louder or withdrawing.

Summary and reflections

This chapter has explored the nature of trauma from an attachment perspective and connected it to the idea of scripts and intentions. It has drawn on the framework of attachment strategies as a form of regulation of emotional deactivation and hyperactivation. The chapter has also explored how both processes are necessary and how security and self-protection involve utilising both types of activation. These ideas have been considered in terms of trauma theory and especially the connection between activation of flight–fight systems and attachment strategies. The chapter has discussed how highly dangerous events can trigger inflated states of physiological arousal, impeding reflective capacities. This has been connected with the concepts of *scripts* and *intentions* to suggest that traumatic states for parents may mean that unconscious scripts and conscious intentions are employed in extreme forms. It has also been suggested that they may operate in conflict with each other and that high arousal (i.e. flight–fight responses) may mean that the inconsistencies and conflicts between unconscious scripts and intentions are not detected. A number of cases, especially of Maria and her family, have been employed to illustrate these ideas. The chapter has considered the sense of failure that may be triggered for parents when they experience that, despite their best intentions, they are repeating patterns they wished to alter, and the experience of futility and failure when they have worked hard to overcome their traumatic experiences but find that these still exert a hold over them.

The next chapter will illustrate therapeutic implications and orientations to working with families, using the concepts of scripts and intentions. It will draw on the ideas considered in this chapter – for example, that an important ingredient is for family members to relearn or reprogramme the automatic triggering of their flight–fight responses. It will argue that central to this is creating a therapeutic secure base such that parents and children can feel safe, become calm, and have their reflective processes facilitated. This can involve a reduction in arousal, a change in unconscious scripts, a revision of conscious intentions, and an increased awareness of the discrepancies between scripts and intentions.

7 Therapy with families: Trauma, scripts and intentions

Introduction

This chapter will draw together the various clinical implications discussed in the preceding and offer a multi-level therapeutic framework. Therapeutic formulations using the idea of scripts as being driven by unresolved traumatic states will be described in relation to a variety of clinical problems, and the chapter will suggest that this formulation offers the basis for an alternative to the medical (diagnostic) model that meets families' concerns regarding blame. A key theme will be that exploring trauma, scripts and corrective intentions allows for a non-blaming therapeutic approach to formulation and assisting families with their problems; an approach that allows an exploration with family members of how family dynamics may be involved in the development of problems without implying blame. The chapter will outline how the construction of a secure base provides a platform of safety from which families can explore their attachment scripts and corrective intentions and promote positive change. There will also be a discussion and an illustration in case studies of the double sense of failure parents may feel when, despite their best intentions, they find themselves repeating unwanted patterns and appearing to contribute to the development of problems. Here, sympathetically acknowledging parents' positive intentions is core to facilitating positive change. Throughout, case studies will be used to illustrate applications of the approach, with an exploration of the positive potential and challenges involved.

Double sense of failure

Many families face a sense of failure and failed expectations. Medical or diagnostic orientations locate problems within one member of the family – the child – and as not significantly related to family dynamics. Within this framework, families may attend family therapy sessions predominantly in order to be assisted to work together to help manage the diagnosed illness or disability. For example, in relation to autism or psychosis, there may be a belief that the condition cannot be cured or significantly relieved but that family members can learn to cope with these conditions more effectively. It is to some extent surprising, however, that many families attend therapy with their own formulations in tow that there may be aspects of their lives together or of the parents' childhood experiences that have a bearing on the problems they're experiencing. My experience is that parents want to consider the role of their childhood experiences in regard to their parenting but, if possible, they want to consider this without feeling blamed – or, perhaps more accurately, without them being drawn into blaming themselves. In my clinical work, I find it helpful not to challenge a medical understanding of the conditions with which the families are attempting to cope. However, I typically find that families hold other, subjugated explanations and, as they come to trust me and my colleagues, they gradually feel more safe and able to discuss relational and other explanations – the door begins to open.

To illustrate: in the previous chapter, a key aspect of the piece of work with Olivia (Case study 6.1), and other cases discussed earlier in the book, in common with many families with whom I have worked, was a sense of shame and failure. For Olivia, this shame and sense of failure was interspersed with a disbelief that, despite her best intentions, she was not only failing to resolve Dan's 'angry and abusive' behaviour but appeared to be reproducing a similar traumatic experience to that experienced in her own childhood. The pattern of this sense of failure is illustrated in Figure 7.1.

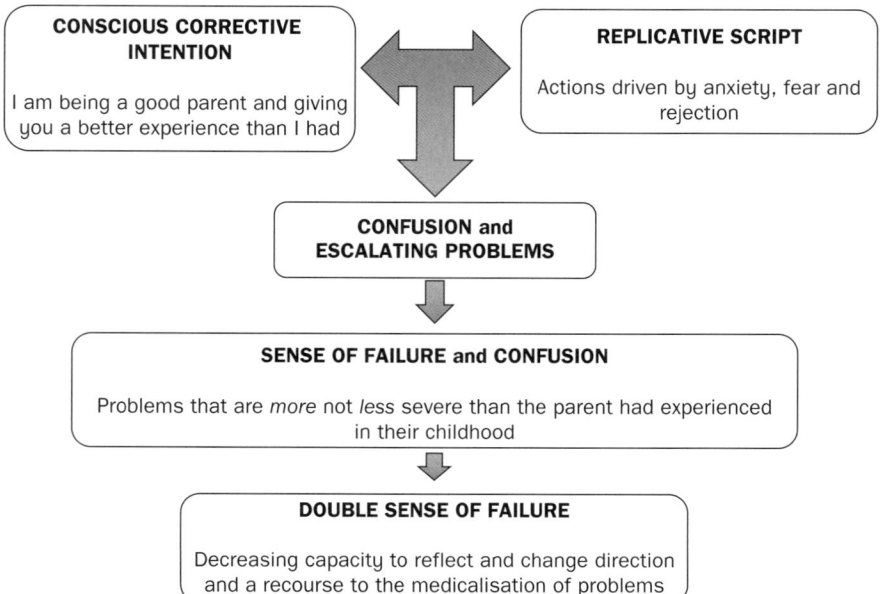

Figure 7.1 Double sense of failure of corrective scripts

In our parenting, we may intend to alter what we felt was unhelpful, unpleasant, painful or even dangerous in the parenting we experienced. We may also attempt to repeat some of what we experienced to be positive aspects of our early family life. Unfortunately, in some cases, as we explored in Chapter 6, these conscious intentions may conflict with or be distorted by unconscious attachment scripts. With Olivia and Dan (Case study 6.1), Olivia's corrective intention, embodied as her wish to have a family that was free of anger and violence, appeared to make her extremely sensitive to Dan's apparent anger. This appeared to lead Dan to feel rejected by her, escalating his angry protests and resulting in the emergence of a pattern of dangerous anger that Olivia so hoped to avoid.

This idea of a double sense of failure captures the central message of this book. It contains a profound irony that out of striving to do the best for our children, what may result is the reverse. For many parents with whom I have worked, this seems an untenable idea, and part of the dilemma is that even if parents become aware that this is a possibility, it may be very hard for them to alter their attachment response patterns. This is especially the case when their attachment scripts and corrective intentions are driven by powerful traumatic states. It is as if the trauma from their childhood has been abusive twice over: once as part of their own childhood and now again, despite their best intentions, it appears to be having a damaging effect on their children.

There are a range of possible solutions to this dilemma:

- One is for parents to hold on to the idea that they have successfully overcome their earlier experiences with the implication that the child's difficulties are not connected with their parenting. The idea that the problems have a neurological or 'illness' basis can have a good fit with this narrative. The parents are able to hold on to the idea that their corrective and replicative intentions are effective but the child's 'illness' means that they cannot apply them or that their intentions are applied but the illness overwhelmingly negatively influences the child's response. We saw examples of this in the previous chapter, for instance where a parent felt they could not be as emotionally close to their child because of the child's autism.
- Another possible solution is to consider developmental pathways and the length of time that the problems have been seen to exist. I have been fortunate to work in an early intervention family therapy service in the west of England. Here, families were referred by their family doctor, social services or by self-referral and they were not required to have severe problems or a member with a diagnosis in place, such as ADHD, autism or anorexia. Using my non-blaming approach, it was much easier to consider with families their family context, including the parents' childhood experiences and how these might impact on their problems. Within a few sessions, I was often able to move to a discussion with the parents of their attachment scripts and their corrective and replicative intentions. Parents typically found this to be a helpful and validating conversation as it emphasised and recognised their positive intentions and sympathised with their dilemmas in not being able to achieve these.

- One final possible solution is for parents to come to recognise the dilemmas and contradictions in their understandings. As we saw in Chapter 1 (Therapy extract 1.1), Brenda struggled with not being able to achieve her positive intentions:

> I don't know how much goes back to the early years . . . was told he needs a strong male model. Wish I could get into his head. He needs me most, when I'm angry with him [tearful] . . . when he's done something wrong and I'm shouting, that's when I should be able to go to him, tell him he's wanted. But I can't do it, and I don't know how to do it – and I know I should.
> (Adapted from author's personal clinical work and research.)

Brenda, though feeling exasperated and at a loss, was moving towards an awareness of the contradictions between her rational understanding and conscious intention to support Mark and her unconscious script that led her to shout at him. Rita, who we met in Chapter 5 (Therapy extract 5.1), had a similar realisation, which she described as the conflict between her 'head and heart'. Her conscious intentions were to be caring for her emotionally fragile adopted daughter; but, she had an embodied sense of disgust at the little girl's tantrums and angry outbursts. Brenda appeared to feel safe to express her exasperation and sense of failure in a relatively open manner. This was despite the fact that her adopted son was engaging in a variety of behaviours that were very worrying for the parents such as drug use, minor criminal activities and staying away without letting them know where he was. The situation may be very different, though, when problems have persisted or escalated for many years. The problems may present as much more severe and hence the amount of potential blame may appear greater for families for not resolving these problems earlier. If families feel threatened and blamed, which occasionally unfortunately has occurred in family sessions I have witnessed, their response might be something like:

> Are you suggesting that we have caused his self-harming, disordered thinking or anorexia?

Moments like this can be difficult to repair. They may make the therapist feel that they are being perceived as persecutory and the family to feel misunderstood. If this occurs, it is usually helpful to discuss this and, in my experience, what often emerges is that families have had many experiences of feeling blamed, for example by neighbours, other professionals, staff at schools and so on. Reassurance that this is not the intention of the therapy can be helpful and can often lead to the family articulating how they have also been blaming themselves.

What's at stake: Blame and the duration of problems

For some families, problems have persisted for considerable periods of time. There is potential for positive change over time but also a danger that problems become entrenched and that family life becomes used to or organised around the problems.

In some services, such as NHS child and adolescent mental health services (CAMHS), families cannot usually access therapy unless the problems are severe. In some conditions, such as autism, families may have to wait for several years to gain a diagnosis and this may mean that the difficulties deteriorate and that in waiting for a diagnosis, other considerations and gaining other possible sources of support may be put on hold. There is a lot at stake further down the line in the developmental pathway of problems. It is also likely that the problems, when they eventually become diagnosed, are regarded as indicative of some form of illness. To suggest to families that this is not the case risks the therapist appearing to be in an antagonistic position to the family and the authorities who support a medically based diagnosis. Unfortunately it can also imply that we professionals are in disagreement with each other, leaving families wondering who to trust. As mentioned in Chapter 2, this can also result in a move towards increasing use of self-diagnosis with reference to material on the internet. I consider these feelings and actions to be an understandable response to the stark sense of disappointment and failure parents may feel that their positive intentions to produce children who are healthy and well-behaved has not appeared to work. These intentions are generally still in place even if somewhat subjugated.

Pause for thought 7.1

Many mental health services are organised on the basis of a medical diagnosis of different conditions. For example, there are services for eating disorders, ADHD, autism, self-harming and so on.

- What are your thoughts about the potential benefits and disadvantages of this?
- What do you think might be a more effective alternative?
- What has been your experience or that of others you know regarding access to services?

One of the potential disadvantages is that families may have to wait until a problem is severe enough to gain entry, for example to CAMHS. As noted, there is the danger that this delay in gaining help results in a deterioration of the problems. On the other hand, some families' problems ameliorate; this is called 'spontaneous recovery'. There may be various explanations for this. For instance, in one piece of research I conducted, I found that some fortuitous source of assistance or support became available. Contrasting arguments are that gaining a diagnosis can lead to being referred to the appropriate services that are geared to offer the specialist support that a particular problem requires. The orientation guiding this chapter is that the various diagnoses share a common base in trauma and attachment disruptions and that early intervention rather than waiting for specialist assistance helps alleviate the risk of deteriorating attachment connections and family dynamics.

Flexible versus rigid intentions

Intense and rigid corrective and replicative intentions can set parents up to fail in not being able to achieve the extremely high standards that they are setting themselves. Further, parents who have experienced highly dangerous events that have led to them becoming traumatised may develop rigid and inflexible corrective intentions. Their interactions with their children may trigger powerful procedural and sensory memories such that the drive to be different – their corrective intention – becomes *compulsive*. It is not uncommon to hear some parents say they do not want to do *anything* the same as their parents. This can serve to obscure them from responding to feedback from their children about how they are experiencing their parenting. In effect, it can short-circuit feedback in their interactions. My experience has been that helping parents to become aware of this can be helpful. However, it can take considerable time before they are able to surface from the anxiety of feeling blamed such that they are able to seriously consider such processes. An important ingredient is that parents are able to feel safe in the therapeutic situation and trust that the therapist is not intending to blame them or lead them to blame themselves.

Parents' intentions need to have a flexible quality to be able to accommodate information and adapt to what therapists are trying to do. Attempting to apply intentions based on our childhood experiences is complex for many reasons, not least that historically, expectations about family life, roles, children, and parents' rights and responsibilities are fluid and changing. Parents often say things like, 'I was never allowed to speak to my parents like that, so disrespectfully'. But children witness many ways of talking with parents in the media (etc.) and there is a need to be able to, within reason, adjust to these historical changes. A particularly striking example can be where parents move between cultures and import expectations from their country of origin into their new culture. For example, in one family I worked with from Iraq, the parents felt their teenage daughter was extremely disrespectful towards them and that she was engaging in inappropriate activities, such as wearing clothing they viewed as 'sexually provocative', smoking and drinking. They became so anxious and angry that they physically beat their daughter and social services became involved. In the family sessions, the parents were initially emotionally agitated, tearful and angry. As they became calm and started to feel safer, they were able to describe some of the trauma they had experienced in Iraq and how they were living with a sense of constant danger. It became apparent that, rather than attempting to stifle and control their daughter's freedom – whatever the actual effect of their actions – they were enacting a corrective intention to keep her and the family safe, something they had been unable to achieve in the dangerous context of Iraq. In my clinical and personal experience, many refugee families also live in a continued state of arousal, a flight–fight mode that may make them susceptible to applying rigid and inflexible intentions fuelled by traumatic states.

Exploring corrective and replicative intentions from a secure base

An essential component of assisting families to discuss their intentions and family dynamics is to help co-create with them a secure base, which they may be able to use to explore and experiment with different scripts and intentions. There is no simple recipe for how, as therapists, we can help achieve this. Some families approach therapy with considerable anxiety and a reluctance to enter into a discussion of relationships and feelings; others are much more able to express their feelings but struggle to organise their thoughts and develop coherent explanations of the causes of events or the consequences of people's actions. Therapy has to proceed carefully to initially fit with the particular parents' attachment orientation and to assist them to explore both their thoughts and emotions at a pace that feels comfortable for them.

There have been interesting developments in family therapy using approaches that invite multiple families to work together in groups, known as 'multi-family therapy' (Asen and Scholz 2010). The concept of the therapeutic relationship and the construction of a secure base has traditionally been thought about in terms of a therapist and a team developing this with a family. I have found multi-family therapy to be a remarkably powerful way of facilitating a sense of safety and trust. In this, families act as consultants to each other. They share their experiences of failure and success and their intentions. This can help to reduce the sense of failure and frustration and that their positive intentions have not been recognised. Thinking of different ways to help create a sense of safety is paramount so that families can engage in honest and sincere explorations and take risks in revising scripts, intentions, and the patterns of actions and solutions they have been attempting. Multi-family work has been incorporated into the family intervention that my colleagues and I have developed for families with a child diagnosed with autism, known as Systemic Autism-related Family Enabling (SAFE) (Dallos and McKenzie 2015). Families are invited to work together, for example in pairs, to discuss the challenges they have faced with coping with autism and to share what they have found to be helpful. Sharing their experiences and using specific techniques, such as mapping problematic sequences, has often been helpful for the families. However, importantly the families have described that the overarching benefit was that they felt less blamed and isolated with their struggles.

Many families initially arrive for family therapy feeling frustrated, disappointed, sad, hopeless or angry. In essence, they often do not feel safe as a family and may therefore be anxious about the therapy. Frequently, these anxieties are over-riding their abilities to be reflective and families want to focus on describing the nature of their problems rather than issues inherent in their family dynamics. This has been described as families being 'problem-saturated' or overwhelmed by a view that the problems are governing their lives. Focusing on helping families to feel less anxious is therefore essential.[23] Systemic family

---

[23] I have described the process of attempting to foster a secure base within an attachment, narrative framework in more detail elsewhere (Dallos 2006; Dallos and Vetere 2009).

therapy (SFT) focuses on starting to identify with families their 'attempted solutions' or what they have tried to improve matters at home. Typically, this has revealed that such attempts serve to make things worse or it transpires that the parents have tried these solutions so sporadically that it has become hard to discriminate between what works and what does not. Discussing what they have attempted helps the therapist to avoid repeating suggestions and advice that they may already have been given and have found unhelpful. It also sets the stage to move on to a discussion of their corrective or replicative intentions for the future. Alternatively, a discussion regarding corrective and replicative intentions can be introduced even into the very first session to underline that, as therapists, we understand and recognise the parents' positive intentions. This can function to provide a sense of relief for them, a sense that we understand their aims and that our work with them will not be blaming. However, there is a double edge to this, since a discussion of how their intentions derive from their childhood experiences of being parented can still also appear, especially for families who are anxious and sensitive to feeling blamed, to be implicating them as responsible for not resolving these earlier traumas more effectively or for carrying that baggage into their parenting habits. In my experience, though, this is rarely the case.

Exploring intentions and scripts from a secure base

Exploring intentions and scripts in families often takes place in a sensitive atmosphere where the potential for feelings of blame may rapidly enter and subvert exploration. There is a risk that the exploration can prompt a defensive process whereby the parents feel a need to justify themselves in terms of a narrative such as, 'I have tried so hard to be better, so it cannot be my or our fault that things are going wrong'. Parents are exposing themselves when they explain their intentions in that it reveals their hopes and sadness that things are not working as they had hoped. The following case study, featuring a young girl, is offered to illustrate this point and how an exploration of scripts and intentions can take place with a family (See Figure 7.2).

Case study 7.1: Denise and her family (Part 1: Background)

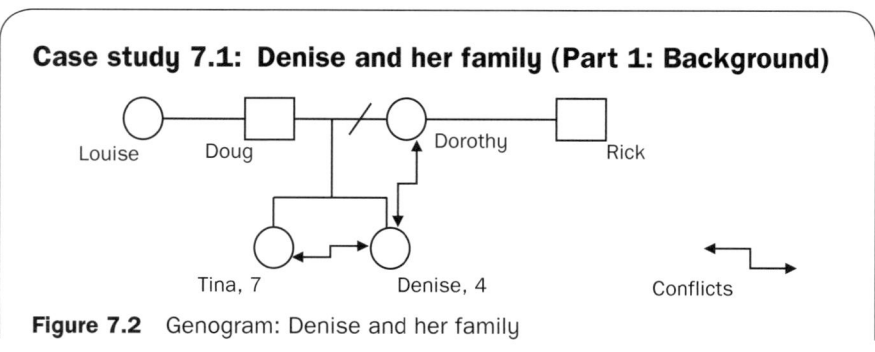

Figure 7.2 Genogram: Denise and her family

The family attended for family therapy in a CAMHS setting because Denise, a young girl, was described by her father, Doug, and stepmother, Louise, as 'rude', 'uncooperative' and, at times, 'angry' towards Louise and her sister, Tina. She was also resisting taking her insulin medication to control her diabetes. Denise's birth parents, Doug and Dorothy, had been experiencing conflicts, as Doug reported, Dorothy had been drinking heavily. She decided to move out and left Denise and Tina with their father. Both parents had found new partners and Louise moved in a year previously to become their stepmother.

The referral for family therapy had come from Doug and Louise, hence this part of the family system was convened; though, I held in mind the possibility of seeing Dorothy and her new partner, Rick, if this was necessary.

Source: Adapted from Crittenden et al. 2014.

Pause for thought 7.2

Reflect on your thoughts and feelings about the information you have read about this family so far.

- What thoughts do you have about the attachment dynamics in this family?
- What are the separations and losses that the family members have experienced?
- What feelings of blame do you imagine might be prevalent in this family?
- Can you speculate about what attachment scripts and potential corrective or replicative intentions might emerge as the therapy proceeds?

Case study 7.1: Denise and her family (Part 2: Therapy sessions)

The sessions started with introductions and an explanation that in the family sessions, I would not seek to blame anybody but would work with the parents to assist them with their concerns. Each was invited to talk about themselves and their interests and then to explain their view of the problems and what they hoped might be the benefit of attending therapy. Doug and Louise both expressed that they were concerned about Denise's angry outbursts, mainly towards Louise and, at times, towards Tina. Meanwhile, Denise held two soft toys, a cool blue sea-horse and a vibrant, red and orange tiger. I explored with her how maybe these showed both her sadness and her anger. A characteristic pattern of family conversation started to emerge whereby Doug and Louise criticised Dorothy:

Louise: 'She [(Dorothy)] has her own problems, she has a problem with alcohol.'

Denise: 'No she doesn't, she never used to . . .'

Doug: 'When she drinks, her personality changes, that's all, Denise.'

Tina: 'When she looks after us, she'll often make us stay up late and she'll drink quite a lot – it's quite scary.'

Denise: 'Yeah, it's scary, but you can't . . .'

RD: (to Denise) *'What does that feel like, when other people say she lets you down?'*

Denise: 'It makes me feel quite sad sometimes . . . 'cause people say things like— it's hard to explain.'

RD: *'What happens to that sadness? Does it turn into something else, does it turn into other feelings?'*

Denise: 'It turns into anger. Sometimes if I get angry, it turns into— like the last few times, I have been in my room and I get a bit . . .'

Denise seemed to play a toll in defending her birth mother, whereas her sister appeared to have aligned herself with her father and stepmother. The session progressed to explore further how Denise's anger may have been related to her sense of split loyalties between her Dorothy and Doug. It was mentioned that she often became angry with her Louise and Tina after talking on the phone to Dorothy or after having spent the weekend with her. However, despite encouraging this insight, Doug and Louise returned again and again to complaining about Dorothy's behaviour and the session was feeling like it was becoming repetitive and stuck. I was aware of thinking about why the choice had been made for the girls to live with a father who was away from home a lot and clearly would not have much time to be with his girls.

Corrective intentions

With Denise occupied with a drawing activity, I invited Dough to talk about his family background, including his corrective intentions. This produced a dramatic change in the tone and content of the session:

RD: (to Doug and Louise) *'Can you say a little bit about your family backgrounds?'*

Doug: 'Nasty . . . with my own children, I've always wanted to be a full-on parent because I never got it. My parents were never interested in anything I did. My mum and dad just fell out . . . I went to live with my dad.'

RD: '*So it's a bit similar to what happened to your own children?*'

Doug: 'Yeah, but then my dad just dropped me at my grandparents and my grandparents brought me up . . .'

Denise: 'That's not very nice.' <walking over to her daddy and gently touching his knee before walking away to get on with her drawing>

This passage and the subsequent conversations indicated that Doug's childhood had been unsettled and unhappy and he had repeatedly felt rejected and unloved. Denise seemed to recognise this as she went over to comfort her dad as he described his saddening childhood. This suggested that he had experienced a traumatic childhood that had resulted in him holding a powerful corrective intention to be a more loving and available parent to his daughters. Doug went on to describe a corrective intention of wanting to be emotionally available and loving, providing a safe home for his girls. Eventually, emotions were softened in the session and the repetitive blaming and criticism of Dorothy ceased. For Doug, he felt able to accept comfort and acknowledgement from us, the therapists, and from his daughter.

Source: Adapted from Crittenden et al. 2014.

Pause for thought 7.3

- Consider for a few moments the potential benefits of helping Doug to express his experiences for him and the family.
- What potential dangers or risks do you see in this?
- How do you imagine Louise and Tina responded to Doug's disclosure about his unhappy childhood?

You may have seen various benefits and risks in the previous sequence. Possibly Louise, who was responsible for much of the parenting in the family, could have felt undermined by this focus on her husband. She might have questioned why the therapists are focusing on his problems rather than Denise being difficult and rude. As Doug disclosed his feelings, she might have chosen, for example, to say something like, 'Yes, Doug had an unhappy childhood – but what has that got to do with Denise's bad behaviour?'

Preparing the ground for change: Validating the parents

We can see this family in terms of multiple attachment patterns, scripts and intentions. My colleague and I had previously asked Louise about her childhood experiences and she told us that her childhood had been fine and there were no difficulties with her parents. While not wanting to operate from a position of suspicion, we regarded such a description as potentially indicative of a wish to avoid discussing this topic at that point in time. Our formulation was that for Louise, this question, asked at this point in the therapy, might have implied some blame of her parenting. Why were we asking about her childhood when she was keen to tell us about *Dorothy's* shortcomings as a parent? It was vital that she felt validated and understood by us, and we were careful to validate her positive intentions to apply the positive experience that she had learnt through her childhood. In fact, we regarded Louise as central to the functioning of the family, since she was taking on most of the parenting of the girls. We discussed how frustrating it must have been for her, as a responsible parent, to see the Dorothy unable to cope. Alongside this, we discussed that it might be possible that she was an important point of security for Denise and that Denise could trust her enough to show her some of her distress and frustration. At the same time, we displayed sympathy for how it must have been for her, despite her good efforts, to get a lot of the flack. This helped to ensure that the family therapy felt safe for Louise and allowed the critical moment of Doug revealing his childhood difficulties to be a constructive experience for the family. If, in contrast, Louise had criticised and been angry with us, she could have dismissed this conversation as irrelevant to the current situation. However, she did not do this and instead allowed this softening to take place, which I believe encouraged her to reflect on what her childhood experiences had been like. Another important issue for her, which was not appropriate to explore in these sessions, was whether she wanted to have her own children and what ideas she had about being a parent and, importantly, how these contrasted with the mother that Dorothy appeared to be. For Denise and her family, it appeared that the discussion of intentions had triggered some important changes, which can happen in the process of family therapy sessions. However, in some cases there are significant traumatic events that have occurred, which may not be appropriate to discuss in front of children, especially if they are younger.

Denise's difficult behaviours ultimately subsided, and she became more co-operative regarding her medication. The family became more open to discussing

Figure 7.3 Denise and Tina's drawings
Source: Crittenden et al. 2014

other important attachment issues, for example Denise's sense of loss of her health and her normal childhood due to the diabetes. My colleague and I continued to validate their parenting and positive intentions, and Doug and Louise subsequently decided they did not need further sessions. The girls left us their drawings as a gift (see Figure 7.3).

Exploration of scripts and intentions: Utilising the Adult Attachment Interview

As noted earlier, my colleagues and I have developed a manualised attachment-based family therapy approach for families with a child with a diagnosis of mild- to high-functioning autism called SAFE (Dallos and McKenzie 2015). This approach starts with each parent being asked to complete an attachment interview based on the Adult Attachment Interview (AAI). Prior to our research trial, we were concerned that parents might be anxious or resistant to engaging in an in-depth discussion of their childhood experiences. In part, this was driven by our concern that the autism field has developed a significant reaction to family models, such as the refrigerator mother hypothesis attributed to the work of Bettelheim (1967), discussed in Chapter 1. We have been surprised that the opposite has been the case. In fact, most parents have welcomed the opportunity to talk about their childhoods in detail. A further surprise has been that we have discovered, in a sample of 30 families, an enormous amount of unresolved trauma and loss (Dallos and McKenzie 2015; McKenzie and Dallos 2017). These parents have typically never told professionals about these traumatic events in their childhoods or, if any details were mentioned, they were not seen as relevant to their family lives with autism. Our exploration of the parents' childhood experiences has provided an opportunity to explore their attachment scripts *collectively* and their corrective intentions *individually*. This provided a platform for considering these in the wider family context.

Case study 7.2: Robin and his family (Part 1: Background)

Robin and his family (Figure 7.2) were seen as a part of our SAFE (Dallos and McKenzie 2015) intervention. This consists of five three-hour sessions: the first and last are multi-family sessions (six families) and the middle three are separate family sessions with each family. The sessions were conducted by me and a co-therapist.

Edwin, Robin's son, was educationally extremely high-functioning and was attending a prestigious school. One of the key concerns for the family was that they were experiencing frequent meltdowns, but they were willing to explore our intervention to see if it might help them as a family. As part of the SAFE intervention, the parents, Robin and Laura, were invited to take part in an AAI prior to the first multi-family therapy session. Laura described her

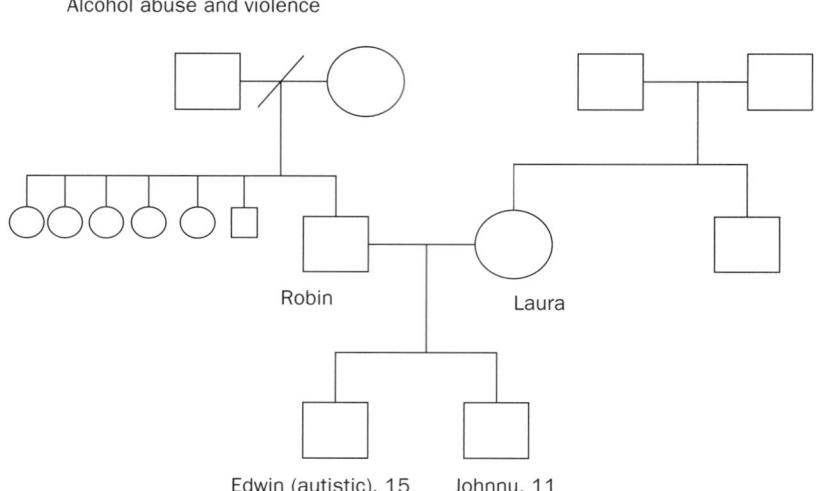

Figure 7.4 Genogram: Robin and his family

childhood overall as safe and loving, one in which she had experienced no significant problems. However, her account revealed relationships were somewhat emotionally distant. Robin, in contrast, described a childhood peppered with traumatic events and these featured an aggressive alcoholic father, who he and his sisters found frightening. He felt that his father was disconnected from the children in any positive way, instead 'just sitting in his chair unless he was really drunk'. He and his sisters were so frightened that his sisters slept with knives under their pillows, as the following extract describes.

> It was just constant shouting and arguing with my mum and dad. It was just constant abuse basically towards me mum, towards me sisters, me mentally . . . I think I've blocked it all out. He got abusive to me sisters and they ran up, grabbed a knife and locked themselves in the bedroom. And me mum taking me up the road and everything where he got abusive.

Robin explained that his mother had to work long hours to make enough money and that she was largely unavailable. He described himself as a 'latch key child' (a child responsible for letting himself into the house after school and taking care of himself until the parents return from work) and was responsible for providing meals for the family from around the age of 11. Robin expressed a strong desire to do things differently with his children, Edwin and Johnny, to be available and kind to them. So much so that he spent most of his time with them. He looked forward to them coming home from school and missed them whenever they were separated. He described how Edwin had several severe tantrums each day and could be difficult. He explained that he felt powerless to manage Edwin's behaviour and felt he could only standby and accept what was happening. He described his role as a parent as 'letting them get away with murder' and 'spoiling them too much' but confided that he felt he was unable to do anything else:

> Umm . . . like I said, I think I'm just too soft, way too soft with them. I fully admit that, you know, they play, you know, they get away with murder 'cause I don't want them to go through it, you know, what I went through.

Source: Adapted from Dallos and McKenzie 2015.

Pause for thought 7.4

Think about this final quote from Robin for a few moments.

- What insights into his childhood and intentions do you think this indicates?
- What are the potential risks for Robin in moving away from this intention and becoming less 'soft'?
- What do you see as the potential negative as well as positive consequences for Laura in relation to her husband's strong intention?
- Why do you think Robin's softness appeared to be more focused on Edwin versus Johnny?

This case presentation is more focused on Robin than Laura, in part because his corrective intentions were very pronounced and they clearly related to a highly traumatic childhood. But a subtler corrective intention can be discerned for Laura. In particular, in contrast to her rather distant and unemotional childhood family, she had a partner who was very loving towards her and kind to the children. Robin changing and becoming emotionally tougher, less 'soft', may have reminded her of the rather cold childhood she had experienced.

I have repeatedly discussed in the book how attachments need to be seen within a wider family dynamic and this is illustrated here in that change in any one member of the family has consequences for other relationships and each person as well as the overall sense of security for the family.

Case study 7.2: Robin and his family (Part 2: Therapy sessions)

Robin found the AAI extremely helpful. He said it was the first time anyone had asked him about these experiences and he found it particularly helpful to reflect on why he was 'too soft' in relation to Edwin. Though not wishing to change his corrective intention of avoiding conflict and anger, he did consider that he was giving in too much and, as a consequence, Edwin was not receiving the guidance and discipline a teenager needed. Some similarities can be seen here to the case of Maria (Running case study in Chapter 6) in terms of a reversal of roles between parent and child: Edwin in some ways appeared to be acting like Robin's father while Robin was enacting a relationship with Edwin similar to the one he had with his father. In effect, Robin was replicating his traumatic childhood attachment script, which was fuelling an extreme corrective intention. This emotional process was very apparent. Robin showed a lot of anxiety in the sessions and was too anxious to attend the initial multi-family session. The family sessions were excruciating for him, but he explained that the chance to discuss his attachment history and corrective intentions was inspiring him to continue for the benefit of his family. This dedication was received with great admiration by his wife, Laura.

In the family sessions, it was apparent that Robin left the parenting to Laura. However, at times she appeared to be operating on her own and felt somewhat undermined by the lack of support from her husband. Although he did not contradict her parenting, it seemed that Edwin was copying Robin in being extremely passive but at other times demanding of and coercing his parents. Robin's corrective intentions appeared to be a vague and admittedly failing strategy of just giving in and mollycoddling Edwin. In addition, Robin appeared to idolise Laura and felt that she knew exactly what to do. Laura was very aware of Robin's highly traumatic childhood and recognised his strong wish not to be aggressive or confrontational with his children. She wanted to provide him with the ideal family, which he had not experienced himself. An unfortunate consequence of this was that she ended up colluding with an extreme corrective intention, which Robin admitted was inappropriate. The bind for Laura may have been that to put her foot down occasionally might have aroused her anxiety that she would upset her husband.

The family's discussions in the sessions were developed to consider how the meltdowns were presenting a problem for all the family. Robin's positive intentions were acknowledged along with a discussion of how it might be possible to help manage Edwin's emotions without fear that this would be repeating negative aspects of Robin's childhood. These discussions seemed to help Laura feel more able to enforce some discipline without fear of upsetting Robin. Important to this process was also an acknowledgement of *Johnny's* needs and that he may have felt ignored in the face of the attention paid to Edwin. This helped Robin to ease his corrective intentions in that he could see that some more control of Edwin's behaviour was necessary for Johnny to have *his* needs met. As a concrete example, they decided that rather than always organising outings to accommodate Edwin's needs, they would do this alternately so that Johnny could choose what to do and where they would go. To their surprise, they found that Edwin fully accepted this plan and welcomed less focus on him and his autism.

Source: Adapted from Dallos and McKenzie 2015.

Building on successes

Since corrective and replicative intentions have the aim of making things better in families, it is very important to support, validate and build on these intentions. Family therapy has tended to focus on identifying and attempting to change problematic patterns or circularities. For some families, it is possible to start with this, but in more severe cases it can inadvertently add to the sense that they are failing and helpless. In contrast, starting with examples of where the family *have* been able to solve problems and positive sequences *have* occurred can provide a sense of safety and acknowledgement of their positive intentions from which exploration of more problematic sequences can flow. In the case of Robin and his family, we identified a positive incident that had occurred and mapped this as a circularity, as seen in Figure 7.5.

Laura stated that she had been surprised at but also very pleased with how calm Edwin had remained in this case of the family's car breaking down.

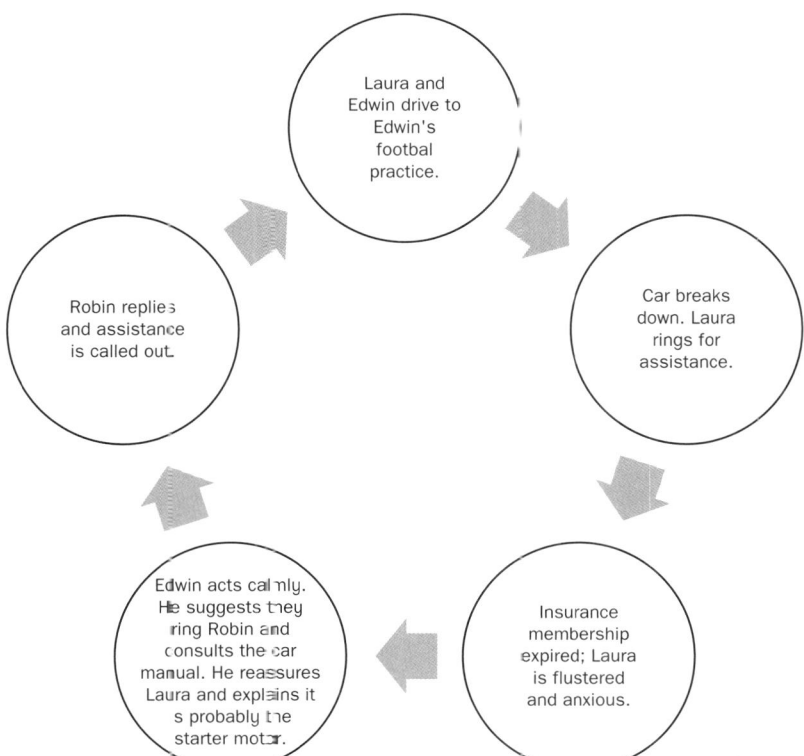

Figure 7.5 Tracking an attachment sequence

Acting out attachment sequences: Role play

Having described and mapped this sequence, we asked the family to role play it, at which point it became obvious that Johnny wanted to be involved. We suggested that he role play making the noises of trying to start a car – 'Urrrrr, Urrrrr' – and he was delighted to do so. Apart from adding some fun to the activity, it highlighted how a corrective intention can have adverse effects on other children in the family. Robin was shy about taking part in the role play but pretended to answer Laura's distressed phone call from the car. This communicated that he could be calm and helpful and that in the session, he could overcome his shyness and anxiety. Laura took the lead and was a highly competent actor, as was Johnny who generally was much more similar to his mother than Edwin, who shared many aspects of his father's personality. Edwin also joined in, primarily in the action-based experience than in the talking parts of the sessions. He was delighted to have his calm reassurance in the car breakdown incident validated and admired by the rest of his family. It seemed that Laura was pleased that Robin took part, though she closely monitored his emotional state. My colleague and I formulated that Robin's attachment script and his corrective intentions could be seen as a relational pattern that could be observed between him and Laura, as illustrated in Figure 7.6.

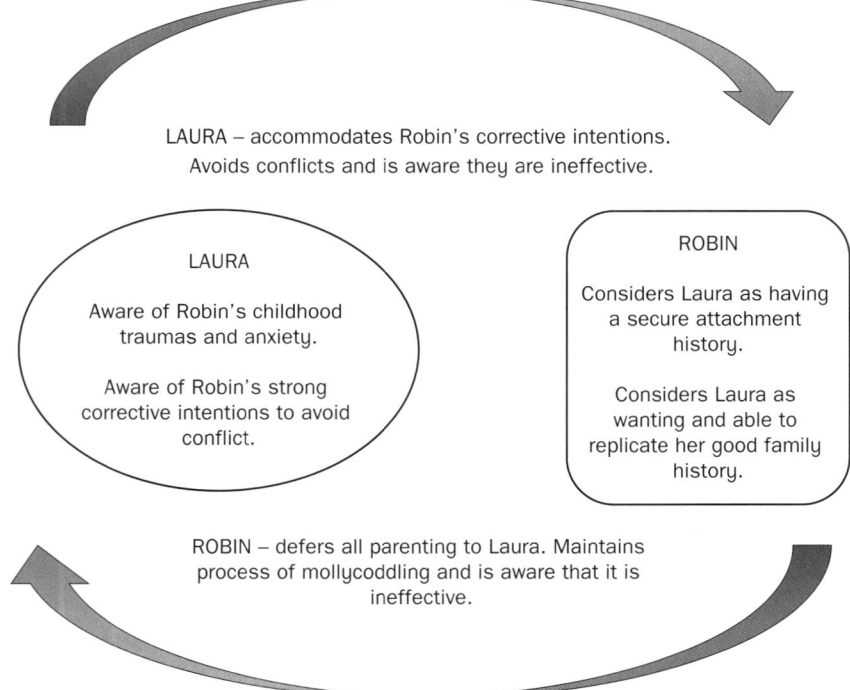

Figure 7.6 Relational dynamic in maintaining ineffective intentions

This representation of the couple's dynamic raises the idea that corrective and replicative intentions are not simply or predominantly intra-psychic, as here they appeared to be maintained by the dynamic between Laura and Robin. Laura appeared to be applying her own replicative intentions, which may have been to be a 'good girl' and be helpful. She was repeating this at considerable cost to herself, since she predominantly bore the brunt of Edwin's meltdowns and was the only one who made any real attempt to manage and contain him. She experienced our validation of 'how hard she was working' and how 'well-intentioned' she was to be a very positive experience. She joked with the other parents in the multi-family therapy session that a lot of the time she was 'knackered' and at the end of the day needed a stiff drink! The other parents expressed sympathy and similar feelings. Their feedback from these sessions indicated that such sharing of their experiences was a validating experience for all of them. Focusing on a positive sequence allowed a discussion of more problematic sequences, though again, surprisingly, once the focus had moved to how their positive intentions were being achieved, fewer examples of negative intentions were mentioned. In effect, the family moved to be less problem-saturated. Role playing sequences invite families to act out their attachment scripts and create new attachment patterns. They also help to transfer these to the whole family system. Robin and Johnny had not been present when this potentially anxiety-provoking event (i.e. the car breakdown incident) occurred but through the role play, they witnessed it, and this helped to transfer it into a new family attachment dynamic. After family therapy, Robin revealed that he felt more confident and that he had recognised that Edwin could cope with being asked to do some things that were difficult for him. Edwin was better able to comply with Johnny's requests for weekend activities and to do things he previously would have refused. Robin also noticed that Edwin had become less agitated and that family life was calmer.

Summary and reflections

This chapter has explored how conscious replicative and corrective intentions are related to the development of positive changes across the generations but can also be related to problematic processes in families. Parents' intentions interact with unconscious attachment scripts and the effects of experiences of danger in our childhoods. Corrective intentions need to be flexible and able to adjust to changing circumstances but also to take into account historical shifts across the generations. This can be extremely difficult when they are driven by experiences of danger and trauma. The chapter has also explored how an exploration of scripts and intentions is an important component of family therapy. The cases have illustrated how a prerequisite to assist families to explore these processes is to help them to feel secure, validated and not blamed such that their arousal system and flight–fight reactions are inhibited and they are able to contemplate and enact more productive ways of managing, or in fact preventing, the development of problems. Additionally, the chapter has discussed how parents may be influenced by competing and contradictory patterns of scripts and intentions if their own parents offered different styles of attachment responses to their childhood needs. These may be compounded by experiences of highly dangerous or distressing experiences that have resulted in traumatic states, which can inadvertently trigger waves of emotional responses that are inconsistent with the level of distress or demand that their child is expressing in the present day, causing family problems. Pervasive dangerous experiences in parents' childhoods can leave them at the mercy of high levels of arousal being generated when they are engaged with their children and conflicts arise. Explicit intentions to do things differently or to use the perceived benefits of one's childhood experiences may become swept away by these high levels of arousal. The case examples have also illustrated how *all* family members need to be considered in effective therapy, which extends attachment theory from a dyadic to multi-person approach. The clinical importance of this was illustrated in the case of Denise and her family. If my colleague and I had not already built a positive relationship with her stepmother so that she felt validated and knew that we were not blaming her for the difficulties, she could have negated the positive aspects of Denise's father disclosing his painful childhood and his heartfelt corrective intentions. This could have stalled the progress of the therapy and limited potential future positive changes.

The final chapter will offer an overview of the key concepts discussed in the book. It will consider some of the implications of the ideas for clinical practice and for future programmes of research. This will include a discussion of some of the theoretical implications, such as the need for attachment-oriented research and practice to incorporate a wider systemic perspective. It will also reflect on the contribution that a focus on intentions can offer to theory and clinical practice. The chapter will return to the question of *diagnosis* and outline how the ideas discussed can offer a constructive alternative that recognises the role of family dynamics as related to the development of problems as well as a positive resource for constructive change.

8 Discussion and reflections

The central aim of this book has been to explore the issue of blame and responsibility in family life, especially when things are not going well. I have suggested that the idea of corrective and replicative intentions held by parents offers a way of thinking about family life as a source of support, comfort and nurturing as well as a source of problems and difficulties. It seems reasonable to suggest that if families can promote growth, they may also unfortunately at times hinder it. Though on the surface this seems a very reasonable proposition, I have discussed how mentioning family dynamics in the causation of difficulties (rather than solely having recourse to a medical diagnosis model) has become imbued with issues of blame of parents and has resulted in a virtual embargo on research into family dynamics as casually related to the development of problems. The aim of this book has not been to hold parents up for any blame, including myself as a parent, but to help advance our understanding of how problems evolve in families to help us to be more able to assist them.

Though the focus of this book has been *family* therapy, the issue of blame is a wider concern for all therapies. It is recognised that seeking help is a risky endeavour and one that many families approach with a heavy heart. They may come with a sense of failure, a sense of loss of a child or the kind of family life they had hoped for. They may have experienced criticism and censure from other family members, people in the community and, sometimes, from professionals. It is vital, therefore, that in the first encounter with families in therapy, we communicate an acceptance and a message that the experience will not be focusing on blame and forms of condemnation. This has been a central focus of this book, and Bowlby's (1988) concept of therapy as being like the provision of a secure base for a child has been a guiding theme. From a sense of safety, we become more reassured, able to think, reflect and generate solutions to our problems. In some ways, the dictum that only the family can solve their own problems is, in a way, right, but they need help to create the context, namely the emotional environment, in which this can happen. Creating a safe and secure context in which therapy can proceed is difficult and complex. What feels safe for one family does not feel safe for another. I have employed attachment theory to help formulate how this coming to feel safe can be enhanced and to identify its ingredients. Attachment theory shows that a consideration of contexts and history is essential. What has happened in the parents' childhoods shapes how they approach the future. Linking this idea with systemic theory, we have considered how this is in turn shaped by how the past combines into current dynamics and family patterns. These shape the influence of the past and can maintain a sense of ability to change or a sense of helplessness and hopelessness – where withdrawing from others and licking our own wounds is the only way we feel able to cope in the present or the future. I have also described how the use of attachment theory is not predominantly a search of the past but how attachment connections are being maintained and reproduced in the current interactions we see in the family unit. Family therapy, using the framework we have explored in this book, is about how past experiences and current dynamics are constantly *inter-weaving*. Importantly, these experiences shape what family members perceive to be likely and possible in their future. We have referred continually to Bowlby's important concept of the internal working model in thinking about how this denotes not just the past but sets up anticipations and strategies for how we will meet future challenges and dangers.

We have explored the general concept of intentions, in particular positive corrective and replicative intentions. These are important for both therapists and families. For therapists, they may hold good intentions that they do not want to blame families and see guiding them towards medical illness explanations of their problems as benign and non-blaming. It can be seen as a sort of Dodo bird verdict in that everyone seems to win: the therapist does not criticise, confront or blame the family and family members do not blame or hold each other responsible. Medication is provided and, if it seems to assist a child by relieving symptoms, such as active behaviour in attention deficit hyperactivity disorder (ADHD), then the diagnosis appears to have been vindicated. Everyone including us as professionals may feel reassured that we are working scientifically and effectively. But as we have discussed, diagnosis and medication *does not always work* or, if it does, the benefits may be relatively short-term. Furthermore, the benefits may be related to other factors such as placebo effects and the reductions in anxiety and guilt, affecting family dynamics, that parents may feel now that something appears to have been done to help them. The temptation to turn to medical explanations at points where families are in crisis and desperate for help is massive. I have two half-brothers who both have a diagnosis of schizophrenia. One of them showed very florid, and frankly frightening, symptoms when he first became distressed. I was tempted to use the word 'ill' here. I recognised at the time that his life, and that of the rest of my family, had been traumatic. Though I was aware that my half-brothers were not simply 'mad' but traumatised, there was very little I could do but to go along with them being medicated and confined to institutions. To try to deal with the extreme levels of distress they were in on my own with a young family was too big a task. Unfortunately, this led to a lifetime of medication and a twilight life for one of them, slightly less for the other for whom I became a long-term carer and provider of support. Looking back, I often wonder how it could have been different and whether things would work out differently now. I am also aware that such retrospective thoughts can be very unsettling for families. As we discussed in various chapters, especially Chapter 7, the longer a problem has persisted and when a diagnosis has been in place for a long time, it can be very upsetting for parents to contemplate that their child's life could have been different. Feelings of guilt may become activated and it is understandably safer to accept that the diagnosis was necessary and that in the circumstances it represented the best solution. Unfortunately, the life of the family and the problems may have various negative self-fulfilling aspects, not least that long-term use of medications may cause serious side-effects and even deteriorations of symptoms. However, to withdraw medication from a child who has been on psychotic medication for most of their life can appear very risky for a family.[24] Studies using the expressed model of intervention, which attempts to train families to reduce the expression of emotional conflicts, blame and criticism have produced evidence that the model can reduce the severity of psychotic symptoms and relapse (Kavanagh 1992). Though not located in attachment theory, this approach can be seen to be consistent with the thesis of this book that when families feel safe, they are able to be calm and have a reduced sense of blame, which has positive consequences for all involved.

Like many of my generation, I read in the 1960s the evocative and inspiring anti-psychiatry literature and was inspired by the writing of R.D. Laing (1964) and others. Later, I came across and was inspired by Gregory Bateson and the Palo Alto Group (1972), from whom systemic family therapy developed. Bateson's concept of the double-bind became employed by Laing in his idea of existential 'knots' in which families could become trapped: this was the fascinating idea that a parent and child could become ensnared in communicational patterns where there were contradictions between what was being said verbally and non- verbally. He described this as a pattern where neither the child nor the parent could ever feel certain that they were loved by or could rely on and be comforted by each other. At the same time, they felt compelled to stay and unable to leave the relationship except by painful means, such as hospitalisation and flights into delusional states. This resonates with the discussion in this book, especially Chapter 3 in the discussion of representational systems. Though continuing to be a source of inspiration, a part of me always remained a little uneasy at what seeped out as some anger towards families and parents from this movement. I discovered later, for example, that Laing continued to be particularly angry with his mother. This, of course, might be a glib thing to say. After all, aren't we all, to some extent? But possibly this was picked up by some parents as a condemnation, that they were being accused of driving their children mad. The approach in this book has been that parents may unfortunately sometimes promote difficulties, but this is generally not their intention. I suspect that Laing's mother likely intended to act, and thought she was acting, benignly and usually in her son's interests. As we discussed in Chapter 3 and elsewhere, a resolved,

---

[24] It would of course be negligent to suggest this without very careful support being put in place, but there is evidence that cessation of medication does not inevitably lead to, for example relapse of psychotic symptoms, and can in some instances be associated with positive changes (Harrow and Jobe 2013; Moncrieff 2006). A family contemplating this would need considerable support and, as this book has emphasised, that reassurance regarding their feelings of blame is a prerequisite.

secure position towards our parents is not rosy coloured but a view that they may have got some things wrong, despite probably being well-intentioned and doing the best as they thought right. We may have some anger towards them but it should not preoccupy us to the point that it clouds our thinking and our strategies for protecting and nurturing our children.

So, 'don't blame the parents', as the book's title exclaims! But, do parents have a responsibility for how and what sorts of problems develop in the family unit? It seems fairly obvious that parents must have some significant influence on how their children turn out. Attribution theories have discovered that parents are much more likely to recognise and admit their influence when they are celebrating success rather than failure (Kelley 1967; Stratton 2003). Certainly, I look back over my parenting and shudder at some of the memories of what I now see as mistakes. Perhaps the biggest regret is that I regarded myself as a caring parent to my children because I spent time with them, delighted in their company and loved them. But I forgot at the time that the conflicts with their mothers was hugely upsetting for them and may have undone a lot of my positive actions as a parent and that I may have made errors in my parenting, too. Children need us to not just love them but, where applicable, show that we love their other parent, in effect to love the relationship that produced them. Of course, there are instances when, for various reasons, a parent may be unsafe or even dangerous and here the other parent may need to ensure the children's safety by guaranteeing a safe distance from this parent (e.g. due to abusive tendencies). However, even in cases like this, children need to have a story about the other parent and have some understanding of why they are behaving as they are, what has happened to them and what sort of a person they are. It is frequent in family therapy that a very negative story can develop about a parent, most typically a father, and frequently the remaining parent(s) and often professionals involved with the family write this father out of the family story altogether, as if he does not exist. In my clinical experience, this is often at a considerable cost to the children who generally want to know about their other parent. Sometimes this is biological curiosity – 'what did I inherit from them?' – but also sometimes a more *relational* curiosity, such as whether they ever think about the child and imagining how they might get on.

As I engage in such reflections, and no doubt also for you as the reader, very powerful emotions arise. In this book, I have argued, inspired by Byng-Hall's (1995) ideas in particular, that one of the things that is most important for me, both personally and as a therapist, is a recognition that my intentions, and generally those of the parents with whom I have worked, were positive. Things may not have worked out the way that I intended, and I can appreciate that and reflect on it once I feel that others, including my therapist, understand my intentions. As we have seen, this issue is complicated by the drive of emotions and memories that unconsciously shape our actions. By analogy, what happens in our parenting is like the waves hitting a beach: a continual merging of waves of emotions and memories shape the sands and the contours of the landscape, our scripts. Continuing the analogy, where these currents or scripts are borne out of significant traumas, they may at times be like tsunamis, sweeping away everything in their wake and wreaking havoc; that is, being unhelpful and counter to effective parenting. The therapeutic secure base helps us to organise and develop ways to prevent our attempts to live our lives by evolving strategies for dealing with the future based on what we have learnt from the past.

This book has employed material from clinical practice and from research with families to illustrate, and hopefully to illuminate, the ideas contained. It is therefore also an invitation for others to return to conduct research on family dynamics. I have suggested that exploring the role of family dynamics in shaping successes and problems is vital to assist the development of the theorical base of therapy and effective practice. Family therapy has arguably adopted a pragmatic position in claiming to suspend judgement regarding causal theories of problems. Laing, for example, used the metaphor of a man in a prison cell finding that his door is open (Laing and Esterson 1964): he does not need to examine his past in order to escape, but we might ask whether, if he does not examine his past, he might very well end up in another prison cell elsewhere.[25] Exploration of causation is not to wallow in and be stuck in the past but to develop plans for facing the future.

Aside from these general reflections, hopefully one of the contributions of this book has been to extend Byng-Hall's idea of scripts to family and other therapies. One distinction that has been repeatedly drawn out is that the concept of a script has contained within it two connected but arguably distinguishable concepts:

1. a script as pattern of action that unfolds in a relatively implicit manner – a form of emotional programming; and
2. the concept of corrective and replicative intentions – these are largely conscious intentions that we hold about aspects of our childhood experiences that we wish to repeat or alter.

Distinguishing these two, I suggest, is important for therapy and, more broadly, for attachment theory. It allows the latter to incorporate a constructionist psychological stance, which emphasises choice and autonomy as opposed to the essentially biologically based and positivist stance that it has been seen to hold. We are not simply determined by our attachment histories and condemned to repeat our patterns. The fascinating point about holding these two facets of attachment scripts and intentions together is that they offer a powerful way of contemplating how the conscious and unconscious forces interact. Of course, this was also the ambition of psychodynamic theory but, as Bowlby argued, attachment theory offers a more empirically based understanding of how early experiences shape both scripts and intentions (Freud 1920; Bowlby 1969).

My colleagues and I have been conducting research with families using these frameworks and many of the examples in this book have come from this research

---

[25] Given what we know about recidivism, this is exactly what frequently happens – and even the familiarity of the same cell seems to appeal and can offer a form of safety and belonging (van der Laan and Eichelsheim 2013).

(Crix et al. 2012; Rea and Dallos 2018). Apart from how stimulating this has been in terms of the material that we have gathered, somewhat to my surprise we have discovered that the families have generally found this research interesting and have not felt threatened by it. We were surprised that many parents found taking part in Adult Attachment Interviews (AAIs) extremely valuable and that it offered them helpful opportunities to reflect on the influence of their childhoods on their parenting. That said, some parents found completing the AAIs challenging and were keen to affirm that their child had a diagnosable illness.[26] Throughout this book, I have discussed many of the reasons for why this is understandable. Of course, there is also the possibility that some conditions, such as severe autism, have clear organic causes. But families were generally willing to consider other possible explanations as well. Coulter and Rapley's (2011) studies on how conversations with families and professionals can happen are illuminating in this regard. They fit with my research and clinical experience that most of the families with whom I have worked clinically and in research are interested in a range of ideas and possibilities to understand their experiences. They want to consider and eliminate different potential explanations, not to assume understanding or to start by attempting to find evidence to support their assumptions. This nicely fits with George Kelly's (1955) idea of 'man the scientist': the idea that we all engage in forming hypotheses about the world and testing the validity of our constructs. It is this curiosity, testing and openness to revision of ideas that forms the core of the scientific method and professionals and 'scientists' do not have a monopoly on the use of this process. As we have explored, there are times when and circumstances where families are distressed, exhausted, feel defeated, frustrated or angry where this sense of curiosity and search for better understandings appears to be diminished. There are also many parts of the world where people experience various prohibitions, including religious and ideological instructions regarding what and how they should think and what it is permissible to speak about publicly or even in the confines of their families. But questioning these constructs is always valuable.

Difference and commonality

A particular focus in this book has been the dominance of the medical illness model of distress. This arguably is a product of Western cultures: the main diagnostic system, DSM-5, is published by the American Psychiatric Association and, although it was compiled by international experts representing 16 countries, was produced predominantly by psychiatrists and some psychologists in the USA. Some have argued that it represents a form of psychological imperialism or globalisation of the Western mind, as Watters (2011) titled his book. For example, concepts of Western psychiatry have been exported, sometimes with deliberate campaigns, for example by pharmaceutical companies to promote the concept of suicide as a form of

---

[26] The structure of this interview and some samples from transcripts of interviews are appended in the appendix.

depressive illness in Japan, where 'suicide' had contained a very different meaning. Promoting depression as a precursor to suicide meant that sales of anti-depressants to *cure* depression could be more effectively marketed in Japan where sales of, for example Prozac, were low. In the Japanese context, suicide has been associated with a sense of dishonour or failure to live up to expectations rather with a manifestation of a form of illness such as depression. It is worth noting that suicide in Western nations is not unequivocally associated with depression and there have been many cases where a person is seen to take their life unexpectedly and to the surprise of family and friends without having previously shown symptoms of depression (Harrington 2001). An important point here is that many professionals, like certain parents, struggle with the medicalisation of psychological distress but there have been few alternatives available. One alternative that I have pursued is to promote the process of *formulation* as opposed to *diagnosis* (Johnstone and Dallos 2013). Different cultures hold different ways of formulating psychological and emotional difficulties, and the Western models are not necessarily the most accurate or most helpful.

This book has employed attachment theory and systems theory as the major conceptual frameworks. Bowlby (1969, 1973) regarded the attachment instinct as a basic evolution-based instinct that was universal. It is of course possible to see that the expression of this instinct may be shaped by different cultures. However, this book has not focused extensively on these diversities and I suggest that a discussion of diversity needs to take place alongside a discussion of commonality. Kelly (1955) has argued that our conceptualisations of the world are bipolar; we understand one thing by contrast to another. So, a discussion of diversity and difference between cultures is made more meaningful by what also appears to be common to them. In this regard, attachment theory has some claim to the notion of offering universal ideas in that attachment is a process we see in all cultures. Attachment appears to be an evolution-based survival mechanism and it would be very surprising to find a culture that does not try to protect its young from danger, to celebrate the birth of infants or to mourn the sadness of losing family members. Even in wartorn and destructive situations, where this can be pushed to the limits, we can see some of the most poignant acts of caring and tenderness. For example, in the refugees fleeing their home countries in unsafe boats. It is certainly my hope, as it was Bowlby's, that attachment theory is increasingly employed as a much-needed theory that fosters a sense of all cultures being connected and similar as well as celebrating variations in our cultures, creativity and arts. Consistent with this, therapies in all their forms across the world may differ, but I think all necessarily contain aspects of Bowlby's ideas. Hopefully, this book adds a little to a position of curiosity and compassion about what happens inside families across the world.

New perspective and integrations

In this book, I have attempted to summarise some of what have been the most relevant and helpful ideas that have emerged from my research and clinical experience.

Most of my clinical work has been with families and children. I have attempted to offer some new ideas but acknowledge that these have been minor in comparison to the monumental contributions that I have built on from Bowlby and Byng-Hall. I regard this book as partly adding some, I hope, helpful conceptual frameworks and some examples of how these can be applied in clinical practice. But the book is not a manual for a particular form of therapy. I think I have summarised and added some new theoretical conceptualisations of the question of blame and responsibility in therapeutic work with families. I imagine my suggestion of working in a non-blaming framework is far from novel, but I hope that I offer some new ideas about how to think about this issue and how to work with families in a way that allows an exploration of parental responsibilities regarding how problems arise and are maintained. Paramount to this is a recognition that nearly always parents are well-intentioned. Though I have employed a systemic family therapy framework, I hope that readers working with other therapeutic models and parents reading this book might be able to connect these ideas to their own models and experiences.

Finally, I have voiced criticism of medical-based diagnosis. Again, like parents, I think most practitioners I have met also have reservations about diagnosis and I have been told by young trainee psychiatry registrars who I have taught that they feel constrained by the extent of the demands on them to prescribe medication and it is not the vision of their role that they wished for on starting the training. While we all operate within the confines of our professional systems, health services, government policies and so on, my view is that more criticism and polemic against diagnosis is important and that it needs to go alongside models of how we can explain the development of problems diagnosed as ADHD, anorexia, autism, depression, psychosis and so on. Without a clear alternative, diagnosis remains the default position. I have contributed to the development of psychological formulation as an alternative and am engaged with colleagues in developing psychological models integrating trauma theory, attachment and systemic theory. I think any such attempt needs to have at its core the issue of parents' intentions and a compassionate stance that problems may develop contrary to parents' best intentions. I emphasise how good intentions may misfire but, also, they can be helpful and facilitate change and development across generations in families. Hopefully, this book will make some contribution to opening up debates and possibilities for research into family dynamics and the development of problems without generating a sense that parents are to blame.

Appendix

Adult Attachment Interview: Structure

Throughout this book, frequent reference is made to this structured interview. The Adult Attachment Interview (AAI) was initially developed by Carol George et al. (George, Kaplan and Main 1985; Crittenden and Landini 2011) and aims to invite adults to describe their childhood experiences of attachment by asking a series of questions in a standardised way. This is in order to facilitate comparing the responses of different people to gain a reliable classification of their attachment strategies. The AAI is deliberately designed to progress from *descriptive* questions to more *evocative* explorations of feelings, emotional connections, and distressing or frightening events that may have occurred. The reason for this is that in order to reveal people's attachment strategies, the attachment system needs to be activated by some degree of threat. The AAI ends with a reflective section inviting the person to consider how their attachment experiences have shaped them as an individual and as a parent. Particularly relevant in relation to this book is that it asks questions exploring *corrective* and *replicative* intentions about what they wish to repeat or change regarding how they were parented.

The structure of the AAI is one that moves between asking for semantic representations – for example, five words to describe the relationship with each attachment figure – and to follow this with a request to provide specific examples for each word. This is to explore to what extent the person is able to utilise all of their representational systems or whether, for example, emotionally toned sensory details are omitted. People who utilise *dismissing* attachment patterns are typically unable to access details of relationships, emotions and sensory material (see Mark later). Those using *preoccupied* patterns tend to be more able to do so, but show incoherence and intrusion of excessive emotion, anger and vivid imagery (see Sandeep later). Likewise, when asked about comfort, the AAI invites specific details of whether and how this occurred. The analysis of the AAI is less concerned with the content of the accounts given than what defensive processes appeared to be employed in providing that content. As an example, a process of idealisation common to dismissing attachment patterns might consist of a semantic statement that their parents *did* comfort them but then a minimal or contradictory episode indicating the contrary, without the person being aware of this distortion or contradiction. The extract from Lillian is intended to illustrate a balance of emotional content, semantic and coherent thinking, imagery and reflective awareness of herself and others. Lillian spontaneously offers integrations and reflections, but Mark does not and, in Sandeep's interview, there is an illustration of responses to questions regarding corrective intentions and you can see that these are rather incoherent and he veers away from the question – this is characteristic of the preoccupied attachment pattern. The final example is from Sally who employed a *dismissing* attachment strategy. Here, it is possible to see that (despite a difficult childhood) she starts by discussing what she will repeat from her parents and then tentatively mentions some corrective intentions and exonerates her parents – that what they did was 'not intentional'.

Part I: Orientation to the speaker's childhood family

- Before we begin, could you orient me to your childhood family? For example, where you were born, who was in your family, where you lived, what your parents did for a living, and whether you moved around much – things like that. I just want to know something about your family before we start.
- Did you know your grandparents when you were a child?
- Were there any other people to whom you were close when you were young?
- What is the earliest memory that you have as a child? Tell me as much as you can remember about it.

Part II: The relationships with attachment figures

- I'd like you to describe your relationship with your mother (or attachment figure #1), as far back as you can remember.
- Now, I'd like you to choose five words or phrases to describe your relationship with your mother (or attachment figure #1) when you were young. This may take a bit of time, so go ahead and think for a moment. I'll write them down as you're talking.
- Okay, let me check, I wrote down: [list the words or phrases]. Is that correct?
- You said that the relationship with your mother was _____. Can you tell me about a specific occasion when your relationship was _____? Try to think back as far as you can.
- Could you now describe your relationship with your father (or attachment figure #2), going as far back as you can remember.
- Now, I'd like you to choose five words or phrases that describe your relationship with your father (or attachment figure #2) when you were young.
- You said that the relationship with your father was _____. Can you give me a memory of a specific occasion when your relationship was _____? Try to think back as far as you can.
- To which parent did you feel closest as a child?
- Why do you think you felt closer to _____?
- Why isn't there this feeling with _____ [the other parent]?

Part III: Direct probes of normative events in which children often feel unsafe

The next set of questions is about some common experiences that children have.

- What happened when you *went to bed* as a child? Can you remember any specific time when you were in bed?
- What happened when you were *ill* as a child? Can you remember a specific instance?
- What about when you were *hurt physically*, what would you do? Can you remember a specific instance?
- When you were *upset emotionally*, what would you do? Can you remember a specific instance?
- If you *needed comfort*, what would you do? Can you remember an instance? Can you recall how your parents would *touch* you? Can you remember a specific time and how that felt?
- Can you tell me about the first time you remember being *separated from your parents*? How did you respond? How do you think your parents felt?
- When you were young, did you ever *feel rejected by your parents*, even though they might not have meant it or have been aware of it? Can you remember an instance? Why do you think your parents did this (or these things)? Do you think they realised that you felt rejected?
- Can you think of a time when your *parents were angry with you*? What happened?
- Can you think of a time when *you were angry with your parents*? What happened?

Part IV: Direct probes of potentially dangerous experiences

In the next set of questions I'll ask about some very difficult experiences that you might have had as a child. First, I'll just ask about the list and you can answer 'yes' or 'no'. Then, if some of these happened, I'll ask you to tell me about them.

- Did your parents ever *threaten you*, for example for discipline, or even jokingly?
- Did they ever *threaten to leave you*?
- Do you have any memories of *frightening punishment or abuse*?
- What about *periods of silence* when people in your family wouldn't speak to each other for a long time?
- Did you ever feel *very frightened* or *not sure that you were safe*?
- Sometimes parents or other people do things that are *not considered acceptable now*. Did this ever happen to you?
- For example:
  - Were you ever *abandoned* so that no one was taking care of you?

- Were you ever *touched or mistreated sexually*?
- Were you *humiliated or deceived* in ways that distressed you when you were young?
- Tell me what happened.
- Do you worry about something like this occurring again? Under what sort of conditions? How likely do you think it is that this could happen again? What would you do to try to recover if it happened again?
- Has this event changed your relationships with other family members? In what way? Why do you think this has happened?
- Can you think of anything good that has come from this experience?

Part V: Loss

The next section is about people who might have died during your lifetime.

- Can you tell me of anyone who died when you were a child? What about as an adult? Can you tell me the circumstances and how old you were?
- Were you present during the death? What happened? If not, how did you find out about it?
- Did you go to the funeral? What was that like for you?
- How did you respond at the time?
- Did you have any warning the death would occur?
- Were there any long-term consequences for you? Have your feelings regarding this death changed much over time? If yes, how?
- How did it affect other members of your family?
- How do you think this loss has affected your approach to your own child?
- Has this event changed your relationships with other family members? In what way?
- Why do you think it has turned out that way? Do you worry about people dying? Under what sort of conditions? Some people think about killing themselves. Have you ever thought about this? Do you have a plan now?

Part VI: Integrative questions regarding childhood in general

- Looking back on it now, do you think your parents loved you? Can you tell me how you know this?
- Taken as a whole, how do you think your childhood experiences have affected your adult personality?
- Are there any aspects of your childhood that you think were a setback or hindered your development?
- Why do you think that your parents acted as they did during your childhood?
- Has your relationship with your parents changed since you have got older? In what way?

- Was it any different in adolescence? Can you give me an example?
- How is your relationship with your parents now?
- How do you think your childhood relationship with your parents or your other early experiences prepared you, as an adolescent and adult, for love relationships? For example, did they affect whether you chose to marry, how you chose your wife (husband/partner), or how you manage your adult love relationships?
- Thinking about your life now, do you have a partner? Children? How do you feel when you separate from your children/your partner?

Part VII: Closing integrative question

- Thinking over all that you have told me, what do you think you have learned from your experience as a child?
- Now that you are an adult, are there any things that you wish to do with your children that are different and/or similar from what your parents did? (Ask for details.)
- I've been asking about your relationships with your parents, as a child and up to now. Is there something more that you wish to add that is important to understand the adult you have become?
- Sometimes, after this sort of interview, you might find that you continue to think about these issues after the interview. If you find yourself feeling uncomfortable or thinking about them too much, please don't hesitate to contact me. In any case, thank you very much.

Adult Attachment Interview: Example of sections

Lillian: Autonomous and secure

RD: *'I would like you to describe the relationship with your parents when you were a child.'*

Lillian: 'As early as I can remember, I didn't have a very good relationship with my mother, I always had a feeling of— I was embarrassed, I was ashamed. I had a bowel problem. They told Mum I was dead when I was about 3 months old and so they did x-rays and it wasn't until years later that they realised that it had done damage to my bowel. It was deformed. No one realised, and they thought that I was a lazy little girl or something when I couldn't control my bowels and I'd come in from outside playing and I would have pooed my pants and she thought I was too lazy to come in. It was still like that when I went to school. School was very traumatic. I grew up one of those children who hated kids. I hated other children. I loved animals, but I hated kids. "Lillian, Lillian the dirty old watermelon" was what I got. I'm laughing now, but it wasn't funny then. Mum used to wash me in the trough and things like that. Perhaps I could understand now but I couldn't then. I think now— Well, Dad worked away from home a lot . . . He had his own business. He was up North a lot. She was mother and father to us three girls and the pressure was on her. She was only 33 or something. She would have got frustrated, especially when there was nothing wrong physically with me. She used to say, "Why do you do it?" and I used to say, "I can't help it, I can't help it". She thought I was lazy. Dad, I always had a good relationship with. He was my idol. I was one of those kids who was going to marry my dad.

RD: *'Describe the changes in your relationship with your parents. What has happened over the years with Mum?'*

Lillian: 'Well, in my early 20s, all this sort of came back to me. I worked in a psychiatric hospital, too – that made a lot of difference. I saw a lot of different people from different families and what had happened to them – most much, much worse than mine. Mine was nothing compared to these people. Just trying to understand where she [(her mum)] was coming from. Was this woman as bad as I thought she was or as I have portrayed her? She can't be. She is my mother. I had to dig around a little and figure things out. My mother would say, "We never had that" and I would say, "Why not? How come?" and she never likes to talk about her past. Even now, she won't. But I had to tell her how I felt and since then we have become closer. I still don't want to live with her. We have real opposite personalities. I love her and she loves me but we couldn't live together, but we are close.'

Mark: Dismissing

RD: *'Describe your early relationship with your parents.'*
Mark: 'There were close relations, very good relations. I suppose in my early years, my mother naturally featured more as my principal carer and provider of meals. Undoubtedly, it is to her that I went on falling over and crying. I always remember both of them being there and supportive. I really have no reservations or major criticism at all about them as parents in the early years. My father, I suppose, became more influential as I grew older. But I think each had a very marked influence upon my life and almost entirely for the better. And I really can't record any negative aspects of that relationship, although, of course, there were many, the usual adolescent conflicts.

'I think tears were very frequent, but I probably ran to my mother – but I am guessing, I cannot remember. I remember cutting my hand badly on a shard of glass and screaming my head off and possibly running back home.'
RD: *'Running back home to your mum?'*
Mark: 'Possibly, I can't remember . . .'

Sandeep: Preoccupied

RD: *'You said that your relationship with your father was violent. Can you give me a memory of a specific occasion when your relationship was violent? Try to think back as far as you can.'*
Sandeep: 'Yeah, there's the classic, like, we'd been rowing about something and I was into Black Widow catapults – do you know what they are?
RD: 'Yeah.'
Sandeep: 'Black Widows have loads of marbles, loads of ball bearings. We had a hallway at the top of the house, really long like 40 metres long, and he [(his dad)] chased me upstairs, something, you know, "raaraaa go to your room, you fucker, raaarraa". I slammed the door of my cell because – they were like cells, he put buzzers in all the rooms for me and brother so he could buzz and get us to go down when he wanted us. So the cell door shuts and my Black Widow was on the side. I thought "fuck you", so he had a dressing gown on, bare legs, I got the Black Widow catapult out, looked down the hallway and just let rip with it – got him right in the back of the calf muscle and it pierced, like blood comes down his leg. I was like [(whispering)] "fuck you". He turned around and comes charging

down that hallway about a thousand miles an hour and my bedroom window was like this and it would only open a little amount and there was like a *really* nasty concrete lintel or slate outside and then a two floor drop onto concrete. I remember thinking, "it's gonna hurt less going out that window than him getting hold of me at this point", so I forced myself out of that window and let myself drop. Took all the skin off my back, landed on the floor and was like, "I'm gone now, brilliant", down through the garden, over the garden fence and then, over the garden, there was a little pony paddock in front and I'd got to the pony paddock and I heard the front door go. I'm thinking, "well, I've got 50 metres on him, there's no way he's gonna catch me before I get down to the stream. If I get down to the stream, I'm gone, I'll go in the woods, he'll never find me". I'm over this fence I'm going down the paddock and look behind me and he's cleared the garden fence already and he's halfway down the paddock, I'd give it. I was good sprinter at school, I'd give absolute beans, but before I know he's just booted my legs out from underneath me and just punches me, like punched me in the field, all the neighbours' houses around, just fucking deck me out'.

RD: *'What happened when you were ill as a child?'*

Sandeep: 'Well, once, my future was completely formed by one thing that happened when I was ill: I had measles and was fucked and I was scratching and sweating and puking, never, never felt so ill, you know? My mum said, "what do you want? What can I get you? I'm going into town, I'll get you anything you want". I said, "I want the new Prince album". She was like, "oh no, not music" 'cause they hated me being into music. I was like, "I want that Prince album. *Sign o' the Times* has just come out" and umm . . . she brought that album for me and that was it, I became a massive vinyl collector from that point and uhh . . . that was the record that started the whole thing. From that point, all the money I had, I was buying records. So that was a good thing. They fucking hated Prince though, this tiny black gay bloke, you know, that I would just pump out as loud as I could throughout the house <laughing> and they be like, "fucking hell, what have we done? Singing about sex and fuckin' shagging Jesus", the maddest stuff. He [(his dad)] would come up or keep his finger on the buzzer, it was like "eeeeeeeeeeeeeeeeeeeeegh!", keep his finger on the buzzer. I'd just turn the stereo up more and he'd keep his finger on this buzzer, it would be like a warfare!'

RD: *'Now that you are an adult, are there any things that you wish to do with your children that are different from what your parents did?'*

Sandeep: 'I'm doing it, I think, just trying to listen an' I'm trying to strike a balance between discipline. I'll show what I put on the fridge actually, this is what's on my fridge at the moment, you know— Like discipline: "you got to do your homework a bit if you don't wanna be scrummin' around for money like me" and "have respect for people, don't swear at people unless they deserve it" but in general umm . . . so this is what's on my fridge, because at school they all watch too much TV, they all listen to shit music, there's no rebellion in them – they're like, kids are pretty vanilla these days. It's like we've succeeded in breaking their will and I want to nurture a bit of rebellion in her [(his daughter)], you know? To say, "that's it, alright?" to not do stuff, to do things differently. You don't have to do everything that everybody tells you, you know, think about stuff yourself.'

Sally: Intentions and dismissing strategy

RD: *'Now think about what you've told me. Are there other things that you want to do differently – umm, you know, from what your parents did? You know, for example, how you are with your children? Would you want to, you know, do you think you try to do things similarly or differently from how they were with you?'*

Sally: 'I think I try and do some things sort of similarly, because they were always . . . they were always there when I needed them. So, I try to be there . . . like, if they need, need something – a cuddle – I sort of try to give them what they need. And I try and teach them responsibility, that they can't always have exactly what they want, right now this minute. And I try and sort of teach them . . . how to do things themselves rather than doing it for them. And . . . those are the kind of similar things. But I do try and make sure that they each get that attention. That if they need any help with something, I'll fight for each and every one of them. Not just kind of . . . someone focused on one. I feel a bit like that's how it was when I was a child . . . I don't feel like it was intentional. But . . . it's just . . . that's how it felt.'

References

Ainsworth, M.D.S. (1973) The development of infant–mother attachment. In B.M. Caldwell and H. Riccuiti (eds) *Review of Child Development Research*, vol. 3. Chicago: Chicago University Press.

Ainsworth, M.D., Blehar, M.C., Waters, E. and Wall, S. (1978) *Patterns of Attachment: A Psychological Study of the Strange Situation*. Hillside, NJ: Lawrence Erlbaum.

Anderson, H., Goolishan, H.A. and Windermand, L. (1986) Problem determined systems: toward transformation in family therapy, *Journal of Strategic and Family Therapy*, 5(4): 1–13.

Asen, E. and Scholz, M. (2010) *Multi-Family Therapy: Concepts and Techniques*. Abingdon: Routledge.

Baerger, D.R. and McAdams, D. (1999) Life story coherence and its relation to psychological well-being, *Narrative Inquiry*, 9: 69–96.

Bassman, R. (2007) *A Flight to Be: A Psychologist's Experience from Both Sides of the Locked Door*. Albany, NY: Tantamount Press.

Bateson, G. (1972) *Steps to an Ecology of Mind*. New York: Ballantine.

Bateson, G., Jackson, D.D., Haley, J. and Weakland, J.H. (1956) Toward a theory of schizophrenia, *Behavioural Science*, 1(4): 251–64.

Beck, A.T. (2002) Cognitive models of depression, *Clinical Advances in Cognitive Psychotherapy: Theory and Application*, 14(1): 29–61.

Bennett, A. (2009) *Alan Bennett Plays 2*. New York: Faber & Faber.

Bennin, F. and Rother, H.A. (2015) 'But it's just paracetamol': Caregivers' ability to administer over-the-counter painkillers to children with the information provided, *Patient Education and Counseling*, 98(3): 331–7.

Bentall, R. (2003) *Madness Explained: Psychosis and Human Nature*. London: Penguin.

Bettelheim, B. (1967) *The Empty Fortress: Infantile Autism and the Birth of the Self*. New York: Simon and Schuster.

Beuler, C. and Welsh, B. (2009) A process model of adolescents' triangulation into parents' marital conflict: the role of emotional reactivity, *Journal of Family Psychology*, 23(2): 167–80.

Bhreathnach, E. (2009) Trauma, sensory processing & attachment: sensory-attachment intervention. Conference paper for the Family Futures Conference: *Innovative Body Based Interventions with Traumatised Children*, London.

Bion, W.R. (1962) *Learning from Experience*. London: Heinemann.

Birns, B. (1999) 1. Attachment theory revisited: challenging conceptual and methodological sacred cows, *Feminism and Psychology*, 9(1): 10–21.

Bowen, M. (1978) *Family Therapy in Clinical Practice*. New York: Jason-Aronson.

Bowlby, J. (1969) *Attachment and Loss, vol. 1: Attachment*. London: Hogarth Press.
Bowlby, J. (1973) *Attachment and Loss, vol. 2: Separation, Anxiety and Anger*. London: Hogarth Press.
Bowlby, J. (1988) *A Secure Base*. New York: Basic Books.
Boyle, M. (1990) *Schizophrenia: A Scientific Delusion?* London: Routledge.
Boyle, M. (2011) Making the world go away, and how psychology and psychiatry benefit. In M. Rapley, J. Moncrieff and J. Dillon (eds) *De-Medicalising Misery*. Chippenham: Palgrave.
Boyle, M. and Johnstone, L. (2014) Alternatives to psychiatric diagnosis, *The Lancet Psychiatry*, 1(6): 409–11.
Breggin, P.R. and Breggin, G.R. (1994) *The War Against Children*. New York: St Martin's.
Bretherton, I. (2010) Fathers in attachment theory and research: a review, *Early Child Development and Care*, 180(1–2): 9–23.
Bruch, H. (1973) *Eating Disorders: Obesity and Anorexia and the Person Within*. New York: Basic Books.
Bruch, H. (1980) Preconditions for the development of anorexia nervosa, *American Journal of Psychoanalysis*, 40(2): 169–72.
Bruner, J. (1990) *Acts of Meaning*. Cambridge, MA: Harvard University Press.
Byng-Hall, J. (1980) The symptom bearer as marital distance regulator: clinical implications, *Family Process*, 19(4): 355–65.
Byng-Hall, J. (1985) The family script: a useful bridge between theory and practice, *Journal of Family Therapy*, 7(3): 301–5.
Byng-Hall, J. (1988) Scripts and legends in families and family therapy, *Family Process*, 27(2): 167–79.
Byng-Hall, J. (1995) *Rewriting Family Scripts: Improvisation and Systems Change*. New York: Guilford Press.
Cecchin, G. (1987) Hypothesizing, circularity and neutrality revisited: an invitation to curiosity, *Family Process*, 26(4): 405–13.
Conners, C.K., Sitarenios, G., Parker, J.D. and Epstein, J.N. (1998) The revised Conners' Parent Rating Scale (CPRS-R): factor structure, reliability, and criterion validity, *Journal of Abnormal Child Psychology*, 26(4): 257–68.
Conrad, P. and Potter, D. (2000) From hyperactive children to ADHD adults: observations on the expansion of medical categories, *Social Problems*, 47(4): 559–82.
Coulter, C. and Rapley, M. (2011) 'I'm just, you know, Joe Bloggs': the management of parental responsibility for first-episode psychosis. In M. Rapley, J. Moncrieff and J. Dillon, *De-Medicalizing Misery: Psychiatry, Psychology and the Human Condition*. London: Palgrave.
Craik, K. (1943) *The Nature of Explanation*. London: Cambridge University Press.
Crittenden, P. (1997) Truth, error, omission, distortion, and deception: an application of attachment theory to the assessment and treatment of psychological disorder. In S.M. Clancy Dollinger and L.F. DiLalla (eds) *Assessment and Intervention Issues Across the Life Span*. London: Lawrence Erlbaum Associates.
Crittenden, P.M. (2006) A dynamic-maturational model of attachment, *Australian and New Zealand Journal of Family Therapy* 27(2): 105–15.

REFERENCES

Crittenden, P., Dallos, R., Landini, A. and Koslowska, K. (2014) *Attachment and Family Therapy*. Maidenhead: McGraw-Hill Education.

Crittenden, P. and Landini, A. (2011) *Assessing Adult Attachment: A Dynamic-Maturational Approach to Discourse Analysis*. New York: Norton.

Crix, D., Stedmon, J., Smart, C. and Dallos, R. (2012) Knowing 'ME' knowing you: the discursive negotiation of contested illness within a family, *Human Systems*, 23(1): 27–49.

Dallos, R. (1991) *Family Belief Systems, Therapy and Change*. Milton Keynes: Open University Press.

Dallos, R. (1996) *Interacting Stories: Narratives, Family Beliefs and Therapy*. London: Karnac Books.

Dallos, R. (2006) *Attachment Narrative Therapy*. Milton Keynes: Open University Press.

Dallos, R. (2015) Don't blame the parents: is it possible to develop non-blaming models of parental causation of distress? In C. Newnes (ed.) *Children and Society: Politics, Policy and Intervention*. London: PCCS Books.

Dallos, R., Bond, N. and McKenzie, R. (In press) *Attachments, Corrective Scripts and Intention*.

Dallos, R. and Denford, S. (2008) A qualitative exploration of relationship and attachment themes in families with an eating disorder, *Clinical Child Psychology and Psychiatry*, 13(2): 305–22.

Dallos, R. and Draper, R. (2015) *An Introduction to Family Therapy*, fourth edition. London: Open University Press.

Dallos, R. and Hamilton-Brown, L. (2000) Pathways to problems – an exploratory study of how problems evolve vs dissolve in families, *Journal of Family Therapy*, 22(4): 375–93.

Dallos, R., Lakus, K., Cahart, M.-S. and McKenzie, R. (2015) Becoming invisible: the effect of triangulation on children's well-being, *Clinical Child Psychology and Psychiatry*, 21(3): 461–76.

Dallos, R. and McKenzie, R. (2015) SAFE Manual: systemic attachment related family enabling. Unpublished manuscript, Department of Clinical Psychology, University of Plymouth.

Dallos, R. and Vetere, A. (2009) *Systemic Therapy and Attachment Narratives: Applications in a Range of Clinical Settings*. London: Routledge.

Dallos, R. and Vetere, A. (2012) Systems theory, family attachments and processes of triangulation: does the concept of triangulation offer a useful bridge?, *Journal of Family Therapy*, 34(2): 117–37.

De Gangi, G. (2000) *Pediatric Disorders of Regulation in Affect and Behavior*. London: Academic Press.

The Division of Clinical Psychology (2011) *Good Practice Guidelines on the Use of Psychological Formulation*. Leicester: The British Psychological Society. Available at: https://shop.bps.org.uk/good-practice-guidelines-on-the-use-of-psychological-formulation.html [Accessed April 2019].

Donaldson, M. (1978) *Children's Minds*. New York: Norton.

DSM-5 (2013) *Diagnostic and Statistical Manual of Mental Disorders*, fifth edition. Washington, DC: American Psychiatric Association.

Dubois-Comtois, K. and Moss, E. (2008) Beyond the dyad: do family interactions influence children's attachment representations in middle childhood?, *Attachment & Human Development*, 10(4): 415–31.

Eells, T.D. (1997) *Handbook of Psychotherapy Case Formulation*. New York: Guilford.

Ensink, K., Normandin, L., Target, M., Fonagy, P., Sabourin, S. and Berthelot, N. (2015) Mentalization in children and mothers in the context of trauma: an initial study of the validity of the Child Reflective Functioning Scale, *British Journal of Developmental Psychology*, 33(2): 203–17.

Fonagy, P., Leigh, T., Steele, M., Steele, H., Kennedy, R., Mattoon, G. et al. (1996) The relation of attachment status, psychiatric classification, and response to psychotherapy, *Journal of Consulting and Clinical Psychology*, 64(1): 22.

Fonagy, P., Steele, H., Moran, G.S., Steele, M. and Higgitt, A. (1991) The capacity for understanding mental states: the reflective self in parent and child and its significance for security of attachment, *Infant Mental Health Journal*, 12(3): 201–18.

Fonagy, P., Steele, M. and Steele, H. (1991) Maternal representations of attachment during pregnancy predicts the organisation of infant–mother attachment at one year of age, *Child Development*, 62: 880–93.

Fonagy, P., Steele, M., Steele, H., Higgitt, A. and Target, M. (1994) The Emanuel Miller Memorial Lecture 1992, The theory and practice of resilience, *Journal of Child Psychiatry*, 35(2): 231–57.

Foucault, M. (1967) *Madness and Civilisation*. London: Tavistock Free Press.

Freh, F.M., Chung, M.C. and Dallos, R. (2013) In the shadow of terror: posttraumatic stress and psychiatric co-morbidity following bombing in Iraq: the role of shattered world assumptions and altered self-capacities, *Journal of Psychiatric Research*, 47(2): 215–25.

Freud, S. (1920) *Beyond the Pleasure Principle* (se, 18: 7–64). London: Hogarth.

Friedlander, M.L., Heatherington, L. and Marrs, A.L. (2000) Responding to blame in family therapy: a constructionist/narrative perspective, *The American Journal of Family Therapy*, 28(2):133–46.

George, C., Kaplan, N. and Main, M. (1985) The Berkeley Adult Attachment Interview. Unpublished protocol. Department of Psychology, University of California, Berkeley, CA.

Gergen, K.J. (1999) *An Invitation to Social Construction*. London: Sage.

Green, D. and Latchford, G. (2012) *Maximising the Benefits of Psychotherapy: A Practice-Based Evidence Approach*. London: John Wiley & Sons.

Grossmann, K., Grossmann K.E., Fremmer-Bombik, E., Kindler, H., Scheuerer-Englisch, H. and Zimmermann, A.P. (2002) The uniqueness of the child–father attachment relationship: fathers' sensitive and challenging play as a pivotal variable in a 16-year longitudinal study, *Social Development*, 11(3): 301–37.

Grunebaum, H. and Chasin, R. (1978) Relabeling and reframing reconsidered: the beneficial effects of a pathological label, *Family Process*, 17(4): 449–55.

Habermas, T. and Bluck, S. (2000) Getting a life: the emergence of the life story in adolescence, *Psychological Bulletin*, 126(5): 748–69.

Hardy, S. and Adnett, N. (2002) The parental leave directive: towards a 'family-friendly' social Europe?, *European Journal of Industrial Relations*, 8(2): 157–72.

Harre, R. and Secord, P.F. (1972) *The Explanation of Social Behaviour*. Oxford: Blackwell.

Harrington, R. (2001) Depression, suicide and deliberate self-harm in adolescence, *British Medical Bulletin*, 57(1): 47–60.

Harvey, J.H., Chwalisz, K.D., Garwood, G. and Orbuch, T.L. (1991) Coping with sexual assault: the roles of account-making and confiding, *Journal of Traumatic Stress*, 4(4): 515–31.

Harvey, J.H., Orbuch, T.L. and Weber, A.L. (eds) (1992) *Attributions, Accounts and Close Relationships*. London: Springer-Verlag.

Hautamäki, A., Hautamäki, L., Neuvonen, L. and Maliniemi-Piispanen, S. (2010) Transmission of attachment across three generations: continuity and reversal, *Clinical Child Psychology and Psychiatry*, 15(3): 347–54.

Holland, S., Dallos, R. and Olver, L. (2012) An exploration of young women's experiences of living with excess weight, *Clinical Child Psychology and Psychiatry*, 17(4): 538–52.

Hudson, M., Dallos, R. and McKenzie, R. (2017) Systemic attachment formulation for families of children with autism, *Advances in Autism*, 3(3): 142–53.

Jackson, D. (1957) The question of family homeostasis, *Psychiatry Quarterly Supplement*, 31: 79–99.

Johnstone, L. and Dallos, R. (2013) *Formulation in Psychology and Psychotherapy: Making Sense of People's Problems*. London: Routledge.

Kanai, A. (2019) On not taking the self seriously: resilience, relatability and humour in young women's Tumblr blogs, *European Journal of Cultural Studies*, 22(1): 60–77.

Kanner, L. and Eisenberg, L. (1956) Early infantile autism 1943–1955, *American Journal of Orthopsychiatry*, 26(3): 556–66.

Kavanagh, D.J. (1992) Recent developments in expressed emotion and schizophrenia, *British Journal of Psychiatry*, 160(5): 601–20.

Keen, T.M. (1999) Schizophrenia: orthodoxy and heresies. A review of alternative possibilities, *Journal of Psychiatric and Mental Health Nursing*, 6(6): 415–24.

Kelley, H.H. (1967) Attribution theory in social psychology, *Nebraska Symposium on Motivation*, 15: 192–238.

Kelly, G.A. (1955) *The Psychology of Personal Constructs, vols. 1 and 2*. New York: Norton.

Kirsch, I. (2013) The placebo effect revisited: lessons learned to date, *Complementary Therapies in Medicine*, 21(2): 102–4.

Kleinman, A. (1988) *The Illness Narratives: Suffering, Healing, and the Human Condition*. New York: Basic Books.

Labov, W. and Waletzky, J. (1967) Narrative analysis: oral versions of personal experience. In. J. Helm (ed.) *Essays on the Verbal and Visual Arts*. Seattle: University of Washington Press.

Laing, R.D. and Esterson, A. (1964) *Sanity, Madness and the Family*. London: Penguin Books.

LeDoux, J. (1998) *The Emotional Brain*. Chicago: University of Chicago Press.

Lewis-Morton, R., Dallos, R., McClelland, L. and Clempson, R. (2014) 'There is something not quite right with Brad...': the ways in which families construct ADHD before receiving a diagnosis, *Contemporary Family Therapy*, 36(2): 260–80.

Main, M. (1991) Metacognitive knowledge, metacognitive monitoring, and singular (coherent) vs multiple (incoherent) models of attachment: findings and directions for future research. In P. Marris, J. Stevenson-Hinde and C. Parkes (eds) *Attachment Across the Lifecycle*. New York: Routledge–Kegan Paul.

Main, M., Kaplan, N. and Cassidy, J. (1985) Security in infancy, childhood, and adulthood: a move to the level of representation. In I. Bretherton and E. Water (eds) *Monographs of the Society for Research and Child Development*, Serial No. 209.50: Nos 1–2. Chicago: University of Chicago Press.

Marvin, R.S. and Stewart, R.B. (1990) A family systems framework for the study of attachment. In M.T. Greenberg, D. Ciccetti and E.M. Cummings (eds) *Attachment in the Pre-school years*. Chicago: University of Chicago Press.

McGoldrick, M. and Carter, B. (2011) Families transformed by the divorce cycle: reconstituted, multinuclear, recoupled, and remarried families. In M. McGoldrick, B. Carter and N. Garcia-Preto (eds) *The Expanded Family Life Cycle: Individual, Family, and Social Perspectives*. London: Pearson.

McHale, J.P. and Fivaz-Depeursinge, E. (1999) Understanding triadic and family group interactions during infancy and toddlerhood, *Clinical Child and Family Psychology Review*, 2(2): 107–27.

McHale, J. and Rasmussen, J. (1998) Co-parental and family group-level dynamics during infancy: early family predictors of child and family functioning during preschool, *Development and Psychopathology*, 10(1): 39–59.

McHoul, A. and Rapley, M. (2005) A case of ADHD diagnosis: Sir Karl and Francis slug it out on the consulting room floor, *Discourse and Society*, 16(3): 419–49.

McKenzie, R. and Dallos, R. (2016) 'I just like Lego!' Self-autism mapping as a non-totalising approach, *Context*, 144: 21–3.

McKenzie, R. and Dallos, R. (2017) Autism and attachment difficulties: overlap of symptoms, implications and innovative solutions, *Clinical Child Psychology and Psychiatry*, 22(4): 632–48. doi: 10.1177/1359104517707323.

McKenzie, R., Dallos, R., Stedmon, J., Hancocks, E., Vassallo, T., Myhill, C. and Ewings, P. (In press) SAFE, a new therapeutic intervention for families of children with autism: study protocol for a feasibility randomised controlled trial, *BMJ Open*.

Mikulincer, M., Shaver, P. and Pereg, D. (2003) Attachment theory and affect regulation: the dynamics, development, and cognitive consequences of attachment-related strategies, *Motivation and Emotion*, 27(2): 77–102.

Mikulincer, M., Shaver, P.R., Sapir-Lavid, Y. and Avihou-Kanza, N. (2009) What's inside the minds of securely and insecurely attached people? The secure-base script and its associations with attachment-style dimensions, *Journal of Personality and Social Psychology*, 97(4): 615–33.

Minuchin, S. (1974) *Families and Family Therapy*. Cambridge, MA: Harvard University Press.

Minuchin, S., Rosman, B. and Baker, L. (1978) *Psychosomatic Families: Anorexia Nervosa in Context*. Cambridge, MA: Harvard University Press.

Moncrieff, J. and Timimi, S. (2011) Critical analysis of the concept of adult attention-deficit hyperactivity disorder, *The Psychiatrist*, 35(9): 334–8.

Montague, I., Dallos, R. and McKenzie, R. (2018) 'It feels like something difficult is coming back to haunt me': the association between a child's autism spectrum disorder meltdown and a parent's adverse childhood, *Clinical Child Psychology and Psychiatry*, 23(1): 125–39.

The National Institute for Health and Care Excellence (NICE) (2014) *Psychosis and schizophrenia in adults: prevention and management*. Clinical guideline [CG178]. Available at: https://www.nice.org.uk/guidance/cg178 [Accessed April 2019].

The National Institute for Health and Care Excellence (NICE) (2018) *Attention deficit hyperactivity disorder: diagnosis and management*. NICE guideline [NG87]. Available at: https://www.nice.org.uk/guidance/ng87 [Accessed April 2019].

Oatley, K. and Johnson-Laird, P.N. (2011) Basic emotions in social relationships, reasoning, and psychological illnesses, *Emotion Review*, 3(4): 424–33.

Olson, D.H. (1986) Circumplex model VII: validation studies and FACES III, *Family Process*, 25(3): 337–51.

O'Reilly, M. and Lester, J.N. (2015) Building a case for good parenting in a family therapy systemic environment: resisting blame and accounting for children's behaviour, *Journal of Family Therapy*, 38(4): 491–511. doi: 10.1111/1467-6427.12094.

Palazzoli, M.S. (1974) *Self-Starvation: From the Intrapsychic to the Transpersonal Approach to Anorexia Nervosa*. London: Human Context Books.

Palazzoli, M.S., Boscolo, L., Cecchin, G. and Prata, G. (1978) Hypothesising-circularity-neutrality: three guidelines for the conductor of the session, *Family Process*, 19: 3–12.

Palazzoli, M.S., Cecchin, G., Prata, G. and Boscolo, L. (1980) *Paradox and Counter Paradox*. New York: Jason Aronson.

Palazzoli, M.S., Cirillo, S., Selvini, M. and Sorrentino, A.M. (1989) *Family Games: General Model of Psychotic Processes in the Family*. New York: W.W. Norton.

Perry, B.D., Pollard, R.A., Blakley, T.L. and Vigilante, D. (1995) Childhood trauma, the neurobiology of adaptation, and 'use-dependent' development of the brain: how 'states' become 'traits', *Infant Mental Health Journal*, 16(4): 271–91.

Piaget, J. (1955) *The Child's Construction of Reality*. London: Routledge and Kegan Paul.

Powell, B., Cooper, G., Hoffman, K. and Marvin, B. (2013/2014) *The Circle of Security Intervention: Enhancing Attachment in Early Parent–Child Relationships*. London: Guilford Press.

Radin, N. (1982) Role sharing fathers. In M. Lamb (ed.) *Non-Traditional Families: Parenting and Child Development*. Hillsdale, NJ: Erlbaum.

Rea, S. and Dallos, R. (2018) Good intentions: exploring narratives of preferred parenting in families of a young person who has experienced a first episode of psychosis (FEP), *Journal of Constructivist Psychology* (in press).

Read, J. and Gumley, A. (2008) Can attachment theory help explain the relationship between childhood adversity and psychosis? *Attachment: New Directions in Psychotherapy and Relational Psychoanalysis*, 2(1): 1–35.

Ritter, T.J. (1917) Mother's remedies, *Nursing*, 556: 565.

Rogers, C.R. and Truax, C.B. (1965) The therapeutic conditions antecedent to change: a theoretical view. In C.R. Rogers (ed.) *The Therapeutic Relationship and its Impact: A Study of Psychotherapy with Schizophrenics*. Wisconsin: University of Wisconsin Press.

Rosenthal, R. and Jacobson, L. (1968) Pygmalion in the classroom, *The Urban Review*, 3(1): 16–20.

Royal College of Psychiatrists (2019) *Anorexia and bulimia*. Available at: https://www.rcpsych.ac.uk/mental-health/problems-disorders/anorexia-and-bulimia [Accessed April 2019].

Rutter, M., Kreppner, J., Croft, C., Murin, M., Colvert, E., Beckett, C. et al. (2007) Early adolescent outcomes of institutionally deprived and non-deprived adoptees. III. Quasi-autism, *Journal of Child Psychology and Psychiatry*, 48(12): 1200–7.

Sadock, B.J. and Sadock, V.A. (eds) (2010) *Kaplan and Sadock's Pocket Handbook of Clinical Psychiatry*. Philadelphia, PA: Lippincott Williams & Wilkins.

Schank, R.C. (1982) *Dynamic Memory: A Theory of Reminding and Learning in Computers and People*. Cambridge: Cambridge University Press.

Schank, R.C. (1999) *Dynamic Memory Revisited*. Cambridge: Cambridge University Press.

Schank, R.C. and Abelson, R.P. (1975) Scripts, plans, and knowledge, *IJCAI*, September: 151–7.

Schank, R.C. and Abelson, R.P. (1977) *Scripts, Plans, Goals and Understanding*. Hillsdale, NJ: Erlbaum.

Schindler, A., Thomasius, R., Sack, P.M., Gemeinhardt, B. and Kustner, U. (2007) Insecure family bases and adolescent drug abuse: a new approach to family patterns of attachment. *Attachment & Human Development*, 9(2): 111–26.

Siegel, D. (2012) *The Developing Mind: How Relationships and the Brain Interact to Shape Who We Are*, second edition. New York: Guilford Press.

Simon, P. (2019) *Lancet Psychiatry's controversial ADHD study: errors, criticism, and responses*. Available at: https://www.madinamerica.com/2017/05/lancet-psychiatrys-controversial-adhd-study-errors-criticism-responses/ [Accessed April 2019].

Slade, A., Grienenberger, J., Bernbach, E., Levy, D. and Locker, A. (2005) Maternal reflective functioning, attachment, and the transmission gap: a preliminary study, *Attachment & Human Development*, 7(3): 283–98.

Solomon, J. and George, C. (1999) The measurement of attachment security in infancy and childhood. In J. Cassidy and P.R. Shaver (eds) *Handbook of Attachment: Theory Research, and Clinical Applications*. New York: Guilford Press.

Solomon, J. and George, C. (eds) (2011) *Disorganized Attachment and Caregiving*. New York: Guilford Press.

Stedmon, J. and Dallos, R. (2009) *Reflective Practice in Psychotherapy and Counselling*. Maidenhead: McGraw-Hill Education.

Stratton, P. (2003) Causal attributions during therapy I: Responsibility and blame, *Journal of Family Therapy*, 25(2): 136–60.

Strickland-Clark, L., Campbell, D. and Dallos, R. (2000) Children's and adolescents' views on family therapy, *Journal of Family Therapy*, 22(3): 324–41.

Thapar, A., Cooper, M., Eyre, O. and Langley, K. (2013) Practitioner review: what have we learnt about the causes of ADHD?, *Journal of Child Psychology and Psychiatry*, 54(1): 3–16.

Timimi, S. (2002) *Pathological Child Psychiatry and the Medicalization of Childhood*. Hove: Brunner-Routledge.

Timimi, S. (2005) *Boys: Anti-Social Behaviour, ADHD and the Role of Culture*. Basingstoke: Palgrave Macmillan.

Timimi, S., Gardner, N. and McCabe, B. (2011) *The Myth of Autism*. Basingstoke: Palgrave Macmillan.

Timimi, S. and Timimi, L. (2015) The social construction of attention deficit hyperactivity disorder. In J.N. Lester and M. O'Reilly (eds) *The Palgrave Handbook of Child Mental Health*. London: Palgrave Macmillan.

Tomm, K. (1988) Interventive interviewing: Part 3. Intending to ask circular, strategic or reflexive questions, *Family Process*, 27(1): 1–17.

Tulving, E. (1972) Episodic and semantic memory. In E. Tulving and W. Davidson (eds) *Organisation of Memory*. New York: Academic Press.

Ugazio, V., Fellin, L., Pennacchio, R., Negri, A. and Colciago, F. (2012) Is systemic thinking really extraneous to common sense?, *Journal of Family Therapy*, 34(1): 53–71.

van IJzendoorn, M.H. (1995) Adult attachment representations, parental responsiveness, and infant attachment: a meta-analysis on the predictive validity of the adult attachment interview, *Psychological Bulletin*, 117(3): 387–403.

van IJzendoorn, M.H., Goldberg, S., Kroonenberg, P.M. and Frenkel, O.J. (1992) The relative effects of maternal and child problems on the quality of attachment: a meta-analysis of attachment in clinical samples, *Child Development*, 63(4): 840–58.

Waters, E. and Cummings, M.C. (2000) A secure base from which to explore close relationships, *Child Development*, 71(1): 164–72.

Waters, E., Merrick, S., Treboux, D., Crowell, J. and Albersheim, L. (2000) Attachment security in infancy and early adulthood: a twenty-year longitudinal study, *Child Development*, 71(3): 684–9.

Waters, H.S. and Waters. E. (2006) The attachment working models concept: among other things, we build script-like representations of secure base experiences, *Attachment & Human Development*, 8(3): 185–97.

Watters, E. (2011) *Crazy Like Us: The Globalisation of the Western Mind*. London: Hachette.

Watzlawick, P., Beavin, J. and Jackson, D. (1967) *Pragmatics of Human Communication*. New York: Norton.

Watzlawick, P., Weakland, J. and Fisch, R. (1974) *Change: Principles of Problem Formation and Problem Resolution*. New York: Norton.

Weakland, J. (1976) Toward a theory of schizophrenia. In C.E. Sluzki and D.D. Ransom (eds) *Double Bind: The Foundation of the Communicational Approach to the Family.* New York: Grune and Stratton.

West, M.L. (1997) Reflective capacity and its significance to the attachment concept of the self, *British Journal of Medical Psychology*, 70: 17–25.

White, M. (1995) *Re-Authoring Lives: Interviews and Essays.* Adelaide: Dulwich Centre Publications.

White, M. and Epston, D. (1990) *Narrative Means to Therapeutic Ends.* New York: Norton.

Winnicott, D.W. (1965) *Maturational Processes and the Facilitating Environment.* New York: International.

Winnicott, D.W. (1971) *Playing and Reality.* London: Tavistock.

World Health Organization (WHO) (2016) *International Statistical Classification of Diseases and Related Health Problems*, 10th revision. Geneva: World Health Organization.

Zubin, J. and Spring, B. (1977) Vulnerability: a new view of schizophrenia, *Journal of Abnormal Psychology*, 86(2): 103.

Index

AAI *see* Adult Attachment Interview
adaptability, attachment scripts 99–100
ADHD *see* attention deficit hyperactivity disorder
Adult Attachment Interview (AAI) 11, 102
  attachment scripts 145–8
  examples 166–9
  intentions 145–8
  reflection use 158
  Strange Situation procedure 88–9
  structure 161–5
adult attachment representations attachment scripts 78–81
aims of this book 153
anorexia 14–15, 18, 19–21, 25, 27–9, 31
anxious–ambivalent scripts, attachment scripts 79
assessment and diagnosis, paediatrician–parent conversation 49–51
attachment 11, 21–2
  attachment theory 24, 53–5
  behavioural patterns 55–7
  Bowlby, John 53–4
  family systems 53–5, 58–60
  internal working model (IWM) 71–87
  narratives styles 67–9
  triangulation 81–3
attachment insecurity
  family systems 15, 21–2, 55, 58–60
  insecure attachment scripts 79
  triangulation 60–5, 81–3
attachment scripts 71, 74–87
  adaptability 99–100
  Adult Attachment Interview (AAI) 145–8
  adult attachment representations 78–81
  anxious–ambivalent scripts 79
  attachment styles 100–105
  avoidant scripts 79
  Byng-Hall, John 75, 83–6, 157
  competing attachment scripts 129–30
  contradictory attachment scripts 129–30
  corrective intentions 100–107
  corrective scripts 93–5
  exploring 140–3
  family processes 104–105

improvisation 99–100
inconsistent attachment scripts 81
insecure attachment scripts 79
intentions 74–81, 100–107, 121–2
interactive model, trauma 130–1
internal working model (IWM) 81–3
key propositions 76
memory systems 73–4, 78
multiple scripts 104–105
narratives 91–6
replicative intentions 100–107
replicative scripts 93–5
secure base 140–3
secure base scripts 78–81
trauma 109–132
triadic processes 104–105
types 77, 97–9
attachment sequences 149–51
  role play 150–1
  tracking 149
attachment strategies 55–60
  behavioural patterns 55–7
  defensive processes 66–7
  trauma 114–15
attachment styles 100–105
attachment theory 153–4, 159
  internal working model (IWM) 81–3
attention deficit hyperactivity disorder (ADHD) 29, 44–6, 48–50, 154
  diagnosis 35–6, 38, 40
  medication 44–5
  methylphenidate 44–5
  responding to 26–7
autism 22, 35–7, 39, 101–102
  diagnosis 35–7, 39
  problems 6–7
  Self-autism Mapping (SAM) 7
autonomy
  autonomous choice 93–5
  internal working model (IWM) 83–6
avoidant scripts, attachment scripts 79

Bateson, G. 21–2
blame
  approaches to addressing 23–4

INDEX

duration of problems 136–7
in families 12–32
managing 27–8
problems 19–23
responding to 18
role 1–2, 3–7
role of the mother 23
self-blame 16–17
Bowlby, John 6, 15
attachment 53–4
Byng-Hall, John 4–5
attachment scripts 75, 93–6, 157
multiple scripts 127

causality, linear/circular 13–14
causation 7–8, 34
problems 47, 109–111
role of families 46–7
change, preparing for 143–5
change and continuity 88–90
choice, internal working model (IWM) 83–6
circle of security 54–5
commonality and difference 158–9
competing attachment scripts 129–30
conscious intentions 89–90, 95–9
unconscious scripts 96–7
continuity and change 88–90
contradictory attachment scripts 129–30
corrective intentions
attachment scripts 100–107
criticisms 101
disorientation 126–7
exploring 139–40
secure base 139–40
trauma 122–4, 126–7, 128
corrective scripts 4, 9, 10
attachment scripts 93–5
double sense of failure 134–6
intentions 121–2
trauma 119–27
cortical integration, trauma and stress 113–14, 115
cultural values, intentions 107–108

deviance, construction 44–7
diagnosis 33–51
attention deficit hyperactivity disorder (ADHD) 35, 38, 40
autism 35–7, 39
family diagnosis 37–8, 43
fibromyalgia 41
genetically based vulnerability 35–7
history 33–8
medical-based diagnosis 107, 126, 129, 133, 137, 154–5, 158–9, 160

paediatrician–parent conversation 49–51
problems 35–7
self diagnosis 37–8
difference and commonality 158–9
disability, *vs.* illness 38–9
discourses and families 47–51
dismissing (deactivating) strategies, trauma 116, 128
distress, construction 44–7
dominant constellations of explanations 29–31
double sense of failure 133–6
corrective scripts 134–6
dynamic personal construct system, internal working model (IWM) 83–4

eating disorder, triangulation 62–5
emotional problems
causes 47–8
families and discourses 47–8

FACES (Family Adaptability and Cohesiveness Evaluation Scale) 43
failure feelings 16–17
double sense of failure 133–6
families and discourses 47–51
emotional problems 47–8
Family Adaptability and Cohesiveness Evaluation Scale (FACES) 43
family diagnosis 37–8
Family Adaptability and Cohesiveness Evaluation Scale (FACES) 43
solution-focused approach 43
family narratives
memory systems 65–6
working models 65–6
family processes
attachment scripts 104–105
multiple scripts 127–30
family relationships, importance 156
family systems
attachment 53–5, 58–60
attachment insecurity 15, 21–2, 55, 58–60
triangulation 60–5
family therapy models 24–9
fathers' influences 105–106
fibromyalgia, diagnosis 41
formulation
definition 40
history 33–8
systemic family therapy (SFT) 39–44

guilt
approaches to addressing 23–4

labelling and the relief of guilt: the medical model 25–8
relational approaches and the relief of guilt: the narrative response 28–9
responding to 18

illness, vs. disability 38–9
'illnesses'
see also mental health
problems as 3, 6–7, 27–31
improvisation, attachment scripts 99–100
influence 12–15
mutual influence 13–15
insecure attachment scripts 79
insecurity, attachment see attachment insecurity
intentions 7–8, 12–15, 154
see also conscious intentions; corrective intentions; positive intentions; replicative intentions
Adult Attachment Interview (AAI) 145–8
attachment scripts 100–107, 121–2
corrective scripts 121–2
cultural values 107–108
exploring 140–3
flexible vs. rigid 138
ineffective intentions 150–1
secure base 140–3
trauma 121–2
internal working model (IWM) 71–87
attachment 71–87
attachment scripts 81–3
attachment theory 81–3
autonomy 83–6
choice 83–6
dynamic personal construct system 83–4
memory systems 73–4, 115
reflective functioning 83–7
representational systems 73–4
trauma 115
triangulation 81–3

loss and trauma 111–14

medication, attention deficit hyperactivity disorder (ADHD) 44–5
memory systems
attachment scripts 73–4, 78
family narratives 65–6
internal working model (IWM) 73–4, 115
representational systems 73–4, 78
mental health
see also 'illnesses'
concept development 34

methylphenidate, attention deficit hyperactivity disorder (ADHD) 44–5
mode of expression, changing 106–107
models
family therapy 24–9
medical models of problems 25–8
multi-family therapy 139
multiple scripts
attachment scripts 104–105
Byng-Hall, John 127
family processes 127–30
triadic processes 127–30
mutual influence 13–15

narratives, attachment scripts 91–6
narratives styles, attachment 67–9
new perspective and integrations 159–60
non-blaming stance, problems 109–111

outline of this book and pedagogy 8–10

paediatrician–parent conversation, assessment and diagnosis 49–51
parents, validating 143–5
positive intentions 90–1
systemic family therapy (SFT) 91
post-traumatic stress disorder (PTSD), trauma 112
preoccupied patterns 104
preoccupying (hyperactivating) strategies, trauma 117
problems
autism 6–7
blame 19–23
causation 109–111
cause 2–7
diagnosis 35–7
duration 136–7
emerging in families 15–23
emotional problems, causes 47–8
as 'illnesses' 3, 6–7, 27–31
medical models of problems 25–8
non-blaming stance 109–111
responsibility 19–23
role of families 46–7
terminology 2–3
PTSD (post-traumatic stress disorder), trauma 112

reflective functioning, internal working model (IWM) 83–7
relational process, trauma as 118–19
replicative intentions
attachment scripts 100–107

criticisms 101
exploring 139–40
secure base 139–40
trauma 124–6, 128–9
replicative scripts, attachment scripts 93–5
representational systems
internal working model (IWM) 73–4
memory systems 73–4, 78
responsibility
approaches to addressing 23–4
in families 12–32
problems 19–23
role 1–2, 3–4, 6–7
role play, attachment sequences 150–1
roles
blame 1–2, 3–7, 23
families' 46–7
mothers' 23
responsibility 1–2, 3–4, 6–7

SAFE (Systemic Autism-related Family Enabling) 139, 145
SAM (Self-autism Mapping) 7
schizophrenia 21, 37, 39, 154–5
scripts, attachment *see* attachment scripts
secure base, exploring from
attachment scripts 140–3
corrective intentions 139–40
intentions 140–3
replicative intentions 139–40
secure base scripts, attachment scripts 78–81
secure–balanced (balanced activation) strategies, trauma 117–18
self diagnosis 37–8
Self-autism Mapping (SAM) 7
self-blame 16–17
self-protective strategies, trauma 115–18
dismissing (deactivating) strategies 116, 128
preoccupying (hyperactivating) strategies 117
secure–balanced (balanced activation) strategies 117–18
SFT *see* systemic family therapy
solution-focused approach, family diagnosis 43
Strange Situation procedure 55, 68–9, 76
Adult Attachment Interview (AAI) 88–9
stress and trauma, cortical integration 113–14, 115

suicide, interpretations 158–9
Systemic Autism-related Family Enabling (SAFE) 139, 145
systemic family therapy (SFT) 13–14, 29–31, 99–100, 139–40
formulation 39–44
positive intentions 91
systemic theory: formulation and formulating 41–4

trauma
attachment scripts 109–132
attachment strategies 114–15
corrective intentions 122–4, 126–7, 128
corrective scripts 119–27
dismissing (deactivating) strategies 116, 128
disorientation 126–7
indications 111–12
intentions 121–2
interactive model, attachment scripts 130–1
internal working model (IWM) 115
and loss 111–14
post-traumatic stress disorder (PTSD) 112
preoccupying (hyperactivating) strategies 117
reactions 112–14
as relational process 118–19
replicative intentions 124–6, 128–9
secure–balanced (balanced activation) strategies 117–18
self-protective strategies 115–18
trauma and stress, cortical integration 113–14, 115
triadic processes
attachment scripts 104–105
multiple scripts 127–30
triangulation
attachment 81–3
attachment insecurity 60–5, 81–3
eating disorder 62–5
family systems 60–5
intergenerational consequences 64–5
internal working model (IWM) 81–3

unconscious scripts, conscious intentions 96–7